48/10

Imagination and Its Pathologies

edited by James Phillips and James Morley

The MIT Press
Cambridge, Massachusetts
London, England

This book was set in Bembo on 3B2 by Asco Typesetters, Hong Kong, and was printed and bound in the United States of America.

Library of Congress Cataloging-in-Publication Data

Imagination and its pathologies / edited by James Phillips and James Morley.
    p.   cm.
  Includes index.
  ISBN 0-262-16214-8
  1. Imagination. 2. Mental illness. 3. Imagination (Philosophy) 4. Psychiatry—
Philosophy. I. Phillips, James, 1938– II. Morley, James, 1957–
BF408 .I455   2003
153.3—dc21   2002035586

Contents

Contributors   vii

Introduction   1
James Phillips and James Morley

I   Pathologic Imagination in Light of Philosophic Reflection

1   Imagination: Looking in the Right Place (and in the Right Way)   21
Paul B. Lieberman

2   Imagination and Its Pathologies: Domain of the Unreal or a Fundamental Dimension of Human Reality?   37
Edwin L. Hersch

3   Narrative and the Ethics of Remembrance   51
Richard Kearney

4   Imagination, Fantasy, Hallucination, and Memory   65
Edward S. Casey

5   The Texture of the Real: Merleau-Ponty on Imagination and Psychopathology   93
James Morley

II   Pathologic Imagination and Psychodynamic Thought

6   The Creative Role of Fantasy in Adaptation   111
Ethel Spector Person

7   The Madonna Imago: A New Interpretation of Its Pathology   133
M. C. Dillon

8   The Impossibility of Female Mourning   147
Jennifer Hansen

9   Depression, Depth, and the Imagination   175
Jennifer Church

10   The Unconscious as a Hermeneutic Myth: A Defense of the
Imagination   187
J. Melvin Woody

III   Pathologic Imagination Applied to Creative and Clinical
Phenomena

11   A Phenomenological Psychological Approach to Research on
Hallucination   209
Amadeo Giorgi

12   Narrative in Play: The Structure of the Imagination in
Psychotherapy with Young Children   225
Robert S. Kruger

13   On the Dialectics of Imagination: Nijinsky's Sublime Defeat   233
Pascal Sauvayre and Barbara Forbes

14   Was St. Anthony Crazy? Visionary Experiences and the Desert
Fathers   253
Greg Mahr

Index   263

Contributors

Edward S. Casey, Ph.D.
Professor of Philosophy
State University of New York at Stony Brook

Jennifer Church, Ph.D.
Professor of Philosophy
Vassar College
Poughkeepsie, NY

M. C. Dillon, Ph.D.
Professor of Philosophy
State University of New York at Binghamton

Barbara Forbes
Associate of Feldenkrais Guild of North America
Private Practice of Feldenkrais Therapy
New York, NY

Amadeo Giorgi, Ph.D.
Dean of Faculty at the Saybrook Institute for Humanistic Psychology
San Francisco, CA

Jennifer Hansen, Ph.D.
Assistant Professor of Philosophy
Gettysburg College
Gettysburg, PA

Edwin L. Hersch, M.D.
Private Practice of Psychiatry
Toronto

Richard Kearney, Ph.D.
Professor of Philosophy at Boston University and University College Dublin

Robert Kruger, Ph.D.
Private Practice of Clinical Psychology
Westport, CT

Paul B. Lieberman, M.D.
Associate Clinical Professor of Psychiatry
Brown School of Medicine
Providence, RI

Greg Mahr, M.D.
Attending Psychiatrist
Henry Ford Health Sciences Center
Detroit, MI

James Morley, Ph.D.
Associate Professor of Clinical Psychology
Ramapo College of New Jersey
Mahwah, NJ

James Phillips, M.D.
Associate Clinical Professor of Psychiatry
Yale School of Medicine
New Haven, CT

Ethel Spector Person, M.D.
Training and Supervising Analyst
Columbia University Center for Psychoanalytic Training and Research
Professor of Clinical Psychiatry
Columbia College of Physicians and Surgeons
New York, NY

Pascal Sauvayre, Ph.D.
Associate
William Alanson Institute for
Psychoanalysis
Private Practice of Psychoanalysis and
Clinical Psychology
New York, NY

J. Melvin Woody, Ph.D.
Professor of Philosophy
Connecticut College
New London, CT

Introduction

James Phillips and James Morley

. . . imagination is not just one faculty on a par with others, but, if one would so speak, it is the faculty instar omnium *(of ultimate prominence). What feeling, knowledge or will a man has depends in the last resort upon what imagination he has. . . . Imagination is the possibility of all reflection, and the intensity of this medium is the possibility of the intensity of the self.*
Søren Kierkegaard

In September 1944 a woman in Mattoon, Illinois, complained to the police that someone was secretly spraying gas into her bedroom and paralyzing her. Other citizens then claimed to have glimpsed the elusive "gasser," and the episode quickly reached newspapers all over the United States. However, in the absence of any real evidence to support the existence of the "gasser," the story dissipated as quickly as it had unfolded. As related by the historian George Rosen, "[a]fter ten days of excitement . . . all the victims had recovered, no substantial clues had been uncovered, the police fell back on 'imagination' to explain the reports, and some newspapers turned up with stories on mass hysteria. The 'phantom gasser' was gone and the episode over." (Rosen 1968, 1–2)[1]

The year is 1944—almost the present—but the invocation of imagination to explain the woman's apparent delusion is nothing new. Such a popular view of pathological imagination has in fact been around for a long time. The story serves to remind us that this commonsense view of imagination gone awry is still with us. To trace its genealogy in the modern era, we may turn back to John Locke, whose treatment of madness and imagination in his *Essay concerning Human Understanding* did much to shape an understanding still operative in Mattoon in 1944. Like Hobbes, Locke accorded minimal importance to the imagination, falling back on the notion of a faded or decaying sense image. He did, however, find a place for it in explaining madness.[2] Striving to distinguish the intellectual defective from the truly mad in the categories of his faculty psychology, he wrote:

In fine, the defect in naturals seems to proceed from want of quickness, activity, and motion in the intellectual faculties, whereby they are deprived of reason; whereas madmen, on the other side, seem to suffer by the other extreme. For they do not appear to me to have lost the faculty of reasoning, but having joined together some ideas very wrongly, they mistake them for truths; and they err as men do that argue right from wrong principles. For, by the violence of their imaginations, having taken their fancies for realities, they make right deductions from them. Thus you shall find a distracted man fancying himself a king, with a right inference require suitable attendance, respect, and obedience; others who have thought themselves made of glass, have used the caution necessary to preserve such brittle bodies. Hence it comes to pass that a man who is very sober, and of a right understanding in all other things, may in one particular be as frantic as any in Bedlam; if either by any sudden very strong impression, or long fixing his fancy upon one sort of thoughts, incoherent ideas have been cemented together so powerfully, as to remain united. But there are degrees of madness, as of folly; the disorderly jumbling ideas together is in some more, and some less. In short, herein seems to lie the difference between idiots and madmen: that madmen put wrong ideas together, and so make wrong propositions, but argue and reason right from them; but idiots make very few or no propositions, and reason scarce at all. (Locke 1959, 207–208)

Locke's explanation of madness through a faulty mixing of ideas by a deranged and violent imagination prevailed through the ensuing centuries and was a direct influence on the great nineteenth-century reformers of psychiatric institutions, the Tukes in England and Pinel in France.[3] And as indicated in the opening vignette, Locke's explanation stretched even to Mattoon in 1944. Moreover this explanation, with its empiricist philosophical underpinnings, fit neatly with the burgeoning natural sciences, and the result was what we might call the received tradition of scientific psychiatry as it developed in the modern era. To illustrate this point, and to bring ourselves fully into the actual present, we may turn to the *Diagnostic and Statistical Manual of Mental Disorders*, fourth edition (the DSM-IV), the quasi-official voice of contemporary psychiatry. In DSM-IV a delusion is defined as "[a] false belief based on incorrect inference about external reality that is firmly sustained despite what almost everyone else believes and despite what constitutes incontrovertible and obvious proof or evidence to the contrary" (American Psychiatric Association 1994, 767). While the

DSM-IV definition does not specifically mention imagination, the definition is clearly consistent with—and derivative from—Locke's description of the madman's "by the violence of their imaginations, . . . tak[ing] their fancies for realities." There is thus a continuity from Locke to DSM-IV and the police of Mattoon—a continuity based on the notion of madness and delusion as resulting from deranged imagination. The notion is so commonsensical that it is hard to 'imagine' any other view of pathological imagination—or for that matter, of its implied opposite, 'normal' imagination. It will be the challenge of this volume to demonstrate how much more complex is the relation of imagination to pathological phenomena than is suggested by this straightforward, 'commonsense' view.

The relationship between madness and imagination was not always as described above. While there was not a formal 'psychiatry' in the premodern era, what we may call 'archaic psychiatry' also understood mental illness in the context of the imaginary, but not the imaginary as deficiency state that we find in Locke and the modern tradition. What we now call the 'supernatural' can be described as a mytho-poetic system in which psychopathological phenomena are represented. 'Mythical consciousness', as studied by Ernst Cassirer, functioned according to other principles than those we associate with instrumental rational thought (Cassirer 1955). For one thing, the imagination of mythic consciousness was imbued with a strong emotional bond with nature. As Cassirer writes:

What is characteristic of primitive mentality is not its logic but its general sentiment of life. Primitive man does not look at nature with the eyes of a naturalist who wishes to classify things in order to satisfy an intellectual curiosity. He does not approach it with merely pragmatic or technical interest. It is for him neither a mere object of knowledge nor the field of his immediate practical needs. We are in the habit of dividing our life into the two spheres of practical and theoretical activity. In this division we are prone to forget that there is a lower stratum beneath them both. Primitive man is not liable to such forgetfulness. All his thoughts and his feelings are still embedded in this lower original stratum. His view of nature is neither merely theoretical nor merely practical; it is *sympathetic*. If we miss this point we cannot find the approach to the mythical world. The most fundamental feature of myth is not a special direction of thought or a special direction of human imagination. Myth is an offspring of emotion and its emotional background imbues all its productions with its own specific color. (Cassirer 1942, 82)

Although we must be cautious in judging what passes for "normal" and "mad" in archaic experience, we can locate instances of our understanding of madness in ancient cultures—always represented, however, in that culture's particular "supernatural" framework. In the ancient Hebrew Book of Samuel, Saul appears, from our psychological point of view, to have suffered from a depressive and paranoid condition. While his mental deterioration seems related to his interpersonal conflict with the prophet Samuel, the bible ascribes it to his disobedience toward God, as represented by the prophet. Following his bitter quarrel with Samuel, "the Spirit of the Lord departed from Saul, and an evil spirit from the Lord tormented him" (I Samuel 16: 14). Saul's experience was quite consistent with the Hebrew conviction that madness is brought on by God. Moses, for instance, warns his people that if they "will not obey the voice of the Lord your God or be careful to do all his commandments and his statues . . . the Lord will smite you with madness and blindness and confusion of mind" (Deuteronomy 28: 15, 28). The story of Saul, in addition to offering an example of madness in the biblical setting, also offers a suggestion about ancient treatment—in this case David's soothing music, again presumably experienced in a supernatural context: "And whenever the evil spirit from God was upon Saul, David took the lyre and played it with his hand; so Saul was refreshed, and was well, and the evil spirit departed from him" (I Samuel 16: 23).[4]

A similar supernatural agency as the cause of madness can be found in Homeric Greece. Indeed, for Homer there is little sense of personal agency of any kind. The gods are at the origin of most human activity, all the more so when the action is "irrational." As Simon puts it: "Overall, there is no notion that mental disturbances arise from a disorder or derangement within a mental structure, since there is no notion of a structure." (Simon 1978, 66). Typical is an episode that Simon describes from the *Odyssey*:

At the opening of Book 23 of the *Odyssey*, the faithful old nurse Eurykleia runs to tell her mistress, Penelope, that Odysseus has returned and has killed the suitors. Penelope, who has been asleep, is incredulous at first and answers:

Dear nurse, the gods have driven you crazy. They are both able
to change a very sensible person into a senseless
one, and to set the light-wit on the way of discretion.
They have set you awry; before now your thoughts were orderly.
Why do you insult me when my heart is heavy with sorrows,
by talking in this wild way . . . ? (Simon 1978, 65)

Finally, few texts chronicle the premodern conception of madness as effectively as the sixth-century Irish saga *Sweeney Astray*. In this narrative the pagan king Sweeney brutally insults the saintly cleric Ronan Finn who, as God's embassador on Earth, delivers a profound curse upon him:

His Brain convulsed
his mind split open.
Vertigo, hysteria, lurchings
and launchings came over him,
he staggered and flapped desperately,
he was revolted by the thought of known places
and dreamed strange migrations.
His fingers stiffened,
his feet scuffled and flurried,
his heart was startled
his senses were mesmerized,
his sight was bent,
the weapons fell from his hands
and he levitated in a frantic cumbersome motion
like a bird of the air.
And Ronan's curse was fulfilled. (Heaney 1983, 9)

The text continues to account Sweeney's "strange migrations" as a creature of the air who blows across the Celtic landscape in unrelenting psychic torment, ensnared in the flights of imagination, and unable to return to "known places." As in the Bible and the *Odyssey*, Sweeney's is not a psychological affliction of guilt but a supernatural one of punishment.

As the archaic age of myth gave way to the philosophical "enlightenment" of the European world, the role of imagination suffered precisely because of its associations with the so-called primitive minds of less rational "barbaric" societies—no less women, children, and (of course) the insane. Thus began the slow devaluation of imagination that culminated with Locke and the empiricists. Plato, while ironically writing in one of the most imaginative styles ever, initiated the Western tradition of viewing imagination as the lowest form of knowledge and not to be trusted. Aristotle, in turn, inaugurated the Western convention of limiting imagination to an intermediary faculty between sense perception and abstract cognition. This gave imagination the status of go-between but denied it an autonomy from these other two faculties. Following Locke and Hume, finally, this trend toward a denigration of imagination was reversed by Kant, who accorded great metaphysical significance to the imagination. This was what, in fact, inaugurated the Romantic movement which strove to revitalize the mythic imagination. As Kearney has traced the history of imagination in the Western world, he describes the modern movement, culminating in the Romantic period, as one of a transformation from merely mechanically 'mimetic' imagination to that of creatively 'productive' imagination (Kearney 1988). It is not surprising that the founding figures of the Romantic

Pathologic Imagination in Light of Philosophical Reflection

A number of papers deal with theoretical aspects of our theme. These papers do not deal directly with either specific pathologic conditions or with therapeutic uses of imagination—although, indirectly, they are often of relevance in both areas. An appropriate place to begin is with Paul Lieberman's "Imagination: Looking in the Right Place (and in the Right Way)." Lieberman introduces our theme with a Wittgensteinian, ordinary language approach that asks, not what do words mean, but how are they used. Wittgenstein's (and Lieberman's) argument is, of course, that we will learn more about a word or a concept through investigating its actual use than through plumbing its "meaning." Lieberman approaches imagination in clinical work in this manner. "A set of philosophical moments or intrusions into clinical work arises, I think, around issues of imagining, imagination, imaginary and related concepts. Following Diamond's suggestion, looking at how we actually use our words for these concepts may help both by orienting us to clinical phenomena which can be difficult to understand, and by supplying therapeutic tools." Lieberman plunges into the apiorias of imagination-in-use with a clinical example, a schizophrenic patient who, noticing a frog in her bedroom, concludes that someone had read her mind and put the frog there to send her a message. Lieberman frames the philosophical issue in terms we are familiar with from Locke and the police of Mattoon: "This, I believe, is the moment at which the clinical situation becomes a philosophical one. The patient believes that someone put a frog in her room. The therapist thinks that her belief is imagination. This can easily deteriorate into a (more or less subtle) confrontation: each person trying to convince the other of his or her correctness." He argues that this view of delusion and imagination is a theoretical position that both distorts the clinical reality and is therapeutically bankrupt. He then proceeds to a detailed examination of our actual experience and use of the vocabulary of imagination.

Edwin Hersch's "Imagination and Its Pathologies: Domain of the Un-real or a Fundamental Dimension of Human Reality?" provides a companion piece to Lieberman's paper in that, while challenging the same constricted view of the imagination targeted by Lieberman, he counters it with a vision inspired by continental, as opposed to Wittgensteinian, philosophy. Hersch organizes his analysis around two approaches to imagination: the tradition of natural science and empiricist philosophy, and the

:ollective cases of historical crime." In the psychological domain Kearney examines both Freud's case history of Dora and the recent debate over remembered child abuse to make his case. In the historical realm he focuses on the ethics of remembrance in the case of the Holocaust. In making his argument Kearney is taking strong issue with those figures who blur the distinctions between aesthetic and historical narrative and thus minimize the reference of narrative to the real world (e.g., Donald Spence in psychoanalysis, Roland Barthes in literary theory, and Hayden White in history).

The two final papers in the section demonstrate how the phenomenological tradition can offer productive contributions toward our topic. Casey shows how the descriptive method of phenomenology can be applied to circumscribing the various forms of imagination generally. Thus he locates pathological hallucination as a unique experiential structure within a spectrum of possible imaginary experiences. Casey provides a comparative phenomenological topology, or index, that allows us to understand what is common to all forms of imagining but, more important, the constituent qualities that differentiate the various forms of imagining. For example, while imagination, memory, hallucination, and fantasy can be distinguished from ordinary perception through the constituent of *belief* in an alternatively real experience, the quality of hallucinatory belief, like perception, feels *involuntary* to the person who is hallucinating. Imagination, memory, and fantasy demonstrate a quality of control that is not present in pathological imagining. Casey's article provides a useful introduction to classical phenomenology for psychiatric researchers who seek a suitable context for description and diagnosis of imaginary psychiatric phenomena.

Working within a continental framework very similar to Casey's, Morley takes up the philosophical psychology of the French existential phenomenologist Maurice Merleau-Ponty. This essay explicates the centrality of imagination to Merleau-Ponty's theory of perception and, further, applies Merleau-Ponty's gestalt figure–ground framework to comprehending the confluence of both the imaginary–real and the pathological–nonpathological spectrums. According to Morley, Merleau-Ponty asserts that it is an act of *faith* which is precategorical to all experience and is thus equally foundational to both perceptual and imaginary acts of consciousness. From this, Morley argues that the imaginary and the real can never be perfectly severed from one another and that the attempt to do so is, in fact, pathology itself. Healthy-minded imagination, like wholesome perception, is tolerant of the ambiguously mixed nature of our human existence;

tradition of phenomenologically oriented philosophy. In tl
tion the imaginary is viewed rather negatively, "as either so
is entirely lacking in external reality, as something 'merely
as 'an image' which is meant to be a 'substitute' representat
re-presentation) of something externally real (or a combin
realities) which are nevertheless not 'really' present." From thi
based as it is on a correspondence theory of truth, pathologic
such as delusions and hallucinations are seen as subjective, or r
nomena that bear no correspondence to objective reality. In th
tion Hersch reminds us that for the empiricist tradition the ima
its "normal" presentation already deficient; in its pathologic pr
it is then deficient to a second degree. In his exposition of t
nental tradition Hersch focuses on Heidegger and the latter's noti
human being as essentially future directed. "We always 'pro-ject'
or 'throw ourselves forward in time' toward *anticipated future po*
Accordingly our initial apprehension of objects is to see them in t
their possible utility in providing what we seek." In this understan
the human being, imagination is, as it were, built in to our consti
That is, living toward the future "must be guided (consciously or n
our *imagination* (i.e., of what is not yet, but might become)." Since i
nation is part of the structure of consciousness, it cannot be seen as i
ently deficient. Further, treatment will not be focused on "tryin
exorcize the patient of the imaginary." Rather, it will take the approac
trying to understand the patient's projects, working out with the pat
what makes sense and what is pathologic or problematic.

Kearney's "Narrative and the Ethics of Remembrance" focuses
imagination in the form of narrative construction. Given the enormous ro
of narrative and narratology in contemporary discourse—whether literar
historical, or psychodynamic—and the fact that the subject is usually no
associated with the question of the imagination, this is a very timely piece
In a very subtle analysis, calling on a variety of literary examples, Kearney
makes a fundamental point—namely that while issues of "telling and not
telling," distortion of historical sequence, and even rank lying, are all part
and parcel of literary narrative, the same cannot be said of psychoanalytic
and historical narrative. In the latter areas the effort to make the narrative
correspond to reality *does* matter. "The moral implications of such an
imaginary/real distinction in the operation of narrative memory are crucial
not only for psychological cases of abuse but also for the more public and

it accommodates to a world that is never perfectly real or imaginary. It exhibits trust in the face of our ambiguous condition. Psychopathology, in this understanding, is itself a failure to sustain faith, trust, or belief in both the imaginary and the real as evidenced by a doomed striving for absolute certainty.

Pathologic Imagination and Psychodynamic Thought

The next section focuses in the interplay between the psychodynamic tradition and pathological imagination. As Laplanche and Pontalis note in their esteemed *Dictionary of Psychoanalysis*: "An explaination of ... the subject's fantasy life is precisely the goal to which Freud's efforts, and the efforts of psychoanalytic thought as a whole, are directed" (Laplanche and Pontalis 1973, 315). Certainly psychoanalysis is the psychiatric paradigm most concerned with the subject matter of imagination. Thus it should be no surprise that several of our authors have used that tradition as a backdrop to our topic. While none of the articles expound a commitment to orthodox or classical Freudian thought, they all present a fresh reading of the relation between contemporary psychoanalytic thought and the pathological imagination.

In relation to the other papers in this section, Ethel Person's "The Creative Role of Fantasy in Adaption" hues closest to traditional psychoanalysis. However, as her focus is on *conscious* fantasy as opposed to *unconscious* fantasy, she moves away from the traditional Freudian emphasis on fantasy as conflictual to a new emphasis on fantasy as creative and adaptive. She begins by noting that daydream fantasizing is "situated within the context of the imagination." Imagination is, however, the larger category. "Fantasizing is a unique kind of imagined thought that serves a psychological or emotional purpose rather than a primarily pragmatic one." In a first section she reviews some of the early history of psychoanalysis, explaining how, with the abandonment of the seduction theory of hysteria, Freud turned toward unconscious fantasy as the preferred territory of psychoanalytic exploration. The consequences of this were an emphasis on the connection between fantasy and psychic conflict, a loss of interest in conscious fantasy, and finally a disregard for the adaptive, nonconflictual uses of fantasy. When he did deal with conscious fantasy, Freud worked with two different models: a dream model, in which conscious fantasy remains tied to conflict, and a play model, in which Freud is able to recognize other functions of conscious fantasy. Person then offers a classification of conscious fantasies into transient daydreams, repeating fantasies, and generative fantasies. Finally, after illustrating her major points with fantasy case material from a particular patient, she ends the paper with an extended discussion of shared fantasies, especially those that are culturally transmitted.

In his "The Madonna Imago: A New Interpretation of its Pathology," Dillon serves a challenge to some key elements of Freud's understanding of infantile development and the role of the mother in that process. He points to two related doctrines that have a baleful influence on much of Freud's theory. The first is that of the mother as the first love object. The second is that of primary narcissism. Both presume a degree of separateness of mother and child that is not present in the earliest infancy. In an argument that is at once psychological and philosophical—and that does not admit of final direct adjudication, both because of infantile amnesia and because the reflective capacity of the infant-adjudicator is precisely what is in question—Dillon asserts that the mother is separate from the infant only from the point of view of an adult observer, and that she is more accurately described as "a global presence whose being is not yet distinct from the infant's own being." Similarly Dillon argues that the notion of primary narcissism—or any narcissism—is a metaphor that presupposes a degree of reflection of which the infant is not capable, reflection that involves a separation and a refinding of oneself in the other. Dillon then questions how Freud is able to develop the 'tender emotions' out of the self-seeking instincts with which the infant begins its life. Finding notions such as sublimation inadequate to this task, he proposes that if the earliest mother-infant relation is reframed as one of primordial indistinction or syncretism, Freud's problem tends to vanish. The tender emotions are now seen as a natural development out of the early syncretism. Reviewing further stages of the developmental process, Dillon shows how this reframing of the mother-infant relationship changes our view of adolescent and adult development. We should note that Dillon's interpretation of the maternal imago is consistent with some recent innovations of psychoanalytic theory: for instance, Winnicott's view of the mother-infant indistinction, as exemplified in his adage, "There is no such thing as a baby," and much recent work in interpersonal theory in psychoanalysis.

With Hansen's "The Impossibility of Female Mourning" we turn to the French psychoanalytic sphere, with a focus on Julia Kristeva and Luce Irigaray. Hansen approaches the subject of imagination from the insight enunciated by both Nietzsche and Freud that the only relief from the core pain of human existence is that offered by the imaginative productions of art. In their respective terms each describes the relief through art not as a resolution or overcoming but rather as a kind of narcosis. Hansen then moves to Kristeva for her reflection on the issue of pain and relief through art. Following Kristeva, she focuses on melancholia "as an archetypal manifestation of the subject's battle with suffering." Kristeva understands melancholia as a stemming from the primary loss of the early maternal love object. The melancholic spends his or her life longing for this lost, unnameable object. Later losses reopen the world of the primary loss. In contrast to Nietzsche and Freud, Kristeva views the work of art as more than a mere narcosis. She "sees the work of imaginative production as not merely numbing painful affect but effectively countering it. The work of art acts not as an 'antidepressant' which dulls affect but as a 'counterdepressant' which cures." The problem with Kristeva's theory, according to Hansen, is that she accepts Freud's position that women are less able to sublimate than are men. Thus the very group that is statistically more depressed has less access to the available resolution—or, to turn the same point around, there are more depressed women because of their failures in sublimation through imagination and art. Unsatisfied with Kristeva's gloomy conclusion, Hansen turns finally to another French psychoanalyst, Irigaray, who both adds the necessary sociological dimension to the discussion of women and depression and also calls for a rethinking of Freud's phallocentric view of feminine development.

Church in her "Depression, Depth, and the Imagination" begins in French phenomenology with Sartre and ends in French psychoanalysis with Kristeva. On the way she passes through German thought with Kant and Freud. In a paper that is resourceful in its integration of different sources (and that consequently could have been comfortably placed in the first section), she begins with a phenomenological description of depression, emphasizing the lack of spacial and temporal depth in the experience of the depressed individual. Asking the question how such experience—or lack of the usual experience of depth—is possible, she recognizes this as a "Kant-ian" question and notes that for Kant it is the imagination that effects the synthesis of experience. The depressive's failure to experience a world in depth is then seen as a failure of imagination. She then notes that this analysis leaves out the emotional dimension of depression, wondering then whether a Kantian analysis is satisfactory. Kant's third *Critique* is then evoked, with its emphasis on the free play of imagination in aesthetic appreciation. At this point in her train of thought Church turns to Freud for further illumination of her theme. She focuses on Freud's notion of sublimation as the way of coping with loss and failed desire, and she interprets sublimation as an exercise of the imagination. Now from a Freudian perspective, then, the depressive's failure to achieve a fully spacialized world is again seen as a failure of imagination. She turns finally to Kristeva's work on depression and describes, as in the previous paper, Kristeva's invocation, via art, of imagination as the most therapeutic response to depression. She concludes: "The parallels, then, between Kant, Freud, and Kristeva are notable. All three emphasize the importance of imagination in mediating not only sensibility and understanding ... but conscious and unconscious mind as well."

In the final chapter in this section, "The Unconscious as a Hermeneutic Myth: A Defense of the Imagination," Woody approaches the classical psychoanalytic unconscious from the perspective of imaginative thought as developed by the philosophers Ernst Cassirer and Suzanne Langer. Following the lead of those thinkers Woody makes a sharp distinction between verbal and nonverbal—or discursive and nondiscursive—forms of representation. He then focuses in on the psychoanalytic notion of the unconscious as an area in which the dialectic of the discursive and the nondiscursive/imaginary is played out. According to Woody, the psychoanalytic unconscious is a product of the "intentional fallacy"—that is, the effort to explain puzzling behavior or symptoms in the present by assuming "unconscious" intentions that exist in that black hole called the unconscious. It is the same fallacy that is at work in the misguided effort to "explain" the meaning of a poem or painting by reverting to the artist's intentions or biography. If, then, there is no unconscious, what are we left with? "What remains is the use of images, the metaphoric and metonymic allusions, the condensations and the overdetermination—and we can recognize all of these as functions that are characteristic of the *imagination*, that same imagination that is at work in the play of children, in fantasies, fairy tales and myths, and in the creation of works of art." The dream or symptom, then, like a work of art, rather than in need of interpretation/translation into discursive language, may be the most adequate (albeit imaginary, nondiscursive) representation of the emotional state of the patient. Woody does not dwell on the therapeutic implications of his analysis, although they are clearly present. The implied direction is toward less emphasis on the verbal dimension of psychotherapy and a greater emphasis on the creative use of imagination in therapy.

Pathologic Imagination Applied to Creative and Clinical Phenomena

The four papers in this section focus on specific cases and specific symptoms and conditions. They all demonstrate the complex tapestry through which imagination is woven into both symptom and treatment, and they all give ample evidence that viewing pathological phenomena as "faulty" imagination is a gross oversimplification. All four papers, not surprisingly, raise diagnostic issues as well as those of treatment. The first two are oriented toward phenomenological psychiatry; the second pair take a clinical perspective on creative and religious psychopathology.

In "A Phenomenological Psychological Approach to Research on Hallucinations" Giorgi confronts head-on the understanding of hallucinations that would follow from the Lockean, empiricist account. He begins with an autobiographical account of a schizophrenic who reports her therapist's saying, "You've gotten rid of major symptoms. You realize that you had schizophrenic hallucinations and that the Operators did not exist." Working out of the standard tradition, the therapist views his patient's hallucinations as products of deranged imagination. What is obvious to the therapist is not obvious to Giorgi. What is the patient seeing? A real thing not present? A quasi-thing? Giorgi goes on to "suggest that the very effort of trying to determine whether hallucinations are pathological manifestations of the imagination or distorted perceptions is already indicative of objective thought and thus operates on a level that will block a fully adequate understanding of the phenomenon of hallucinations. In opposition to the objectivist approach, Giorgi attempts to follow the phenomenological philosopher Merleau-Ponty in understanding hallucinations as operating at the level of pre-objective thought. At this level, when the focus is not just on the reality status of the hallucinatory phenomena, they may be viewed as 'presences' rather than as existences or realities. Further, for the patient to accept the presences as somehow 'real', the so-called real world must itself recede in the patient's experience. The patient is then living at a pre-objective level. The presences may be described further. Belonging to a quasi-world, "they are 'thin' in duration and in space; they lack the articulateness of the world that the real carries; they are short-lived; they are inarticulate phenomena that lack the relations of true causality and so on."

In Giorgi's (and Merleau-Ponty's) account of hallucinations imagination is clearly present, but it is not that stripped-down version we are familiar with in the empiricist account. Imagination is here at the same time pathologic and creative, deficient and productive.

In "Narrative in Play: Structures of Imagination in Psychotherapy with Young Children" Robert Kruger explores the clinical value of conceptualizing the various way young children structure their play as narratives and how psychopathology can be treated through these narratives. By developing an understanding of the phenomenological elements of symbolic (pretend) play and how these are organized into stories, the child therapist can fashion a powerful tool for enabling children to come to terms with conflict and trauma. Kruger argues that a case can be made for viewing all symbolic play as a pastiche of stories which, much like dreams, fairy tales, thematize the currently salient wishes, worries, and concerns of the young child. He points out, however, that in psychotherapy sessions, unlike in novels, these tales are usually not overtly articulated but simply acted out. It is the therapist's job to assist in putting words to the flow of the child's playful actions, thereby placing them in a perspective that permits alternative stories to be told. It is these alternatives, structured and restructured through the therapist's interpretations and questions, that help the child to resolve anxieties and conflicts, thus diminishing pathological symptoms. Kruger develops his theme more theoretically by applying the analytic tools of linguistics to therapeutic narrative, and he illustrates his points finally with actual case material.

The final two papers of this section explore the complex relationship between pathologic imagination and creative and religious expression. Taking examples from across history and culture, one examines the psychotic break of one of the most famous artists of the early twentieth century, the second focuses upon one of the most important mystics of the early Christian church.

In their paper, "On the Dialectics of Imagination: Nijinsky's Sublime Defeat," Sauvayre and Forbes discuss the question of pathologic and creative imagination in the case of Vaslav Nijinsky, the great ballet dancer who shocked the art world when forced to retire at the peak of his career due to schizophrenia. Viewing creative imagination in terms of a dialectical tension between raw emotion and symbolic expression, they consider successful artistic expression to be dependent on a balance of the two poles. "The creative movement is lost whether the mind's collapse is into the realm of cold logic and secondary process ... or into the raw unformulated world of primary process." Vaslav Nijinsky illustrates both the creative tension as well as its collapse into madness. In this study they analyze in detail both phases of Nijinsky's life, and at the same time they raise and discuss the larger question: whether there is an natural or necessary correlation between madness and creativity. In the terms of their discussion this question is whether the creative balance between primary and secondary process renders the artist, as the individual who is more in touch with the former than most of us, more vulnerable to psychosis.

In "Was St. Anthony Crazy? The Visionary Experiences and the Desert Fathers," Greg Mahr transports us into another historical epoch, that of the early Medieval Europe. Focusing on Athanasius's *Life of St. Anthony*, he takes up the visionary experiences of the desert fathers of the fourth-century Egypt. Known as the "athletes of God," these men who abandoned urban life for a life of solitude and prayer were admired for their great capacities for fasting and continuous prayer. Mahr describes the visionary experiences of Anthony as what we would clearly call hallucinations. For example, Anthony and his fellow monks wrote copiously of their battles with seemingly 'imaginary' adversaries comprised of devils and demons. He then develops an elaborate analysis of these phenomena from a contemporary psychiatric perspective by interpreting them as "culture-bound" hallucinations that can be distinguished from the hallucinations seen in schizophrenia and mania. He concludes that such culture-bound hallucinations are powerful experiences that can be turned in both creative and destructive directions.

Notes

1. Rosen takes his account from Douglas M. Johnson (1945, 175–186).

2. Kearney writes: "Basil Willey informs us: 'Locke's philosophy was the philosophy of an age whose whole effort had been to arrive at 'truth' by exorcising the phantoms of imagination, and the truth standards which the eighteenth century inherited through him involved the relegation of the mind's shaping power to an inferior status.' So wary was Locke of the irrationalist effects of imagination on the scientific ideal that in his *Thoughts concerning Education*, he actually counselled all parents who discovered a 'fanciful vein' in their children to 'stifle and suppress it as much as may be.' The romantic poets who came after Locke were, not surprisingly, quite enraged by his attitude. Blake accused him of 'petrifying all the Human Imagination into Rock and Sand'; Coleridge of reducing the mind to a cold mechanism; and pursuing this romantic legacy of denunciation, Yeats would later claim that 'Locke took away the world and gave us its excrement instead'" (Kearney 1988, 164).

3. "Drawing upon John Locke's theory of the workings of the human understanding, such reformers characteristically stressed that the madman was not utterly bereft of reasoning power (such was the idiot); nor had his reason been totally destroyed by the anarchy of the passions. Rather he was a creature in whom the faulty associating of ideas and feelings in the mind had led to erroneous conclusions about reality and proper behaviour. Madness was thus essentially delusion, and delusion sprang from intellectual error. Mad people were trapped in fantasy worlds, all too frequently the outgrowth of unbridled imagination. They needed to be treated essentially like children, who required a stiff dose of rigorous mental discipline, rectification and retraining in thinking and feeling. The madhouse should thus become a reform school" (Porter 1987, 19).

4. The episode is related in Rosen (1968, 21–37).

References

American Psychiatric Association. 1994. *Diagnostic and Statistical Manual of Mental Disorders*, 4th ed. Washington, DC: American Psychiatric Association Press.

Cassirer, E. 1942. *An Essay on Man*. New Haven: Yale University Press.

Cassirer, E. 1955. *The Philosophy of Symbolic Forms: Mythical Thought*, vol. 2. New Haven: Yale University Press.

Heaney, S., trans. 1983. *Sweeney Astray: A Version from the Irish by Seamus Heaney*. New York: Farrar Straus Giroux.

Johnson, D. M. 1945. The "phantom anesthetist" of Mattoon: A field study of mass hysteria. *Journal of Abnormal and Social Psychology* 40: 175–86.

Kearney, R. 1988. *The Wake of Imagination: Toward a Postmodern Culture*. Minneapolis: University of Minnesota Press.

Laplanche, J., and J.-B. Pontalis. 1973. *Dictionary of Psychoanalysis*. London: Hogarth Press.

Locke, J. [1689] 1959. *Essay concerning Human Understanding*. New York: Dover, book II, chapter XI.

Porter, R. 1987. *A Social History of Madness: The World through the Eyes of the Insane*. New York: Weidenfeld and Nicolson.

Rosen, G. 1968. *Madness in Society: Chapters in the Historical Sociology of Mental Illness*. New York: Harper Torchbooks.

Simon, B. 1978. *Mind and Madness in Ancient Greece: The Classical Roots of Modern Psychiatry*. Ithaca: Cornell University Press.

I

Pathologic Imagination in the Light of Philosophic Reflection

Imagination: Looking in the Right Place (and in the Right Way)

Paul B. Lieberman

The title and much of the inspiration for this essay are taken from a paper of Cora Diamond's entitled "Rules: Looking in the Right Place" (1989). In that paper, Diamond discusses ideas summarized by Ludwig Wittgenstein's remark that we should not look for the meanings of words but for their uses. She cites, in this same vein, a remark of Rush Rhees that "rules of grammar are rules of the lives in which there is language" (12–34).

What I think Diamond is pointing to in Wittgenstein's philosophy is this. We tend to have the following idea about the meanings of words: there are objects, call them meanings, that are what the word refers to. These objects or meanings are held by us in our minds. They are the mental objects that correspond to objects in the ordinary sense in the world. Propositions are made up of combinations of these mental objects. And when the combinations in the mind correspond to the states of affairs in the world, then the meanings refer and the propositions are true.

Now, since Wittgenstein, this model has seemed unsatisfactory, in part because of his having shown that it cannot explain what we wish it to explain, namely how words mean or refer to things. The reason it cannot explain this is that no object, inner or mental, can automatically refer to anything. The meanings must be actively related to the objects, and there are always an infinite number of ways in which such inner objects or meanings can be projected onto, or related to, the world. What singles out the "right" projection must itself be an intentional act, and this seems to presuppose the connection between meaning and object meant, which is to be explained (Wittgenstein 1969).

Thus, since Wittgenstein, we have been more apt to say that the way in which meaning "happens" is that our forms of life, our behaviors and practices, are what determine meanings, not the having of inner ideas in the head. Put in somewhat different terms, we are now apt to talk about "assertability conditions": if we are in particular circumstances and use words in their commonly accepted ways, they thereby have our common meanings and we are warranted in using them. We all participate in the shared language games that make these uses correct. So, instead of correlating words with objects in the head, we correlate them with practices and with assertability conditions.

This is the view that Diamond believes to be widely held of Wittgenstein, for example, by Saul Kripke. It is, however, a view that Diamond believes to misrepresent what Wittgenstein was really interested in and really doing. It is also, as Rhees put it, to miss the *philosophy* of Wittgenstein.

Instead, Diamond suggests: don't look for the assertability conditions, don't look for what gives us the right to use words as we do, don't look to ground or found words on sets of external behavioral criteria. Instead, look at how we actually use words. For example, don't look for the external behavioral conditions that give us the grounding or justification for saying that it is now 3 o'clock—the operational definition, as if Wittgenstein were a verificationist. As Diamond notes (1991), Wittgenstein is not a verificationist because he is not giving an analysis either of what words mean or what justifies someone in claiming to speak correctly (in both cases the verificationist answer would be: following our commonly accepted patterns of behavior). Instead, look at the many things we actually do concerning clocks and time: coordinate our activities, mark the starts and ends of events, measure our ages and correlate these with things that to happen to us, and so on.

Now, what we seem to lose by this external referentiality seems to be immense: we seem to lose, as it were, the fact of time itself, the essence of time. It is as if there were some central fact about time—the fact that makes our assertions about time meaningful and true—and we are simply overlooking it. We are, it seems, talking about incidentals, whereas what we seem to want to do is, as Wittgenstein says, to "penetrate phenomena," to get at their core and, as it were, nail them in place. But this, I believe, Diamond is saying, is what Wittgenstein is saying we must give up.

What we gain by giving this up is a new attention to what is already before our eyes but which, it seems, we tend to ignore: our verbal and nonverbal practices, forms of life, language games. The picture of meaning has held us captive. Freed from it, we may be more able to see our lives more clearly.

Now, for Wittgenstein, and for Diamond, it is philosophers who are limited by misleading pictures of how the mind is related to other aspects of reality. But, I would like to suggest, it is also a problem for patients and for clinicians. There are many times in the course of treatment, in the course of thinking about ourselves and our patients, when we come upon problems that are really forms or instances of philosophical problems and when we, as clinicians, can be in the state philosophers come to when looking for inner meanings or for assertability conditions, trying to attach them to our words and when they, and we, would do better to give up asking that type of question, and to look at actual practices—how words weave their way through our complicated forms of life.

A set of such philosophical moments or intrusions into clinical work arises, I think, around issues of imagining, imagination, and imaginary and related concepts such as belief. These words and the situations in which we use them can involve us in certain intellectual paralyses that are very similar to those of philosophers. I believe that an analysis of the sort Diamond proposes, for such words as "imagination," "imaginary," and "imagine" may help us in clinical situations. It may help both by orienting us to clinical phenomena that can be difficult to appreciate or understand, and by supplying therapeutic tools.

To provide a point of reference, I would like to sketch briefly a case in which imagination appears to play an overly prominent, in fact psychotic, role.

The patient was a single woman in her late twenties. She had a history of two prior psychotic episodes and was most probably suffering from schizophrenia, paranoid type, although she had graduated from college, was a talented artist, interested in people (though she had trouble understanding them), and had a depressive rather than predominantly odd or "blunted" affect. She was now, having tapered her antipsychotic medication and recently having had several stressful encounters with old friends, heading rapidly into another period of psychosis.

One afternoon, she told me, she left her house to sit alongside a stream nearby. When her mother came out to ask what she was doing, the patient replied that she was, "looking at the frogs and fish." That night, when she was getting ready for bed, the patient noticed that, somehow, a frog had actually made its way into her room. This apparently really happened, according to her mother.

The patient took this incident to show that someone, having somehow read her mind or overheard her comment earlier that day, had deliberately put the frog into her house. She did not think that the only person who might really have done this, her mother, would do such an odd thing. Rather, she believed that this was some kind of message—or, perhaps, a sign that forces outside of herself were signalling to her and preparing to send her messages in some other way.

When I suggested, in a session later that week, that the frog's appearance could more plausibly be understood as a coincidence—admittedly a strange and even eerie one—the patient considered this possibility but could not accept it. It still seemed more likely to her that encrypted messages and occult forces were about.

This, I believe, is the moment at which the clinical situation becomes a philosophical one. The patient believes that someone put the frog in her room. The therapist thinks that her belief is imagination. This can easily deteriorate into a (more or less subtle) confrontation: each person trying to convince the other of his or her correctness. That would be the clinical example of trying to satisfy Cartesian doubt, trying to separate dream from reality, trying, in other words, to find criteria or assertability conditions that would make (prove) one's position impregnable.

But, if Diamond is right, this task is misconceived. It is the wrong activity in which we should be engaging. What we should be doing, instead, is trying to clarify, put into perspective, and develop a perspicuous representation of the many, varied roles of imagination and imaginary activity in our lives. As Diamond points out, this appears to be simply changing the question and ignoring the core problem. Yet, if Diamond and Wittgenstein are right, this change of activity—what, I think, Stanley Cavell (1979) is also referring to when he talks of leading our words back from their metaphysical to their ordinary uses—is what should be done to help.

Now, when we say that this person—that anyone—is imagining, what kind of phenomena are we talking about and in what way(s), and for what purposes are we talking about them?

First, I think, as this example illustrates, when we say someone is imagining, we are saying that they are 'seeing things' in situations, or drawing inferences about situations (interpreting them), or reacting to situations as if there were elements in them that are not believed/thought by others to 'really be' in those situations currently. This is true not only in cases where imagination seems to be false—as in this clinical example—but in situations where it is neutral (e.g., as when I think of someone or something not now here) and even when it is inspired (e.g., as Galileo's imagining, correctly, that shadows on the telescopic image of the moon represented mountains—and implied a new world view).

Thus, imagining shares features of perception and, typically of seeing, in that it seems to present us with a kind of information about the world (e.g., in contrast to experiencing feelings or sensations). Imagination refers to things in the world.

We use terms like "accurate," "vivid," and "lively" to characterize someone's imagination—depending on how convincing or detailed or realistic their reports are of what they imagine. We speak of seeing in the imagination, seeing in the mind's eye, imagining clearly or dimly— expressions that all analogize imagining to perceiving.

Wittgenstein emphasized that what is imagined, as well as what is seen, share the important feature that each can be represented by a picture (Wittgenstein 1980, 13–28). In other words, imagination, in contrast, per- haps, to feeling or thinking or believing, is part of a network of activities that includes picturing—and this would seem to imply that we imagine from a particular point of view, and also that we simply do present or rep- resent what we imagine in visual terms.

This quality of imagination as seeming—like perception—to inform us about the world is also shown by our characterization of what is "in" the imagination, or the imaginary, as passively appearing to us: an image pops into my mind, I can't stop seeing it. Conversely, I may try to imagine something and fail. Even when someone, for example, when instructed to imagine a scene or person (e.g., in therapy) tries and succeeds in doing so, he does not "feel himself to have" full control over what the content of his image is. If I imagine, for example, my old home, then, I want to say, the content of the image, "what it looks like," is determined not by me but by the home itself.

Not only can we think of what we imagine as appearing to us, or not fully under our control. There is also the experience that what is imag- ined has an inevitability, a logic of its own: even when we recognize that something is an image or imaginary, it still has a power; "it" leads us along. Musical expressions, conversation or the unfolding of a play or movie illustrate this logic. Often the logic will only be recognized when a sequence of notes, ideas, or plot twists has occurred. Is this pattern in the creation or in us? Meyer Shapiro writes of our imagination being "satisfied" (1996). If we think of this satisfaction as a function of the appropriate completion of what is in the imagined external world, then we are capable of appreciating the logic. If we think of the satisfaction as due to our natures, then it is an objective fact about us. Either way imagination can, it seems, pull us along; it has a power in it (though one we can resist or ignore or turn away from).

Finally, imagination, like perception, tends to support belief. If I am imagining something, then I am tending, on that basis, to believe it (though I may not, in fact, believe it). If I cannot imagine something, on the contrary, then, on that basis, I tend not to believe it. For example, I cannot imagine how a frog could be produced in someone's bedroom, or why, or what message was being meant, or how a mind could be read. My conceptions of the world are limited: I cannot imagine this to be happening. But another person might; my patient did, or seemed to. As we will discuss, however, I can believe that she is not really imagining, not really forming any clear conception of what she thinks she imagines.

But, although there are such analogies between the ways in which we think about imagination and the ways in which we think about perception, especially seeing, there are also a number of differences. Imagination, as shown in the clinical example, involves selective attention to and interpretation of what is perceived. It is not just seeing but "seeing as"—that is, interpreting or reading a situation in a certain, but not inevitable, way. Wittgenstein emphasized that imagination does not provide us with information about the world. We cannot imagine what we are now, currently, perceiving. We cannot see an object that is in front of our eyes *as* that very object. The reason he says this seems to have to do, precisely, with the fact that while what is imagined does have a certain tenacity or power, we can modify what we imagine. We can, at least, fight against the intrusion of imaginary thoughts and images. This fighting against indicates, according to Wittgenstein, that imagination is subject to the will in ways in which perception is not, and therefore that imagination precisely does not inform us about reality.

Additionally imagination differs from perceiving in the ways in which the language games of each are played and extended. Seeing is connected with looking: leaning forward, outlining, and pointing. Imagining, by contrast, is usually connected with telling. When I wish to share what I imagine, I may try to describe it more clearly and vividly, find analogies, suggest similarities, ask you to "picture yourself" in my position. In the theater, in children's play (Winnicott 1971), in conversation, and in the psychotherapeutic situation (Loewald 1980), sharing one's imagination with someone else involves participation in these ways rather than observation.

Participation in these circumstances—children's play, conversation, theater, and therapy—involves a willingness to focus on certain features of the situation and to ignore others. Imagination and sharing of what is imaged often require ignoring limitation.

Thus imagination shares features with perceiving but also diverges from it. Additionally, I think, a number of features of imagination— features of the language games in which "imagination" is used—suggest that imaginary activities and "products" are both personal and external, simultaneously.

Imagination has the characteristic feature that it "belongs" to the person doing the imagining. What contrasts it from perception is that what is "seen" or believed to be in a situation is exactly not what other people would, ordinarily, agree was in the situation. Instead, there is an element that is introduced by the person doing the imagining.

But there is an important *quality* to this 'element' which is 'introduced into' or 'seen in' the situation by the person who is imagining. This quality is that the person often both recognizes that this image or interpretation or way of seeing the situation is coming from himself—recognizes, that is, that others may not and perhaps usually will not agree that it is in the situation, or see it in the situation—and yet believes that he is 'more right,' seeing more accurately or fully than the consensual interpretation. Imagination thus can seem to provide a view or understanding of the world that, while personal and recognized as not readily acceptable to others, is yet more true, in the sense of giving an understanding or insight about the world felt to be important, enriching, organizing of experience, or even deeply meaningful. This characteristic of imagination—that it seems to be at once personally introduced into the situation and yet really to be there and to be deeply meaningful—is marked in a number of ways.

One is in our attitudes toward showing or telling people what we imagine. This attitude is often highly ambivalent: we want to show or tell because we have discovered something important, yet we don't want to show or tell because we "know" that other people will or may fail to appreciate what we have seen, fail to have an appropriate reaction, or even criticize us as "just imagining," having "let our imagination run away with us," and so on.

Wittgenstein emphasized that we tend to tell people our dreams. Even when we withhold telling, we still feel there is something to be told, therefore to be shared. He does not, as far as I know, elaborate on why this tendency is worth mentioning, but one explanation is that he is pointing out this quality of the imagination: that it is recognized to be both private, or at least personal, in myself, and also to have meaning that can be shown, shared, and that will be more generally interesting. We take an interest in our dreams. In dreams, for example, what is illuminated is not 'only' something about my personal psychology or history but something remarkable about the ways in which the mind works—that it can refer to history, for example, in these persistent but disguised ways and therefore that, as it were, imagination is everywhere. This is clearly also true in the theater, where imaginary works can inform and deepen our experience. Even children's play can throw into relief features embodied by the games themselves: heroism, action, creativity, adventure, noise, and so on.

The fact that we are interested in what we imagine, that it is natural to tell what is in the imagination is an indication that imagination seems to show us something important. It is worth telling about. Telling, or speaking, implies an intention to make oneself understood, or known, thus to be heard and acknowledged. The fact that it is natural to tell what we imagine therefore shows that we wish it to be acknowledged—therefore that we believe that it has a wider sphere of interest than just myself.

There are other ways in which imagination occupies an ambiguous position between what is subjective—what is brought to situations by the person—and what is objective—what is really there. An examination of what is imagined can show something about how subjective and objective are distinguished.

One such feature of imagination involves the area of authority or ownership for what is imagined. And this, in turn, leads to the ways in which issues of interpersonal authority and credentials are interwoven into our practices involving the imagination.

Consider the question of who decides whether or what someone is imagining, or whether it is true. When I express pain, for example, there is usually no question that I have felt it. Similarly, when I report a dream, there is no question: I am the final authority. No one else is entitled to tell me what, at least on a manifest level, I dreamt.

By contrast, there are also clearly times when I can be shown not to be imagining what I say I am imagining. I may not (really) be imagining anything at all. This could occur, for example, when I say I am imagining something which is impossible: a round square, for example, or a "private language" whose words refer to sensations only experienced by me. I can also be corrected: I say I am imagining a particular event or person but, from my description, it is apparent to someone else that I am wrong: it is another event or person, or I am imagining it or them inaccurately. To make this kind of correction of me requires that you have certain credentials. Typically, when you correct my report—"You are not imagining A (your birthday party) but B (Christmas)"—you can say this based on the fact that, for example, you were there, so you can recognize my description. You can, in this example, again, typically by further description or by narration, show me wherein I am wrong. Interestingly it seems this kind of dialogue can occur even when the person or event is unreal, that is, truly imaginary. For example, "I can just imagine what it would be like to win the lottery." "Oh, no, you just think you can imagine that. Really: it would be beyond your wildest dreams," or "Really: there would be complications you never thought of." And here, again, more description is offered.

A similar kind of dialogue, with similar interactions around authority, evidence, and credentials can go on in discussing delusions, or neurotic beliefs. Whether I am really imagining anything at all, the content of what I am imagining, and whether what I am imagining is true are all subject to this kind of dialogue or conversation. And this conversation has generally accepted rules: rules for demonstrating, elaborating, describing, claiming to have credentials, trying to put oneself in another person's place or frame of mind, providing a wider context, giving examples. And there seem to be interconnections among these several questions: not only that if I *cannot* imagine something, then I *am* not, but also, as we already noted, if I am imagining it, then I am tending, on that basis, to believe it (though I am not necessarily believing it). Many such conversations, however, will be inconclusive. There do not seem to be preordained, guaranteed points at which agreement must occur.

The clinical/philosophical point, I think, is this: as a therapist, I recognize the kind of activity that discussing imagination is. I appreciate the issues of agreement and authority, credentials and convincingness, that are involved. I remember that it is not appropriate, that it can be hurtful, to invoke such authority when invited to participate in the games of children—and that, in adults too, the products of the imagination are invested, by the person whose imagination it is, with value. That is to say, the world can be seen in this certain way, and reporting it has some, not merely personal, value or importance. Questions of proof do not always arise. Rather it is a question of developing, incorporating, and sublimating those forms of life into others which are "more realistic." In this way, as in others as we have seen, the sharp contrast between what is imagined and what is real is not established more clearly but dissolved. We may also need to remember that attributing something to the imagination can be reassuring, and that failing to accept reassurance can be the heavy price paid for maintaining one's conviction.

To try and summarize this brief analysis. We tend to have an idea—what I think Wittgenstein would call a picture—of what imagining or imagination is. According to this picture, imagining is having an idea or belief, perhaps an inner picture, in the mind. It may or may not correspond to reality. But it is created by the subject, and it exists in his or her mind, independently of whether it so corresponds—as a picture can exist that is not a picture of anything.

But when we look at how we use these words, what we find are complex relationships between subjective and objective, inner and outer, personal and consensual. It is true that we do (can)not imagine what we are currently perceiving. But drawing or finding the boundary of each co-determines the other. What I think is possible or real determines whether I believe someone (else) is imagining, what content I can accept (their) imagination as containing, and whether that imagination corresponds to reality. The process of finding this boundary follows a grammar of authority, credentials, evidence, convincing. But it may and often will not be settled conclusively. Imagination has qualities of perceiving—a logic seemingly residing in it, a power to convince or tendency to produce belief, the property of being able to be represented by a picture, the capacity to put us into contact with (giving us access to, or informing us about) important, true, or meaningful aspects (ways of viewing) the world. Yet imagination also has an important personal element that distinguishes it from seeing or other forms of perceiving: we acknowledge that others may not 'see'

Similarities to perceiving	Informs about reality
	Uses visual terminology (e.g., imagines clearly)
	Can be pictured
	Perspectival
	Seems to arise externally
	Has 'power' to influence belief
	Has 'logic' independent of the imaginer supports belief
Dissimilarities to perceiving	Is nonconsensual, 'in' the person
	Draws attention to selective features
	Cannot be currently perceived
	Does not inform about reality
	Is subject to the will
	Is not clarified by looking but by telling more analogy, describing wider context and participation
Other features as a 'bridging' or 'transition' concept	Seems in subject and in world simultaneously
	Is 'personal' yet convincing
	Involves the natural role of telling/ sharing what is imagined
	Can give insight, depth, meaning to (as if: in) external reality
	Is authorized by interpersonal, not internal standards
	Provides 'conclusions' that are not inevitable
	Invites participation

Figure 1.1
Some features of imagination

(imagine) as we do; we do not share an image by looking or visually focusing but by other means: describing, suspending disbelief, telling stories, offering analogies, inviting participation.

Imagination thus plays varied roles in our lives. It involves ways of relating oneself to the world—for example, by emphasizing aspects of it, or orienting oneself to the world. Imagination is a form of connection that melds inner, personal experiences and external reality. It involves certain kinds of relationships to other people. A comment of Luis Bunuel's presents some similar sentiments, I think:

Our imagination and our dreams are forever invading our memories; and since we are all apt to believe in the reality of our fantasies, we end up transforming our lies into truths. Of course fantasy and reality are equally personal and equally felt, so their confusion is matter of only relative importance (cited by Diamond 1989).

To conclude, then, let us return to the clinical example presented earlier and ask: How would Wittgenstein's philosophy, applied to imagination, help orient us to this patient? Could a Wittgensteinian interest in how the "phenomena of imagination" are woven into her life affect the clinical approach we might take?

If we are influenced by the kind of analysis of imagination I have tried to outline, we will, I think, tend to increase our attention to the "fine shades of behavior" that indicate the presence and action of imagination weaving through the life of the person. What is imagined is a kind of seeing that seems both 'in' the world and 'read into' the world. It has a power to convince, and a logic to which it adheres. It tends to support belief, although both the imagining person and others may admit that only she or a few other like-minded people will accept as true what is being imagined. What is imagined says something that the imagining person recognizes to be unusual about her/himself but that she would also like to claim as being something important and something worth telling others about. Imagination involves a *commitment* by this person to ways of seeing and thinking about the world: what she imagines commits her to beliefs about what is true and false, possible and impossible. Such imagined beliefs are therefore embedded within a web or net of other beliefs, as Wittgenstein and many other contemporary philosophers have emphasized.

This catalog of putative facts about our concept of imagination does not include truth conditions or assertability conditions for identifying when imagining is going on, or how it can reliably be distinguished from accurate perception or belief about reality. And this important lack may lead to our first, concrete, clinical conclusion: following this analysis will tend to direct our clinical orientation *away* from one common attitude toward delusional, or imaginary, beliefs—an attitude that might be paraphrased as wanting to say to the patient, "This belief you have is false. You would be better off not believing it." Whereupon, in the clinical situation, there usually follows various efforts, pharmacological and psychotherapeutic, to 'get' the patient to abandon the belief that seems to be so harmful to him or her. Even if that is not the explicit focus of treatment, it is usually an implicit goal. Symptom checklists, for example, used to assess severity of psychopathology, will ask about the presence or absence or degree of delusional beliefs.

But, since this analysis does not include criteria for telling when beliefs are imaginary as opposed to true, it will, I think, tend to focus the clinician's attention in other directions. For example, the clinician will recognize that what is imagined may not have any clear identifying marks that distinguish it from what is truly known or believed. Thus, even if I do not agree with my patient, concretely it may be helpful (because true to our mutually shared understanding of the grammar of imagination) simply to admit this. I may have to acknowledge that I cannot provide a basis for my contrary belief, nor even convincing refutation of hers.

Such an admission of humility may go even further: because imagination seems to come to us from outside of the sphere of our conscious control and because it typically has a logic or power that inheres in it, the therapist may actually have to acknowledge and accept the power of the imaginary, even while she is also turning her face against it as an object of true belief.

Holding what others believe to be imaginary or delusional beliefs says a great deal about how the individual thinks the world is, but it is a viewpoint that, she recognizes full well, others probably will not share. And yet, to her, it is often what is most important that other people recognize and agree to. The imaginary, delusional beliefs are thus ones that she wants to tell. If so, then what seems to be the usual, paranoid behavior of withholding important information should not be taken for granted but should be seen as a sign of something requiring further explanation, such as additional motives (others will think she's crazy) or the expenditure of extra effort (perhaps related to the tension, strain, and irritability which are often part of paranoid individuals' social lives). Having delusional beliefs thus puts someone in a very particular kind of relationship to others. Imagination has a lot to teach us about the roles of conviction, consensus, authority, and interpersonal dependency in our lives as speakers and makers of judgments. Awareness of these dimensions of the grammar of imagination, its roles and rules in our lives, may be clinically useful. The paranoid person, in her relationships to others, is assured, insecure, suspicious, grandiose, isolated, and comforted by the special knowledge which she has. And each quality in this list may call for particular reciprocal responses from the clinician.

In considering more carefully our criteria for imagination, the clinician may also recognize that her patient may be seeing possible connections in the world of which she has never even thought (never even imagined, as we say). The clinician then may be led to *appreciate* several other related facts: one is the nature and extent of the patient's imagination, in a positive sense. This woman, for example, was a highly skilled photographer. Her mind was imaginative. The nature of an individual's imaginativeness may depend on his or her skills or talents: one person imagines visually or narratively, another (e.g., some paranoid people who have training in the natural sciences or engineering) may imagine mechanisms or may borrow concepts from science to explain experience in unusual and novel ways. Recognizing, appreciating, acknowledging, and enjoying these skills will influence the clinician's feeling about the patient. And a clinician so influenced will react to the patient differently from one who is not so impressed.

What an individual imagines will say something, perhaps a lot, about the kind of world s/he inhabits. For example, it may be a world in which minds can be read, or messages left by unseen individuals or groups. This is, of course, to see *intention* in situations where others would only recognize coincidence (if they thought about it at all). It is to see caring activities and examples of human purpose in facts where many other people would not. But, again to refer to the person in our example, it is an unusually indirect kind of action and caring, even if it is benevolent, as in this patient's case (she believed that people were sending her messages to help her in various ways). The clinician may then discuss with the patient, What is it like to live in a world like that? How does one cope? Could it be otherwise?

In listing possible clinical implications of the grammatical analysis of imagination proposed here, we have tried to rely only on those features of imagination that are widely accepted and known by all—parts of its grammar, the rules of life in which imaginative activities play a part. If the grammatical analysis is accurate, the clinical implications of it arise directly from our ordinary criteria for using words or concepts for imagination, imagined, imaginary, belief, and so on. This ordinariness is part of the strength of the criteria, and therefore part of the strength of the clinical interventions based on those criteria. Both patient and clinician will, if the analysis is correct, agree upon the criteria, will mutually acknowledge and agree on the "rules of life" within which imagination, belief, and related concepts are used. This may provide a mutually agreed-upon basis for patient and clinician to begin to talk to one another, about, among many other things, the patient's imaginary beliefs.

Finally, let us consider what often seems the central fact about the imagination, which we have so far not considered directly—its content. After all, what seems most important about this patient's imagination is the fact that she believes *that others are sending her messages in strange and uncanny ways*. In contrast with this troubling belief or perception, paying attention to formal or grammatical attributes of imagination (how it is and is not like seeing, what it says about the world the subject inhabits, how it throws into relief certain issues regarding conviction, authority, community, etc.) may appear a very abstract and intellectualized activity.

But it need not be. When, for example, the clinician admits her inability to prove her own position, or to dissuade the patient from hers, but admits, as well, the logic and power of the imaginary, she is forming a human tie based upon acknowledgment of our shared judgments and mutual limitations. Such admission shares and joins the patient's inevitable mixture of doubt and conviction. Drawing out the implications of an imaginary belief—and, thereby, articulating the world in which such a belief is embedded—is also a sharing and joining. What the clinician and patient participate in, in these situations, are kinds of relationships in which the focus of their shared attention is imagination itself: the public and personal, cognitive, emotional and volitional characteristics that are phenomena of imagination.

This shared attention and interest has, at least, two possible therapeutic implications that address the issue of the troubling delusional content. First, within the relationship, the patient may be led to develop new interests, "routes of feeling," and attachments. She is led out from the isolating, imaginary preoccupation into a shared, if tenuous, relationship with someone else. She may not "give up" any beliefs, but other interests may assume new importance, take more of the center of the stage—such as the interest, shared with the clinician, of acknowledging the workings of such psychological concepts as imagination and belief.

Second, as she, for example, comes to appreciate and accept the groundlessness of her beliefs, of beliefs in general, she may come, naturally, as a normal human reaction, to turn toward and welcome the importance of shared beliefs, community, acceptance of our public criteria. This may feel, to the patient, like a giving up of something (her imaginary, important belief). She is apt to feel that acceptance of shared standards and rules is a shaky basis for belief. Is truth really just a matter of our agreement in judgment? But, though inconclusive, such a resting point may be good enough: a tenuous, but examined and accepted connection to others.

In such encounters, perhaps, Wittgenstein's claim that philosophy is a kind of therapy may be made good.

References

Cavell, S. 1979. *The Claim of Reason*. New York: Oxford University Press.

Diamond, C. 1989. Rules: Looking in the right place. In D. Z. Phillips and P. Winch, eds., *Wittgenstein: Attention to Particulars*. New York: St. Martin's Press, pp. 12–34.

Diamond, C. 1991. Realism and the realistic spirit. In C. Diamond, ed., *The Realistic Spirit*. Cambridge: MIT Press, pp. 39–72.

Loewald, H. 1980. Psychoanalysis as an art and the fantasy character of the psychoanalytic situation. In H. Loewald, ed., *Papers on Psychoanalysis*. New Haven: Yale University Press, pp. 352–71.

Shapiro, M. 1996. *Words, Script and Pictures: Semiotics of Visual Language*. New York: Braziller.

Winnicott, D. W. 1971. *Playing and Reality*. London: Tavistock.

Wittgenstein, L. 1969. *Philosophical Investigations*. Translated by G. E. M. Anscombe. New York: Macmillan.

Wittgenstein, L. 1980. *Remarks on the Philosophy of Psychology*. Translated by C. G. Luckhardt and M. A. E. Aue. Edited by G. H. von Wright and H. Nyman. Chicago: University of Chicago Press.

2

Imagination and Its Pathologies: Domain of the Unreal or a Fundamental Dimension of Human Reality?

Edwin L. Hersch

Varying concepts of "imagination" occur in both everyday language and in clinical usage. It is sometimes seen positively as in "creative imagination" and sometimes negatively as in "it's only in your imagination." Likewise it can be seen as describing a particular *domain* or zone of our experience characterized primarily as one of unreality, fiction, and falsehood, or, alternatively, as an existential *dimension* of our being, namely an essential aspect inherent to all of human reality. It is here argued that these differing notions of imagination reflect two distinct sets of philosophical positions differing from each other at quite fundamental levels. These each have their characteristic implications for our understanding and approach to the definitions and treatment of the "pathological" manifestations of the imagination as well.

This author has previously described a method of analyzing psychological theories in which we begin by trying first to address their most fundamental or foundational philosophical assumptions and then proceed "upwardly" through a series of hierarchical "levels of theoretical inquiry" including the ontological, epistemological, and psychological levels (each of which remains grounded upon the former; Hersch 1996, 2001, 2003). This method will here be used to explicate the two understandings of imagination described above. A brief summary of this approach is illustrated by figures 2.1 and 2.2.

Using this method of theory illustration and comparison, I will now present and contrast two models of imagination derived from two different philosophical traditions. I will call these theories model A and model B for now.

Psychological	*G*	How do people feel, think, behave, interact, etc.? How can we best help them psychotherapeutically?
Field-specific or discipline-specific epistemological	*F*	How do we *validate* knowledge appropriately *in this given field*? What *methodological* approaches are appropriate to it?
	E	What can we know or hope to learn within this *given field* or discipline? What are the *limits or boundaries* to the above?
General epistemological	*D*	How do we *validate* our knowledge? How do we know it is true? What criteria do we use to assess its truth-value?
	C	What is our access to truth or *knowledge* (in general)? Where is truth to be found? How or from what is it constituted?
Ontological	*B*	What is *our position or relation to* that *reality* (if we do assume it exists on level *A*)?
	A	Is there any *reality* independent or partially independent of us? Does any absolute truth exist?

Figure 2.1
Hierarchy of levels of theoretical inquiry and their questions. The bottom levels are the most "foundational" to the others. The chart should be read from the bottom level up: from A to G. Positions at level A form the "grounding" or the conditions for the possibilities of positions on level B; those of B ground C, and so on. Thus, on psychological level G, insights and theories must rest upon a whole series of positions taken on each of the supporting levels, A through F.

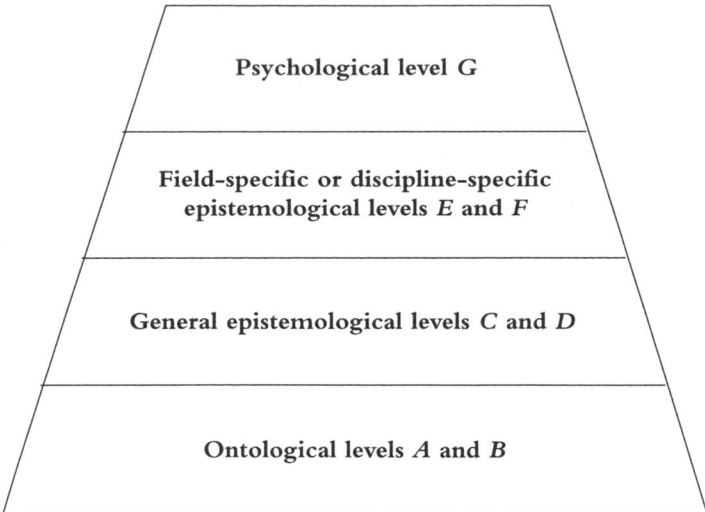

Figure 2.2
Hierarchy of levels of inquiry

Model A

This model represents the more common "natural scientific" or "empiricist" understanding of imagination as found, for example, in the approach of the DSM-IV (American Psychiatric Association, 1994). In this view the imaginary is seen as either something that is entirely lacking in external reality—as something "merely subjective"—or as "an image" that is meant to be a 'substitute' representation (literally a re-presentation) of something externally real (or a combination of such realities) that is nevertheless not 'really' present. Validity or truth is judged in this model by using a *correspondence theory of truth*, which postulates that there is one external, 'real' pure object to which our perceptions, images, and ideas must correspond, match, or accurately reflect in order to be considered as valid (Hanly 1992; Wallace 1988).

Things (or phenomena) are here seen as being real, true, and "objective," or not. There is a domain of the true and another of the false or the imaginary. An ontological disjunction is thus asserted: it is an either/or position with no in-between possible. There can, however, be much epistemological uncertainty as to the correct placement of a given phenomenon into one or the other of these domains; that is, we may not know for sure whether x is true or false, but it must be one or the other.

In such epistemological positions as "objectivism" and "empiricism" it is argued that such absolute realities or facts are accessible to us, in principle, but that we may be deceived in any of our particular validity judgments due to "subjective distortions" and biases.

In this model such clinical phenomena as hallucinations, delusions, illusions, confabulations, and distortions of the past can be seen as "mental" or "subjective" phenomena lacking in correspondence with their objective ideals. Indeed, it is this lack of correspondence with the postulated external and normative reality that comes to define the above "abnormalities" as *pathologies* of the imagination. As such our common psychiatric textbook definitions of these phenomena as "false perceptions," "false beliefs," and more recently "false memories" easily follow (Kaplan and Sadock 1985, pp. 500–501).

Despite the rather uncritical acceptance of the correspondence theory of truth in much of traditional psychological and psychiatric text and practice, it has recently taken quite a beating of criticism in philosophical and related circles. Its position, for example, is outright rejected by many including those calling themselves hermeneuticists, postmodernists, and phenomenologists (Gadamer 1960; Kvale 1990; Merleau-Ponty 1945; Rorty 1989). When we look closely once more at these defining terms like "false perceptions," "false beliefs," and "false memories," we see there are problems with the theory here.

How can a perception, meaning an experience, be "false?" An experience either is or is not present. Clearly, the high *valuing* of the external object, and the supposed requirement that one's experiences correspond with it, are more important in such definitions than is an understanding of the experience of the individual perceiver here. Yet, for psychotherapists, in particular, the individual's experience and feelings are usually of paramount importance. Furthermore in such definitions as above the assumption is that the clinician has a privileged position with respect to the "objective truth" in comparison with the patient—a position that is not always presented with convincing justification (Atwood and Stolorow 1984; Stolorow and Atwood 1992). One could thus be misled into seeing treatment as a process in which one is expected to convince, convert, or enlighten the patient to come over to the clinician's way of thinking. Surely this is not what we strive for in modern clinical practice! So where did we go wrong? What exactly are the underlying assumptions that led us here? And is there a better alternative?

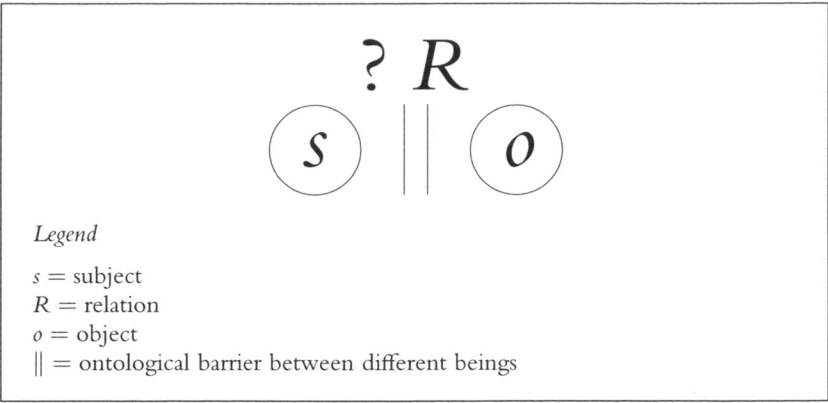

Legend

s = subject
R = relation
o = object
$\|$ = ontological barrier between different beings

Figure 2.3
Model A's Cartesian dualistic paradigm. The subject (s) and the object or world (o) are here seen as two separated types of being, with a puzzling relationship (R) between them.

Analysis of model A by the hierarchical method presents us with a model that is realist on the ontological level but is also (Cartesian) dualistic (Descartes 1641). That is it assumes a radical split between the subject and the object on the ontological level. Figure 2.3 illustrates this split.

On the epistemological level, model A is described as *objectivist*; that is, "*truth*" is seen as coming from the *object side* of the Cartesian split. It also subscribes to a correspondence theory of validity (as described above): to be valid, "knowledge" in (s) must correspond with something of (o).

On the field-specific epistemological level, we find a view of objective or pure facts, or truth, as being (at least potentially) accessible, even in the psychological/psychiatric field, but that such access is seen as limited by a series of subjective distortions that we must weed out as best as possible.

Empirical methodologies dealing with seemingly more "factual" data thus become greatly preferred. Interobserver reliability is to be maximized here even if it comes at the expense of intrapersonal meaning or significance. Thus, even on the psychological level the emphasis here is put on the external, that is, the physical or chemical, the observable, and the behavioral with a corresponding de-emphasis on and devaluing of the "merely subjective," internal, or experiential. The natural scientific values of measurability, reproducibility, prediction and control may be so aggressively pursued in this approach that much of what is most personal and

	Level	Model A's position
Psychological	*G*	Emphasis on the *external* (the physical, observable, behavioral, or the most reproducible)
Field-specific epistemological	*F*	Validity and methodology dictated by measurability, inter-rater reliability, and experimental methods
	E	Objective facts or truth accessible, only limited by subjective distortions. The imaginary as unreal, false, or a source of distortion
General epistemological	*D*	Correspondence theory of validity
	C	Objectivist
Ontological	*B*	*sRo* Cartesian dualist
	A	Realist

Figure 2.4
Positions taken by model A shown on the hierarchy of levels of theoretical inquiry

meaningful to the individual may get swept aside or neglected in the guise of trying to be more "scientific."

The "imaginary" in such a model is likewise devalued and seen as part of the domain of the nonobjective or the untrue. It may be seen here as not only lacking in correspondence to external reality but, even worse, as the source of the undesirable subjective biases that impede or distort our direct access to the (postulated) pure truth. Figure 2.4 summarizes the philosophical positions taken by model A graphically on the aforementioned hierarchy.

Model B

Let us now consider a different model entirely, model B. Model B begins with an understanding of our fundamental relatedness in a world as it comes out of a contrary philosophical tradition to that of model A. Model B is grounded in continental phenomenological philosophy (as opposed to model A's roots in positivism and empiricism). Such central concepts of phenomenology as "intentionality," "temporality," and the "projective" nature of our being from such philosophers as Husserl (1913, 1929), Heidegger (1927), Sartre (1943), and Merleau-Ponty (1945) have provided the basis of this nondualistic ontological position.

On the ontological level model B agrees with model A in being "realist"; that is, it postulates that the external world is not entirely a product of one's mind (Bernstein 1983; Langan 1996). It, however, rejects model A's Cartesian dualistic assumption that subject and object begin as radically separate beings that then must somehow relate to each other. Instead, it favors an intentionality-based model of human *being*, where we are defined not as the isolated *subject* (as above) but rather precisely as a *relation to a world*. That is to say, we are seen as fundamentally and irreducibly in a vector-like relatedness to our world and in time. This is shown in figure 2.5.

Figure 2.5 illustrates the two distinct ontological level paradigms of our relatedness to the world operating in models A and B. We can see in model B's paradigm that (s) and (o) are not separated from each other to begin with, and our mode of existence is seen not as that of an isolated (s) or subject, but as an (R) or an (sR), a 'subject-in-a-vector-like-relatedness-to-an-object (or world)'.

It is argued that these differing positions at this level will have a multitude of consequences at subsequent (higher) levels as well. One such consequence will be quite different and more positive understandings of the nature, place, and value of the imaginary.

If we follow Heidegger's (1927) notions of "care," "instrumentality," and "temporality" closely, our nature is seen as one of "thrown-projection" (Langan 1961). This *future*-directedness which both he and Sartre (1943) emphasize have interesting implications for a theory of imagination. In "caring" the nature of our being is posited as being in a relation to our world such that we are always already wanting something of the world. We always "project" ourselves or "throw ourselves forward in time" toward *anticipated future possibilities*. Accordingly our initial apprehension of objects is to see them in terms of their possible utility in providing what we seek (Heidegger 1927). Our way of being, including our very perception, in this view, is always "caring" or "motivated." But motivation should not here be understood in the sense of our being "pushed" deterministically by our past. Rather, it can be better understood as being "pulled" by our anticipatory

Model A's Cartesian dualistic paradigm

Legend

s = subject
R = relation
o = object
‖ = ontological barrier between different beings

Model B's intentionality-based paradigm

Legend

sR = *subject in* a directional *relation* toward its *o*
o = object or world

Figure 2.5
Schematic comparison of models A and B

projections into the future as *what might be* if we do *x* or if *y* should happen, and so on. But such anticipation must be guided (consciously or not) by our *imagination* (i.e., of what is not yet but might become). In this model then at least some form of imagination must be seen as part of our primordial, fundamental relatedness to the *world in time* starting at the ontological level. That is, if the way we always see things is to see them from within a perspective of wanting certain things or changes and by imaginatively anticipating them, then imagination or the imaginary must be omnipresent from the outset. As such imagination would here appear to be an essential *dimension* or aspect inherent to every human perception or conscious act. It is here seen as part of the very structure of consciousness. Unlike model A, we do not here describe perceptions or ideas as being either imaginary or real, for in this model the imaginary is a fundamental part of all our reality.

On the epistemological level, human perception and knowledge can then be seen to always be limited, perspectival, and somewhat fluid as they will always contain motivational and imaginative components. All perception is thus seen as perception "in the light of our past experiences and our future projects."

Lest we be misinterpreted as simply flipping to the "subjectivist" side of the dualistic split (Bernstein 1983; Orange 1995), it is mentioned here that this model does not deny the "externally based," unyielding facticity or "giveness" aspect of all human phenomena either. The epistemological position that model B is based on is a "co-constitutional" one (Hersch 1993, 2003) in which the truths of human reality are based on a blending or interaction between "given" and "made" elements (Orange 1995). This relational structure of consciousness has previously been likened by this author to a "beam of light" that must shine on some object or aspect of its world for either of them to be seen (Hersch 1993, 1996, 2001, 2003).

With this background a naive correspondence theory of truth (or falsehood) would make little sense as the external, ideal "pure object or fact" of the objectivists does not exist in human perception. Indeed, such an idealized object is only possible because of our ability to form imaginative projections and extrapolations. But surely an imaginary ideal makes a poor measuring stick for determining an experience to be either "real and true" or "imaginary." As opposed to model A's appeal to correspondence with a (likely unavailable) ideal, validity judgments must here rely on other sorts of criteria, including those of the "coherence" and "pragmatic" theories of truth (the former emphasizing the internal consistency of the arguments and findings within a given theory and the latter emphasizing practical consequences and basically what works in practice) (Hanly 1992; Orange 1995).

On the field-specific epistemological level, these alternative positions amount to psychology and/or psychiatry's equivalent to Heisenberg's (1958) uncertainty principle in physics. On the psychological level, the emphasis in this model has swung over to the experiential side of things. Only by trying to understand the patient's experience, projects and interpretations of his/her world (i.e., one's personal situation and context) will we be able to appreciate the meanings and significances of one's "imaginings." And if we dismiss one's imaginings as being "mere fictions," we may miss everything of true significance in his or her life. Model B's position on the hierarchy is shown in figure 2.6.

	Level	Model B's position
Psychological	G	Emphasis on *experiential* phenomena in the historical, temporal, meaningful context of an interpretive and imaginative relatedness to a real external world. Goals of widening range of possibilities (both of action and imagination)
Field-specific epistemological	F	Methodology and validity criteria acknowledging the complexity of mutually influencing elements in a dialogical system. Experiential and external elements, and their interaction all addressed
	E	Interactive, dialogical embeddedness in a world system of meanings and projects. No completely objective uninterpreted facts (uncertainty). No isolated mind. Imagination as inherent to consciousness or perception
General epistemological	D	Coherence, pragmatic, hermeneutic, + some nondualistic modified criteria formerly associated with correspondence (mixture)
	C	Co-constitutional, perspectivalist, "caring," motivated, future-oriented, anticipating
Ontological	B	$\left(\; sR \rightarrow o \;\right)$; nondualistic
	A	Realist

Figure 2.6
Positions taken by model B on the hierarchy of levels of theoretical inquiry

Within the realm of psychological/psychiatric treatment our more humble clinician now is no longer asking whether the patient's experience is true or false but rather raises some questions: In what proportions are the more imaginary and less imaginary elements mixed? Which of his/her projects are most over or under represented or evident in each? What are the likely present and future consequences of such beliefs and perceptions in terms of the patient's projects, relationships and feelings?

In model B we would not call a delusion a "false belief" (as in the true or false mode of model A) but rather would understand it as one in which the imaginative component or particular projects or motives appear to be *dominating* perception and reasoning *to the exclusion of others*. Here we can now put the emphasis on *that which limits one's possibilities* and/or *causes pain, suffering, dysfunction*, and other *undesirable consequences* as defining what is to be regarded as "pathological" and in need of treatment. Treatment will then be reconceptualized not in terms of trying to exorcise the patient of the imaginary. Rather, in accepting the imaginary as a fundamental and valued part of the structure of experience, our goal will be to acknowledge and free up our patient's imaginative and active possibilities in areas where they've become rigid, narrowed, and restricting of other aspects of his/her experience.

The diagnosis of "delusion" includes an examination of how rigidly any alternative possibilities must be rejected by the patient. This may prove pragmatically to be of most consequence. (Of course, by that criterion some dogmatic clinicians might equally well be described as delusional.)

In practice, good clinicians have long recognized there is usually some "kernel of truth" hidden within most delusions. We have also made good use of many important and practically significant findings that were based on natural scientific research methods: for example, that altered dopamine levels in the brain predispose one to the sort of clinical phenomena described above (Kaplan and Sadock 1985). However, while such "externally real" elements remain very important to our understanding, they will never explain away the experiential aspects. As clinicians our ultimate goals are in the area of trying to help *in the experiential domain*, that is to say, to alleviate suffering and foster creative enjoyment and fulfillment. The rest is only our means to that end.

If nothing else, model B may provide a more humble approach to truth questions and foster a more respectful, cooperative, and less epistemologically judgmental tone to our approach to "the imaginary."

Level	Model A	Model B
Psychological		
G	Emphasis on the *external* (the physical, observable, behavioral, or the most reproducible). Goals of prediction and control	Emphasis on *experiential* phenomena in the historical, temporal, meaningful context of an interpretive and imaginative relatedness to a real external world. Goals of widening range of possibilities (both of action and imagination)
Field-specific epistemological		
F	Validity and methodology dictated by measurability, inter-rater reliability, and experimental methods	Methodology and validity criteria acknowledging the complexity of mutually influencing elements in a dialogical system. Experiential and external elements, and their interaction all addressed
E	Objective facts or truth accessible, only limited by subjective distortions. The imaginary as unreal, false, or a source of distortion.	Interactive, dialogical embeddedness in a world system of meanings and projects. No completely objective uninterpreted facts (uncertainty). No isolated mind. Imagination as inherent to consciousness or perception
General epistemological		
D	Correspondence	Coherence, pragmatic, hermeneutic, + some nondualistic modified criteria formerly associated with correspondence (mixture)
C	Objectivist	Co-constitutional, perspectivalist, "caring," motivated, future-oriented, anticipating
Ontological		
B	sRo Cartesian dualist	$\boxed{sR \rightarrow o}$; nondualistic
A	Realist	Realist

Figure 2.7
Positions taken by particular theories shown on the hierarchy of levels of theoretical inquiry

To summarize, the positions of model A and model B can be compared and contrasted hierarchically as seen in figure 2.7.

The two models can be seen to vary on many different levels. As such, it is not surprising that they result in differing views of what the imaginary is, what its value and importance is, when it should be deemed "pathological," and what approaches to it should the clinician take. Hopefully this has provided a demonstration as well as to how our underlying philosophical presuppositions are anything but irrelevant to our clinical practices and that the more aware of them we are, likely the better clinicians we can become.

References

American Psychiatric Association. 1994. *Diagnostic and Statistical Manual of Mental Disorders*, 4th ed. Washington, DC: American Psychiatric Association Press.

Atwood, G., and R. Stolorow. 1984. *Structures of Subjectivity: Explorations in Psychoanalytic Phenomenology*. Hillsdale, NJ: Analytic Press.

Bernstein, R. J. 1983. *Beyond Objectivism and Relativism: Science, Hermeneutics, and Praxis*. Philadelphia: University of Pennsylvania Press.

Descartes, R. [1641] 1961. *Meditations* in *Philosophic Classics*, 2nd ed. Trans. by J. Veitch, ed. by W. Kaufmann. Engelwood Cliffs, NJ: Prentice-Hall.

Gadamer, H.-G. [1960] 1995. *Truth and Method*, 2nd rev. ed. Trans. rev. by J. Weinsheimer and D. G. Marshall. New York: Continuum, 1995.

Hanly, C. 1992. *The Problem of Truth in Applied Psychoanalysis*. New York: Guilford Press.

Heidegger, M. [1927] 1962. *Being and Time*. Trans. by J. Macquerrie and E. Robinson. New York: Harper and Row.

Heisenberg, W. 1958. *Physics and Philosophy*. New York: Harper and Row.

Hersch, E. 1993. A paradigm shift: Explicating a new philosophical model providing a defensible epistemological and ontological foundation for intersubjectivity theory. Paper presented at the 16th Annual Conference on the Psychology of the Self, Toronto, October 1993.

Hersch, E. 1996. Epistemology, ontology and psychotherapy. Paper presented at the First International Conference on Philosophy and Mental Health, Benalmadena, Spain, February 1996.

Hersch, E. 2001. Making our philosophical unconscious more conscious: A method of exploring the philosophical basis of psychological theory. *Canadian Journal of Psychoanalysis* 9: 165–86.

Hersch, E. 2003 (forthcoming). *From Philosophy to Psychotherapy: A Phenomenological Model for Psychology, Psychiatry, and Psychoanalysis*. Toronto: University of Toronto Press.

Husserl, E. [1913] 1931. *Ideas: An Introduction to Pure Phenomenology.* Trans. by W. Gibson, New York: Macmillan.

Husserl, E. [1929] 1973. *Cartesian Meditations.* Trans. by D. Cairns. The Hague: Martinus Nijhoff.

Kaplan, H., and B. Sadock, eds. 1985. *Comprehensive Textbook of Psychiatry IV*, 4th ed. Baltimore and London: Williams and Wilkins.

Kvale, S. 1990. Themes of post-modernity. In W. Anderson, ed., *The Truth about the Truth.* New York: Tarcher/Putnam, pp. 18–25.

Langan, T. 1961. *The Meaning of Heidegger.* New York: Columbia University Press.

Langan, T. 1996. *Being and Truth.* Columbia: University of Missouri Press.

Merleau-Ponty, M. [1945] 1962. *Phenomenology of Perception.* Trans. by C. Smith. London: Routledge and Kegan Paul.

Orange, D. 1995. *Emotional Understanding: Studies in Psychoanalytic Epistemology.* New York: Guilford Press.

Rorty, R. 1989. Ironists and Metaphysicians. In W. Anderson, ed., *The Truth about the Truth.* New York: Tarcher/Putnam, pp. 100–106.

Sadler, J., O. Wiggins, and M. Schwartz, eds. 1994. *Philosophical Perspectives on Psychiatric Diagnostic Classification.* Baltimore: Johns Hopkins University Press.

Sartre, J.-P. [1943] 1953. *Being and Nothingness.* Trans. by H. Barnes. New York: Washington Square Press.

Stolorow, R., and G. Atwood. 1992. *Contexts of Being.* Hillsdale, NJ: Analytic Press.

Wallace, E. 1988. What is truth? Some philosophical contributions to psychiatric issues. *American Journal of Psychiatry* 145: 137–47.

3

Narrative and the Ethics of Remembrance

Richard Kearney

To tell or not to tell? This is the question I propose to explore here. How much of the past should be remembered and recounted? How much forgotten and forgiven? How do we respect the summons of history—personal or communal—to be recollected again and again so that our debt to the past be honored without succumbing to resentment and revenge? And, finally, how does memory itself negotiate a passage between its opposing fidelities to imagination and reality?

I will attempt to address this question in terms of both literary memory and literal (lived) memory. In my discussion, I will weigh the poetic right to recreate against the ethical duty to represent the past as it actually happened (*wie es eigentlich gewesen*).

PAST as Present

I begin with the literary example of *Hamlet*, a play that begins and ends with the question of memory.

"Remember me," says King Hamlet to his son. Tell my story. Carry my memory, my legacy, my legitimacy, into the next generation, to my people, to my children and grandchildren? And why not? Should not every son remember his father. Especially when he was a glorious king, the sun of all the firmament, cut down while still in his prime? Is it not mandatory for any king—and certainly those in Shakespeare's plays—to end their days confiding their secret stories to their sons, transferred with their benediction and their birthright? Of course. And was not young Hamlet born for this indeed, to tell his father's story to the people of the Union: the Union of two nations, Denmark and Norway, sealed by the pearl won by his father in the famous duel with Fortinbras the Elder—the day (lest we forget) of younger Hamlet's birth? Was not Prince Hamlet born to carry on his father's history and avenge his crime?

But there's a rub. First, we can't be sure *who* speaks. Hamlet's friend Horatio, scholar returned from Wurtenburg, says "tis but a fantasy"—or worse "a guilty thing"—that speaks to Hamlet. At best, a ghost one moment there, one moment gone; there and not there, present and absent, the past as present. And when the ghostly, guilt-ridden spirit finally speaks, after much coaxing, he claims he is a creature come, not back from heaven, but hell: from "sulphrous and tormenting flames." He is indeed a "questionable shape."

And there's another rub. If we can't be sure *who* the ghost is, we can't be sure *what* he is saying either. He tells his son, "remember!" Yes. *But what is he to remember?* His father's glories as illustrious monarch, faithful to his people, spouse, and son? No. The irony is that the first thing father tells son is *what he cannot tell him.*

I am thy father's spirit,
doomed for a certain term to walk the night
and for the days confined to fast in fires
till the foul crimes done in my days of nature
are burnt and purged away. But that I am forbid
to tell the secrets of my prison house,
I could a tale unfold whose lightest word
would harrow up thy soul. . . . (act 1, sc. v)

The second thing King Hamlet tells his son is to prevent the "royal bed of Denmark" from being "a couch . . . of damned incest." But here again there are problems, for he adds: "do not contrive against thy mother aught." In other words, another double injunction. First: remember me/ remember me not. Second: intervene/don't intervene.

Freud, as we know from his famous reading of the play in *Interpretation of Dreams* (1900), sees these paradoxes as the betrayal (in both senses of term) of Hamlet's Oedipus Complex. The repressed desire to vilify the father and possess the mother. Lacan (1982) sees the double injunction as a "tragedy of desire." While Nicholas Abraham (1988) reads it as a symptom of the gap left in us by the untold secrets of others who came before us. King Hamlet's "Remember me!" means *both* (1) to commemorate the ghost's memory by honoring his summons to avenge *and* (2) to recall what the ghost-king actually did if he could only say it (which alas he is "forbid"). This contradictory summons represents what might be described as a *tragedy of narrative.* We have a story to tell but can't tell it. Or as the narrator of Beckett's *Molloy* puts it, "I can't go on [telling stories], I'll go on."

Hamlet, on this reading, is a story about the simultaneous necessity and impossibility of stories. Ophelia cannot tell her story until she goes mad (when she tells everything but is no longer herself: "Here's rosemary for remembrance"); Claudius cannot tell his story, even in the confessional, until it is forced from him by the play within the play; Gertrude cannot tell her story because she is ignorant of it (she does not know that Claudius killed the King); Polonius and his fellow courtiers, Rosencrantz and Guildenstern and Osric, cannot tell their stories since they say only what pleases or deceives. Even Prince Hamlet cannot tell his story for as long as conscience makes a coward of him. No, not until, dying of a fatal wound he begs his friend Horatio: "absent thee from felicity awhile to tell my story." Which means that this is a play where no one actually tells their story, no one truly remembers, until Prince Fortinbras arrives too late on the scene, and announces: "I have some rights of *memory* in this kingdom/ which now to claim my vantage doth invite me" (act V, sc. ii).

What exactly these rights of 'memory' are no one tells us. And if they could, one has good reason to suspect the play would not have survived the first act. In other words, the play is about a cover-up, a concealment of a crime (or crimes) that the hero, Hamlet, is trying to uncover and reveal. Numerous psychoanalysts over the years—drawn to the play like kittens to a ball of wool—have read between the lines and dared to tell the untold tale. Namely, as André Green (1982) and Nicholas Abraham (1988) would have it, that King Hamlet has done to King Fortinbras what Claudius does to Hamlet (King and Prince)—poison him to secure the rights of kingship. The 'rights of memory' restored by young Fortinbras in the last act would refer, on this reading, to the final righting of the wrong committed against Fortinbras's own father by Hamlet's father. That King Hamlet's 'foul crime' occurred on Hamlet's birthday is surely no accident, as suggested by the Prince's opening invocation of the "dram of evil"—that "vicious mole of nature in (particular men), /as in their birth, wherein they are not guilty,/ (since nature cannot chose his origin). . . ." (act I, sc. iv) The ethics of remembrance, Shakespeare reminds us, proves more complex than it seems. Indeed, were it *less complex,* one wonders if Shakespeare would have spun his marvelous play at all in the first place. It's true: "the play's the thing in which we'll catch the conscience of the king." But which king are we speaking of? King Hamlet? King Claudius? Hamlet pretender to the throne? Or King Fortinbras who too was to his grave untimely sent?

It's because there's no quick answer to this question that *Hamlet* the play survives to this day, and Hamlet the prince is the most written about person in Western culture after Jesus and Napoleon!

So what's the story? Tell/don't tell! The double injunction that makes us human. The essence of tragedy in literature and life. But there's a difference between literature and life and, I will argue, it's a significant one. Despite certain current views that the imaginary and the real are one and the same, I submit that what is good for literature is by no means always good for life. If at the epistemological level it is often extremely difficult to establish clear referential relations between narrative and world, this does not mean, especially from an ethical point of view, that there is no distinction whatsoever.

Memory in Fiction

But before proceeding with this vexed issue, let me cite one more example of the role of narrative imagination in fiction. I quote here from a recent novel, *The Bend for Home* (1996), by an Irish writer, Dermot Healey, disciple of Joyce and Beckett and fascinated, like them, by the mystery of memory as recounted in fiction. How does the past alter in the telling? How does fiction change the way things were in order to make a story out of how things might have been. (The future anterior is a favourite tense in fiction). And yet in ostensibly distorting truth, poetic lies can tell another kind of truth, sometimes a truer truth. Here are some anecdotes from Healey's novel that capture this enigma.

1. *There's a song by Percy French called "Come back Paddy Reilly to Ballyjamesduff,"*
seemingly written about a cabman who used to collect Mr French, the road-engineer, from the
railway station there. Then the cabman went off to America and things were never the same.
Hence the title. One of the verses goes: "just turn to the left at the bridge of Finea/ And stop
when halfway to Cootehill." But it can't be done. No matter how you try you can't turn left
at the bridge of Finea, unless you go up Bullasheer Lane which leads eventually to the banks
of floating reeds on Kinale. Some make a case for the old Carrick road which passes the
weeping walls of Carrick Church that stands in a quarry, but the Carrick road is to the right.
It's all cod. For the sake of a song Percy French got his geography amiss. Even road-engineers
are capable of giving wrong directions in order to get a couplet true. And that's how I found out
writers not only make up things, but get things wrong as well. Language, to be memorable,
dispenses with accuracy.... To top the coincidence my mother took the turn to the left that
doesn't exist and eventually found herself in Cootehill. These things happen. That's how it is.
She followed the words of the song. (pp. 9–10)

2. *The first real essay I wrote was about rain. I remember reading it out in the De La Salle Brothers School. I stole the lines from a book by Charles Lamb that I found in the attic. Imagination. . . . begins with our first lie. It's hard for me to remember my first lie, since I've told so many. And now I'm at it again. Can I lie here and sidestep some memory I'd rather not entertain, and then let fiction take care of it elsewhere, because that is sometimes what fiction does? It becomes the receptacle for those truths we would rather not allow into our tales of the self. The made-up characters feel their way by virtue of thoughts that novelists deny having. So I'd like to describe my first stab at fame, even though it shames me. It was a combination of lies and a fondness for words that started me. I can still remember the liquid feel of those words for rain. How the beads were blown against a windowpane, and glistened there and ran. The words for rain were better than the rain itself. I wanted to type up words. . . .* (p. 57)

3. Healey goes on to describe, finally, how he achieved his first fame, like Synge's Playboy before him, "by the power of a lie." He describes returning to a wedding in his native Cavan after some months in exile in London. At the wedding reception he finds himself seated beside the editor of the local newspaper, the *Anglo-Celt*, in which he'd published his first short story some years previously. Asked by the editor how the writing was going for him in London, Healey made up a story about having finished a play that would soon be shown on British television. Responding to the editor's more detailed inquiries, Healey invented a string of fibs—it was called *Nightcrossing*, he'd received an advance of one thousand pounds and so on. The dancing started up then and Healey forgot all about the "play he'd never written." He returned to London a few days later but his lie was to return to haunt him. Seated in an Irish pub in Piccadilly a week after the wedding, another ex-pat came in and clamped a copy of the most recent *Anglo-Celt* down on the bar:

"Look," says he.

And there I was on the front page with a cigarette in my mouth over a small headline that read: CAVAN AUTHOR FINDS FAME. . . .

(My friend) would set me questions about the plot, and the more he asked the more I had to invent.

In time I invented a producer from ITV, a Mr Evans, if you don't mind, who lived in Hammersmith. Apparently I saw him from time to time. He went over the shots and camera angles with me. I even eventually set a date when it would be broadcast to the nation—November 10th, let's say. In fact I began to believe in it myself. I believed the script existed. The more of the story I invented, the more real it became. Then I'd suddenly wake out of a dream terror-stricken by my duplicity. Slowly I tried to extricate myself from the lie. There were problems with production monies, I said. There were production difficulties. Something had gone wrong down the line. The date for the broadcast came and went. No one mentioned it.

But in fact I had set myself a duty. Everything I write now is an attempt to make up for that terrible lie. Had I not lied I might never have tried my hand at fiction. The truth is the lie you once told returning to haunt you. (pp. 59–60)

In short, Healey, like Hamlet's ghost, enjoins us to tell our tale but not to tell it as it happened! He contrives to straddle the extremes of telling and not telling.

Poetic Exigency

Healey is responding here to the double injunction of all poetics—tell it
but do not tell it as it was. This double exigency can be interpreted in different ways, of course. On the one hand, there is the Beckettian view that
"silence is our mother tongue," and that all forms of remembering (apart
from involuntary memory à la Proust) are distortions, stories we invent
to ward off the "suffering of being." Hence Beckett's resolve to dismantle
the narrative form, paring his stories down until they become "residua" or
"no-texts"—anti-novels. Seamus Heaney offers a recent ironic variation on
this same tune when he writes: "Whatever you say say nothing." The best
stories are the stories never told—hence Heaney's corollary counsel to
"govern the tongue," to write poetry rather than fiction.

Against this, there is the Joycean tradition that says: tell everything!—
a tradition that produces *Finnegan's Wake* (the text of "allmen") rather than
Beckett's *No's Knife* (the text of "noman"). The Joycean impulse celebrates the fictional re-creation of history in its entirety working to the refrain
of the garrulous washerwomen by the Liffey: "mememormee, mememormee!"

So while the former poetic exigency may be expressed as *tell nothing
whatever you tell*, the latter translates as *tell everything you can tell*.

From Stories to Histories

What is fine for fiction is another matter when it comes to history. Here the
double injunction—tell/don't tell—may have very different resonances and
consequences, especially at an existential and ethical level. It is this contrast
between fictional and historical remembrance that I wish to explore in the
remainder of this chapter. If fiction is entirely free to recreate the past *as it
might have been*, history has a duty to recount the past *as it actually was* (*wie es
eigentlich gewesen*). If it is true, as Paul Ricoeur claims, that "l'imaginaire ne
connaît pas de censure," the same cannot be said of historical narrative. The
difference is crucial, though not always self-evident.

To illustrate this contrast between literary and nonliterary forms of
narrative memory, I will concentrate on some controversial "case histories" in psychotherapy, before briefly touching on the more general
debate about the role of narrative in the recounting of public historical
events.

Suppressed Memory

In psychotherapy the double injunction—tell/do not tell—would seem to be resolved. A cure happens when one gets to the bottom of things, when the suffering subject manages to remember and recount the *whole story*, or at least as much of it as is recoverable and utterable given the lapses of time between the events of trauma and the recall of those events. This at least seems to be Freud's view in the famous case of Dora. Here Freud believed he could cure his patient's hysteria if only he could reconstitute the "missing pieces" in Dora's fragmented narrative. Freud's theory was that hysterics suffer from blockages of memory that result in "hysterical conversion symptoms" such as (in Dora's case) insomnias, depressions, coughing fits, and so on. The psychoanalytic hypothesis was, accordingly, that Dora would be cured once her repressed desires and traumas were recovered in and through narrative—that is, once she succeeded in telling her *full* story. In this instance, her secret desire to marry Herr K. The cure would therefore comprise a narrative cure made possible by the recovery of repressed desire through analytic discourse and transference.

The same applies to Freud's other case histories—Little Hans, the Ratman, the Wolfman, Schneider—a telling concession being that the decisive evidence is revealed more as "creative narrative" than as "scientific fact." But there is an immediate problem, is there not? How are we to know whether the narrative is "true" or not? It was precisely the difficulty of responding to this question that provoked the controversy surrounding Freud's changing views on the seduction theory—at one time suggesting that childhood memories of abuse were real, at other times claiming they were fantasy.

I don't propose to get into the history of this well-rehearsed controversy here. Suffice it to say that from an ethical and juridical standpoint (whatever about the complex epistemological issues of how we can ever *know* the past as past), it *does* and *should* matter whether a recovered memory relates to things that actually happened or not. And this mattering pertains to both the person allegedly abused and to the person who allegedly perpetrated the abuse.

Let me give some examples. We have seen recently, particularly in the United States, a wide debate on the so-called false memory syndrome. This has been documented in a number of highly publicised books, such as Michael Yapko's *Suggestions of Abuse: True and False Memories of Childhood*

Sexual Trauma (1994), Lenore Terr's *Unchained Memories: True Stories of Traumatic Memories, Lost and Found* (1995), Lawrence Wright's *Remembering Satan* (1994), and Mark Pendergast and Melody Gavigan's *Victims of Memory: Sex Abuse Accusations and Shattered Lives* (1996). Even if none of these authors wish to contest the validity of the persistent memory of infantile sexual abuse, some of them cast serious doubt on the use of suggestion and trancework techniques in cases of long-term recovered memory. Wright, for instance, cites the case of a Mr. Ingram, accused by his daughter of performing sexual abuse rites on her after she had recovered a long repressed memory thanks to (1) her reading of some recent literature on Satanic rituals and (2) a number of trancework sessions with psychotherapists. The accused himself confessed to the crimes, after sustained interrogations by police and psychologists during which he was assured that the more he acknowledged the abuse the more clearly his own (repressed) memories of such events would be recovered. As Paul Ingram admitted, "My memory is becoming clearer as I go through all this.... It's getting clearer as more things come out." The basic "suggestibility" premiss of the interrogators was: If you have the *feeling* that such abuse occurred, even if not actually the cognitive awareness, then it did occur. Mr. Ingram was condemned to twenty years of imprisonment before the case was contested and reopened. (One can think of more notorious cases of such suggestion-confessions running from the Salem witch trials, so brilliantly captured by Arthur Miller's *The Crucible*, to the recent investigations of collective Satanic abuse of children in the Orkney Islands off Scotland.)

As a result of certain abuses of the memory of abuse (even if such be the exceptions rather than the rule), the whole notion of psychological memory is being challenged. As Walter Reich argues in his essay, "The Monster in the Mist: Are Long Buried Memories of Child Abuse Reliable?": "Given memory's indispensability and frailty, it's striking that so many of us are ready to play so fast and loose with it. When we uncritically embrace reports of recovered memories of sexual abuse, and when we nonchalantly assume that they must be as good as our ordinary memories, we debase the coinage of memory altogether. What we *should* do is shore up the legitimacy of an imperfect but precious human capacity— the capacity to attest to events that we have always remembered—by resisting the creation of a new category of memory whose products are so often mere inventions conjured by the ministrations of recovery specialists. Instead, too many of us undermine that legitimacy by according to recovered memories, even the most bizarre ones, the same status—psychologically as well as legally—that we accord to traditional forms of memory" (1995, 38).

The undermining of testimonial memory in this way does a grave disservice not only to those falsely accused of abuse but also to those many victims of real abuse. The question of the *veracity* of narratives of childhood abuse—recovered or persistent—is of capital importance (especially, I repeat, from a moral-judicial point of view).

Missing Pieces

Let me return for a moment here to the famous case of Dora. The possibility of "suggestion" is far from absent in this controversial case history—which itself comprises a history of revisions and controversies. As several of Freud's contemporaries and successors noted, the "talking cure" did not actually work for Dora for the probable reason that Freud constructed her story according to his own unconscious identifications—in particular, with the virile Herr K. whom Freud believed Dora secretly wished to marry. Freud's remarks about Dora's resistance to his hypothetical interpretation of her hysterical symptoms may thus actually betray a *countertransference* of his own desires onto his analysand—a complex psychoanalytic phenomenon that Freud himself had not yet come to fully appreciate, as Lacan and others observed. But Freud did, in fairness, have the professional honesty to call this case history a "fragment," thereby at least implicitly acknowledging that the "missing pieces" of Dora's story were never fully filled in or completed by Dora herself.

The question raised by this fragmentary narrative is therefore: *Whose story is it anyway?* Dora's or Freud's? Certain commentators, most notably Claire Kahane in *In Dora's Case* (1990), construe the oblique, truncated, and unfinished character of Dora's story as itself a signal of its singular truth. Hysteria, this argument goes, is by its very nature an experience of fragmentariness and its truthfulness derives from its uncompromising and legitimate resistance to Freud's attempt to play the omnipotent father-god capable of filling in the fissures and fractures of her story in order to sign off a "total account." Dora's narrative has thus become in certain feminist circles a *cas célèbre* of genuine feminine resistance—hysterical or otherwise—to the phallocentric exigency to "tell everything." According to this view, it is precisely the covert, oblique, and obscure elements in Dora's version that constitutes a necessary female refuge from the male imperative to know and appropriate anything alien to it.

This reading is persuasively developed by Jane Gallop (1990) who argues that hysterical discourse is a paradigm of "woman's story" ("Keys to Dora"). And it is also invoked by Stephen Marcus in his literary-psychological account, "Freud and Dora: Story, History, Case History" (1990), where he cites Dora's narrative as a exemplary instance of modernist fiction, displaying four central common features: (1) the impossibility of access to truth, (2) the dissolution of linear narration and its explosion into multiple, often competing, perspectives, (3) the existence of an unreliable narrator (Freud), and (4) the undecidable relation between fiction and reality, both inside and outside of the discourse.

Memory and Ethics

What some of these commentators seem to ignore, however, is that if it is true that at an *aesthetic* level it matters little whether there is an accurate correspondence between narrative and reality, it matters hugely at an *ethical* level. It certainly mattered to Dora—who got worse rather than better thanks to Freud's countertranferential account and to all those other victims of abuse, trauma, or manipulation. What is good for the modernist or postmodernist novel is not necessarily good for actual life. There is, after all, a need to discriminate (as best we can) between the purely story-element of case histories and the history-element as a reality-reference to the past "as it actually happened." The two strands—fiction or fact—are, of course, always intimately interwoven in the narrative text (oral or written), but that does not mean that the strands can never be, at least partially, disentangled and distinguished. Consequently, while I would not for a moment deny that literary analogies between Freudian case histories and modernist fiction can teach us much about the subtle and sophisticated uses of narrative, such analogies do not do justice to the ethical significance of memories of real suffering—memories that the sufferers who recount them wish to be *recognized as true*, that is, as referring to events that did happen.

The moral implications of such an imaginary/real distinction in the operation of narrative memory are crucial not only for psychological cases of abuse but also for the more public and collective cases of historical crime. The instances of revisionism and negationism with respect to the Holocaust and other genocides in history are timely reminders of the fundamental stakes involved. The whole nature of memory as historical witness is at issue here. While revisionist historians like Faurisson and David Irving deny the existence of gas chambers, antirevisionists like Lawrence Langer in *Holocaust Testimonies: The Ruins of Memory* (1991) recall just how fragile and indispensable the role of testimonial memory is. Indeed, Langer's scrupulous distinctions between 'deep memory' and other variant categories of remembering—'anguished', 'humiliated', 'tainted', and 'unheroic'—represents just the kind of typological work that is necessary to answer those who would discredit the legitimacy of personal and historical remembrance. As Walter Reich aptly reminds us:

The institution of memory deserves the respect and protection it can get. One indication of just how vulnerable to manipulation it already is can be appreciated from the fact that Holocaust deniers have managed to receive, in recent years, a respectful hearing on college campuses and elsewhere, despite the existence of mountains of firsthand and corroborated traumatic memories of the Holocaust provided by many thousands of survivors—memories that don't have to be recovered because they are all too vividly, and all too persistently, remembered. Holocaust deniers began to achieve their victory over memory even before efforts were made to establish the new category of recovered memory. If recovered memory continues to remain unchallenged as a new form of memory, then one can only guess how much more vulnerable to doubt and manipulation legitimate memory will become. Memory is one of our most precious human assets. It needs protection from those who, by debasing it, diminish its integrity, even as victims of sexual abuse need protection from those who, by abusing them, diminish their humanity. (p. 38)

Conclusion

Sometimes, some places—Northern Ireland, Bosnia, Rwuanda—it is important to let go of history, to heed Nietzsche's counsel to "actively forget" the past in order to surmount the instincts of resentment and revenge. Other times, other places—Auschwitz being the time and place *par excellence*—it is essential to *remember* the past in order to honor our "debt to the dead" and to ensure that it never happens again. As Ricoeur argues in "The Memory of Suffering": "we must remember because remembering is a *moral duty*. We owe a *debt* to all the victims. And the tiniest way of paying our debt is to tell and retell what happened at Auschwitz.... [B]y remembering and telling, we not only prevent forgetfulness from killing the victims twice; we also prevent their life stories from becoming banal ... and the events from appearing as necessary" (1995, 290).

Narrative remembrance can serve two functions: it can help us to remember the past by representing it (as it "really was") *or* to forget the past by reinventing it (as it might have been). In fiction, the role of reinvention is what matters most—even in historical novels like *War and Peace*. In psychotherapeutic and historical testimony, the function of veridical recall claims primacy. Distinguishing between these two separate, if often overlapping, functions is, I submit, of great ethical importance. As is discerning *when* it is right to remember and *when* it is better to forget—; and, as important, *how much* we should remember and forget. (Genuine amnesty, in forgiving the past, is never mere amnesia.)

These are critical hermeneutic tasks requiring far more detailed analysis than I can provide here. But if the matter is crucial, it is also extraordinarily complex. To be reminded of this, we need only recall the difficulty that arises when one is asked, like Hamlet, to *remember and forget* at the same time. Such a double injunction can lead to great literature—but not always to a great life. Hamlet, the suffering Prince, paid the price with his own life. As have many before and since.

References

Abraham, N. 1988. The phantom of Hamlet. *Diacritics* 18: 171–90.

Freud, S. [1900] 1953. *The Interpretation of Dreams*. Translated by J. Strachey. *Standard Edition, IV*. London: Hogarth Press.

Gallop, J. 1990. Keys to Dora. In C. Kahane and C. Bernheimer, eds., *In Dora's Case*. New York: Columbia University Press, pp. 200–220.

Green, A. 1982. *Hamlet et Hamlet*. Paris: Balland.

Kahane, C., and C. Bernheimer, eds. 1990. *In Dora's Case*. New York: Columbia University Press.

Healey, D. 1996. *The Bend for Home*. London: Harvill Press.

Lacan, J. 1982. Desire and the interpretation of desire. In S. Felman, ed., *Literature and Psychoanalysis*, Baltimore: Johns Hopkins University Press.

Langer, L. 1991. *Holocaust Testimonies: The Ruins of Memory*. New Haven: Yale University Press.

Marcus, S. 1990. Freud and Dora: Story, history, case-history. In C. Kahane and C. Bernheimer, eds., *In Dora's Case*. New York: Columbia University Press, pp. 56–91.

Prendergast, M., and M. Gavigan. 1996. *Victims of Memory: Sex Abuse Accusations and Shattered Lives*. New York: Upper Access Publisher.

Ricoeur, P. 1995. The memory of suffering. In P. Ricoeur, ed., *Figuring the Sacred: Religion, Narrative, and Imagination*. Minneapolis: Fortress Press.

Reich, W. 1994. The monster in the mist: Are long buried memories of child abuse reliable? *The New York Times Book Review*, May 15, 1994, pp. 38–39.

Terr, L. 1995. *Unchained Memories: True Stories of Traumatic Memories, Lost and Found.* New York: Basic Books.

Yapko, M. 1994. *Suggestions of Abuse: True and False Memories of Childhood Sexual Trauma*. New York: Simon and Schuster.

Wright, L. 1994. *Remembering Satan*. New York: Knopf.

4

Imagination, Fantasy, Hallucination, and Memory

Edward S. Casey

It is a remarkable fact that many previous philosophies and psychologies of mind, however perspicuous or profound that they may be in other ways, have failed to provide adequate accounts of basic differences among imagining, remembering, hallucinating, and fantasying. Even the most elementary descriptions of such differences are often lacking. Perhaps it has been presumed that the four acts in question are so closely affiliated as not to need descriptive differentiation. In this vein, they are frequently regarded as sibling acts having the same progenitor: perception. Yet each of the acts is related to perception very differently, ranging from apparent replication (in hallucination) to distinct discontinuity (in imagination). It is not my present purpose, however, to delineate this particular series of relationships. Rather, in this chapter I will concentrate on eidetic differences between imagining, on the one hand, and memory, hallucination, and fantasy, on the other. Each of the latter three acts will be described in terms of its most salient features, features that distinguish it from imagining in fundamental respects.[1] Thus the present project represents an exercise in the comparative phenomenology of mind—a neglected but important part of the eidetics of human experience.

I

Memory and imagination have long been regarded as psychical partners, as mates of the mind. Ever since Aristotle conjoined them under the common yoke of "experience,"[2] philosophers and psychologists have attempted to keep them together in a conjugal state by making two sorts of claims: either that the two acts are in fact one and the same act (though viewed form different perspectives) or that they differ in degree only. The first, more extreme, claim is made by Hobbes:

This *decaying sense*, when wee should express the thing it self, (I mean *fancy* it selfe) wee call *Imagination.* . . . But when we would express the *decay*, and signifie that the Sense is fading, old, and past, it is called *Memory.* So that *Imagination* and *Memory* are but one thing, which for divers considerations hath diverse names. (1968, 89)[3]

Imagination and memory "are but one thing" because both are immediate derivatives of "sense" or sensation, "The Originall of them all" (p. 85).[4] They differ only according to whether more stress is placed upon the *content* or decaying sense (i.e., "fancy it selfe") or upon the decay per se. Otherwise, they are identical—merely two aspects of the same thing. As Vico was to put it almost a century later: "Memory is the same as imagination" because imagination itself is "nothing but extended or compounded memory" (1968, 75 and 313).[5] Yet what both Hobbes and Vico overlook are the felt differences that emerge in the actual experience of the two acts.

The second claim is more difficult to dispute. That memory and imagination differ only in degree is a thesis that has had perennial appeal. It informs the opinion of a contemporary psychologist, who writes that "the difference between [mental images] and memory images is one of degree and not absolute" (McKellar 1957, 23).[6] But the *locus classicus* is found in Hume's *Treatise of Human Nature*, where it is argued that "the ideas of the memory are much more lively and strong than those of the imagination" (1967, 9).[7] Here a difference in vivacity—which is a difference in degree, being a matter of comparative sensory intensity—becomes the criterion for distinguishing imagination from memory. Yet Hume calls this very criterion into question by recognizing borderline cases in which relative vivacity is no longer an adequate basis for distinction: "And as an idea of the memory, by losing its force and vivacity, may degenerate to such a degree, as to be taken for an idea of the imagination; so on the other hand an idea of the imagination may acquire such a force and vivacity, as to pass for an idea of the memory" (Hume 1967, 96).

If memory and imagination are not to be differentiated in terms of relative vivacity alone, how then do they differ? Are there more deep-going differences between the two acts that Hume and others overlook? To single out such differences is not to deny that imagining and remembering possess several features in common. Each act can occur in a spontaneous or in a controlled manner—as ordinary language indicates by distinguishing between "instant" or "involuntary" recall and the effort to "search one's memory."[8] Further each act can alter, compound, or dissociate content that is borrowed initially from perception, though memory is largely restricted to modifying the sequence in which such content was originally experienced. There is, in addition, a similarity of act-forms: we can imagine or remember isolated objects and events, imagine or remember *that* a certain state of affairs took place, and even imagine or remember *how* something happened or was experienced. We should also notice that sensuous imagery is not any more essential to memory than it is to imagination; recollection can occur abstractly, as when I remember the "atmosphere" of a former situation or recall the answer to a problem in mathematics without summoning up any specific number-images.

Beyond those obvious similarities, however, there remain at least five fundamental differences between memory and imagination.

1. *Rootedness in Perception.* Not only *can* memory borrow its content from perception, in most cases it *must* do so. To remember an object or event is almost always to summon back before the mind what was once in fact perceived. (In the relatively few instances when this is not the case, we recall a former fantasy or thought, although there is a tendency even here to remember the perceptual surroundings as well.) The prior perceptions upon which most remembering is founded influence not just its temporal direction (memory is exclusively past-oriented—see point 2) but also its thetic character (see point 5), its corrigibility (recollection, like perception, can be correct or incorrect), and its ability to change is own content (an ability delimited by considerations of fidelity to what was originally perceived). All of these features of remembering reflect memory's basis in previous perceivings, and they represent distinctive divergences from imagining, which is less constricted and more maneuverable in regard to each such feature: we need not imagine what is past or real, and what we imagine is not subject to criteria of corrigibility or of fidelity to former experience.

2. *Link to the Past.* A crucial consequence of the close connection between memory and perception is to be found in the basic temporal character of memory. Just as perception has to do with the *in*-sistence of objects or events that appear or occur in the present, so memory has to do with the *per*-sistence of objects or events that first appeared or occurred in the past. Such persistence is in turn founded upon two facts. First, whatever persists as the specific content of memory must possess a certain minimal obduracy—a perseverance over time, even if this perseverance occurs solely in the mind. Second, the temporal field in which remembered content is presently given to one is ultimately continuous with the particular temporal

field within which this content was first experienced at an earlier and precisely datable point. For both the original field of experience and the present field of recollection (which may resemble each other only insofar as it is
the *same* object or event that is experienced and remembered) form part of a
single temporal continuum. No matter how distant in time the two fields
may be from each other, we are assured that intermediate fields serve to
connect the original field with the one in which our remembering now
occurs. The resulting continuum from past occurrence to present remembrance provides a unified foundation for the persistence of remembered
material.

In imagining, there is a notable absence of both of these factors.
Nothing, strictly speaking persists in imaginative experience, whose content
lacks the fixity and stability of remembered content. In their fluidity and
fleetingness, imagined objects and events exhibit none of the obduracy or
perseverance of the things we remember, and they are not datable and
locatable in any measurably precise fashion. Further there is nothing in
imaginative experience that is meaningfully comparable to a perduring
temporal field in which entities or events can arise, last, and be focused
upon in an intersubjectively confirmable way. Consequently a given imaginative experience does not necessarily intermesh with the imaginer's past
experiences. In fact it is normally quite discontinuous with the temporal
fields in which these experiences took place. Yet, by the same token, precisely because what we imagine is not something that has persisted from the
past and does not belong to a backward-reaching continuum of linked
temporal fields, it is free to arise and develop in a less confined manner than
is what we remember. In exercising memory, we revert, implicitly or
explicity, to particular points of reference as factual-historical supports: I
remember Jones standing on the dock, at such-and-such a time of day, and
so on. These referential points, which help to situate whatever it is that we
recollect, *cannot be transposed* once they are established by the original appearance or occurrence of a given object or event. Imagined objects and
events, in contrast, are not attached to any such fixed original positions and
may be freely transported from one imaginative presentation to another.[9]

3. *Retentionality.* The term "retentionality" brings together two closely
related features that are both inherent in the temporality of memory: retentiveness and the retentional fringe. Neither of these features has any
counterpart in imagination. *Retentiveness* refers to the capacity to retain a

former experience in mind (though not necessarily consciously in mind) so as to be able to recall it on subsequent occasions. Thus retentiveness is a "dispositional" term in the sense that it indicates what memory *puts at our disposition* through its powers of retention. These powers are considerable, and it has even been argued that in some sense we retain everything we have ever experienced. At the very least, we cannot fail to be struck by the way in which many of our prior experiences are preserved in a form that is, in Freud's phrase, "astonishingly intact" (Freud and Breuer 1893–95, 10).[10] At the same time, retentiveness makes possible the assimilation of cognitive, perceptual, and motor skills; once they are thoroughly learned, we need not recollect explicitly *how* we first learned them.[11] Retentiveness, we might say, is the means by which we hold the past ready for reactivation in the present. As such, it is the basis for all explicit recollection.[12]

The *retentional fringe*, on the other hand, is that element or phrase of a just-past experience that lingers on in each successively new "now"; it is the immediately preceding moment as it fades from focus. William James describes the retentional fringe as "the rearward portion of the present space of time" (1950, 647), and Husserl (who terms it "retention" or "primary memory") likens it to "a comet's tail which clings onto the perception of the [present] moment" (1962, 57–59). The retentional fringe is essential to retentiveness, for an experience lacking a retentional fringe would not possess sufficient temporal density or distention to be retained for future recall. Moreover, far form being restricted to a role in retentiveness and recall, the retentional fringe shows itself to be operative in all area of mental life: *every psychical phenomenon has its retentional fringe.* This fringe helps to constitute the felt continuity that is ingredient to some degree in all forms of human experience. For no single characteristic of imagining can a comparable universality be claimed. In fact it is evident that imagining functions more as an alternative to, than as an accompaniment of, other mental acts. None of its essential features figures as an invariant dimension of other types of experience, while it is itself subject to retentionality in both senses of the term: a given imaginative experience is retained indefinitely, and it possesses its own retentional fringe.

4. *Familiarity.* Another distinctive, but more delimited, trait of memory is familiarity, the fact that what we remember is always something with which we are already acquainted to some degree. Unless we were at least minimally familiar with the objects and events we recollect, we could not

be said to re-member them—that is, to put them back together in a way that is faithful to the original experience, as well as becoming once more their contemporary (though now only via an intermediary act of recollection). In short, to be remembered, something must form part of the rememberer's *own* past experience. As James puts it: "Memory requires more than mere dating of a fact in the past. It must be dated in *my* past. In other words, I must think that I, directly, experienced its occurrence" (1950, 650). The familiarity underlying memory thus involves a personal relationship with remembered content, a relationship characterized by what James calls "warmth and intimacy" (1950, 650) and Bertrand Russell "trust."[13]

Familiarity is closely related to retentionality as described above. First of all, familiarity presupposes retentiveness insofar as any object or event with which we are familiar is one whose acquaintance we have retained over a given period of time. Second, familiarity involves the retentional fringe because we could never have *become* familiar with a particular object or event in the first place unless the experience of this object or event had been allowed to linger ("sink down" into our mind, as Husserl says) long enough for familiarity to be established.

As a form of personal relationship with the content of past experience, familiarity decisively demarcates remembering from imagining: familiarity is indispensable to memory but dispensable in imagination. I can imagine something with which I am not at all familiar (i.e., which has never been present in my experience), but I cannot remember anything with which I am not acquainted or familiar in some way and to some extent. It comes as no surprise therefore to discover that a number of philosophers "have regarded this same sense of familiarity as the feature which distinguishes memory from imagination." (Smith 1966, 20).[14] All that needs qualification in this assertion is that familiarity is not the *only* feature that differentiates the one act from the other.

5. *Belief.* By "belief" I refer to the characteristic thetic activity of remembering. In this usage, I follow Hume's lead: "The be*lief* or *assent*, which always attends the memory and senses ... alone distinguishes them from the imagination" (Hume 1967, 86). But if such belief, in line with the critical remarks made previously, is not to be reduced to what Hume calls the "vivacity of perceptions, in what does it consist? Is it only a matter, as James claims, of "feeling" or "emotion"?[15] Also, and more crucially,

involved in mnemonic belief is a specific cognitive operation by which we attribute a particular thetic character to what we recall. When I remember an object or event, and whether I do so with effort or spontaneously, I take this object or event to be something that once actually appeared or occurred in my presence. I accept or take it as possessing the thetic quality of *having-been-part-of-my-past-experience.*

This thetic character is unique to memory and is ultimately bound up with the four characteristics of remembering outlined in preceding sections. It is related, first of all, to prior perceptual experience, for to believe in the empirical existence of something requires that it be (or have been) perceived or at least perceivable. As Freud says laconically, "Belief in reality is bound up with perception through the senses" (1917, 230).[16] Second, belief in the content of memory as having-been-part-of-my-past-experience carries with it the presumption that my present act of recollection is temporarily continuous, through a series of interlacing time-fields, with the original experience I am now recalling; the absence of such continuity might lead me to doubt the authenticity of my memory. Third, belief in the past reality of what I remember presupposes retentionality; I believe that something actually has been because it has been "retained" in both of the primary meanings of this term. Finally, and perhaps most tellingly, I lend mnemonic credence to what I am familiar with through former (and perhaps continuing) acquaintance. To be familiar with the content of memory is to be in a position to posit this content as authentically having-been-part-of-my-past.

As Husserl recognized, the verb "to posit" (*setzen*) is of critical importance in any consideration of thetic activity. To say that I believe in the reality of what I recall is to say that I posit it (i.e., set it forth) as existent-in-my-past-just as I posit the content of anticipation as existent-in-my-future. Both forms of "positing presentification" (to use Husserl's technical term) are thus to be distinguished from the nonpositing presentifications of imagining, picturing, and sign-activity.[17] This suggests a final formulation of the difference between memory and imagination in regard to their respective thetic activities. In remembering, I believe in, or posit, as existing in my personal past that which presents itself (or more exactly, that which is presentified) now in the present; in imagining, I do no such thing: not only do I not posit imagined content as having-been, I do not posit it as existing in *any* sense or at *any* time.

Memory, we may conclude, is the *Janus bifrons* of mind. It gazes (and gazes most insistently) in one direction: toward the pole of perception, from which it derives the features of temporal order, familiarity, and belief that have been expounded in the pages above. But it also looks in a quite different direction: toward the pole of imagination, with which it shares such features as presentification, the option of spontaneity/controlledness, various act-forms, and the nonessentially of imagery. This double directedness of memory appears graphically if we attempt to represent Husserl's classificatory system in a diagrammatic form:

Positing acts	Presentifying acts
Memory	Memory
Perception	Imagination

In contrast with perception and imagination, which are single place-holders, memory appears twice in this schema. It is at once positing and presentifying, just as it is at once reality-bound (in terms of its origin in prior perceptions) and reality-free (insofar as it does not actually present, but only presentifies, an experience of the real). Given such strict ambivalence, it is not surprising that memory has been forced into ambiguous alliances by philosophers and psychologists—being made to side sometimes with perception and sometimes (indeed, more frequently) with imagination. In view of the foregoing analysis, however, it should be recognized as distinct and distinguishable from perception and imagination alike.

II

Hallucination is an experience that presents itself as even more akin to perception than is memory. Many of those who have attempted to determine the nature of hallucinating consider it to be, in fact, a specifies of perception. "Perception without an object" has been a classical definition of hallucination, frequently found in the literature on the subject.[18] Freud remarks that hallucinatory dream-images are "more like perceptions than they are like mnemonic presentations" (1900, 50), and he tries to demonstrate that these images are, in the final analysis, reactivated perceptions.[19] A representative recent pronouncement is that "a hallucination is an internal image that seems as real, vivid, and external as the perception of an object"

(Horowitz 1970, 8). To bear this out, the author furnishes the following report of a full-blown hallucination: "I was staring off into space, the I saw my brother in the corner of the room. His mouth moved but I heard no words. I spoke to him and he didn't answer. He just stood there, about eight feet away form me. Then he kind of fogged up and disappeared" (Horowitz 1970, 8). Such a statement helps us to understand why so many writers on the subject have taken hallucinations to be forms of perception. For the report indicates that the hallucinated brother-figure appeared in the hallucinator's *ordinary perceptual space* ("in the corner of the room"), as if he occupied a position along with, or in place of, everyday objects of perception; it also disappeared from this same perceived area by "fogging up." Here what is hallucinated and what is perceived are on a par, and seem to coexist, with each other.

The perceptual or at least quasi-perceptual status of hallucinations is at once their most striking and their most perplexing characteristic. It may lead us to ask: How can something that is nonperceptual in nature be taken as perceived? Fortunately, a phenomenological investigation need not provide an answer to this question. All that such an investigation must concern itself with is the fact *that* all hallucinations present themselves as perceptions. From this fact, which contrasts so vividly with the situation in imagining where nothing presents itself as perceptual), we may derive the following five features of hallucinatory experience, none of which has an exact counterpart in imaginative experience:

1. *Paranormality*. The vast majority of hallucinations come tinged with the pathological. It is clear that to hallucinate is not just to fall into perceptual *illusional*, which may be a natural and normal part of perceptual experience. It is to depart radically from the usual course of perceiving and to enter into an experience that it is natural to consider abnormal vis-à-vis the usual norms and practices of perception. To be more accurate, though, we should call hallucinating a paranormal activity, where the "para" stresses that the activity takes place "beside" normal perceptual activity. Hallucinations arise *alongside* ordinary perceptions, or they *replace* them for the time being. When this occurs in waking life, the suspicion of pathology is difficult to suppress, whether the hallucination is a positive one (as in the case just cited) or a negative one (as when the Wolfman hallucinated that he had cut off one of his fingers; 1918, 85–86). Even hallucinatory dream-images, which emerge every night in the lives of nonpathological as well as

pathological human subjects, are considered by Freud to be quite analogous
to "hallucinatory wish psychosis" and to furnish a paradigm for psycho-
neurotic symptoms (1917).[20]

Nevertheless, the paranormal character of hallucinating need not be
pathological in any strict clinical or nosological sense. There is a whole
group of hallucinatory experiences that, while potentially disruptive, are not
signs or symptoms of sickness of any kind. These include vivid entoptic
images ("phosphenes"), after-images and eidetic images, hallucinations
induced under hypnosis, déjà vu experiences, various synesthetic sensations,
misreadings of written texts (these are often species of negative hallucination, as in imperfect proofreading), phantom limbs, imaginary companions,
"dream scintillations," and religious visions.[21] None of these varied experiences is inherently pathological, and yet each is a genuine instance of hallucination inasmuch as its perceptual or quasi-perceptual nature is able to
arrest our attention and divert it from absorption in present perceptual experience. By thus competing with ordinary perception, such experiences
remain paranormal. From this we may conclude that whether pathological
or not, hallucinations differ distinctly from acts of imagining. The latter,
lacing thetic commitment to the empirically real, typically do not inter-
fere with or interrupt acts of perceiving. Imagined objects or events never
appear as if existing in the perceptual world. Therefore imagining cannot be
considered paranormal, since it does not distort or divert perceiving or
threaten to take its place. In its inherent innocence, imagination neither
rivals nor replicates perception.

2. *Sensory Vivacity*. It follows from what has just been said that unless
hallucinations achieve a certain sensory intensity, they cannot be compared
with, nor substitute themselves for, perceptions. To invoke "intensity" and
"vivacity" might seem to land us in the same difficulty in which Hume
became ensnared when he tried to distinguish imagination from memory.
But it is not here a question of establishing a *scale* of carefully graduated
sensory intensities on which to locate various mental acts at different points.
Rather, it is only a matter of attesting that *in a given situation* (and therefore
allowing for differences from situation to situation) a hallucination must
display sufficient vividness to allow it to enter into competition with our
ongoing perceptual activity. It must be rich enough in sensory qualities to
claim our committed awareness, to make us believe in it as a bona fide form
of perception. Thus a dream-image need not be as sensuously vivid as a

positive hallucination occurring in broad daylight. In the former case, the level of sensory vividness can be considerably diminished, thanks to what Freud called the "motor paralysis" of sleep. With our normal waking sensory channels mostly closed off, our mind is more easily attracted by a comparatively dim presentation. In the latter case, in contrast, the hallucination must appear vividly enough to be accepted as an acute or possible occupant of the daylight world.[22]

In imagining, there is no competition of any sort with perceiving. For one thing, we can imagine and perceive *concurrently*—so long as we are not attempting to imagine and perceive the same thing in the same respect. Imagined content is not experienced as occupying part of our present perceptual field, much less as taking it over. Further, what we imagine need not be sensory in character. By imagining nonsensuously, we diminish still further the opportunity for any direct competition with perception. To imagine an abstract state of affairs as purely as possible is, ipso facto, to leave the domain of perception—and any domain built upon, or analogous to, perception. Hallucinating, on the other hand, knows no such freedom from perceptual or quasi-perceptual domains. Hallucinations always appear in a specific sensory form, where the meaning of "sensory" includes reference to all of the following factors: "space, time, direction, distance, obtrusiveness, mineness, motion, measurability, and objectivity" (Straus 1966, 284).[23] No such set of strictly perceptual parameters structures the mini-worlds of imagination.

3. *Projectedness.* Still another basic characteristic of hallucinations is that their contents are experienced as "out there," as projected presences existing externally to the hallucinator's consciousness. Thus Freud asserts that a dream (his prototype for all hallucinating), is "a *projection*: an externalization of an internal process" (1917, 233).[24] Further, "dreams construct a *situation* out of [hallucinatory] images; they represent an event which is actually happening" (1900, 50). An event actually occurring in a situation takes place *outside* oneself as its observer; it is located externally to the perceiving self—as if arising *beyond* this self. Since a hallucinated event does *not* in fact occur in an actual situation, it has to be projected by the hallucinating subject as occurring there. "Projectedness" names the resulting pseudo-eternality, which characterizes everything from the elaborate visual displays of LSD hallucinations to "autoscopic" observations of one's own body from an external point in space. What psychologists or physiologists would regard

as located *inside* one's mind or body is projected outward until the equivalent of an authentically perceived object or event is felt to be present.[25]

Imaginative experience does not contain anything comparable to such thoroughgoing projectedness of content. We may speak of "projecting" possible objects and states of affairs in imagining, but such *possibilia* are not projected as constituents of actual situations external to the imaginer. Far from inhabiting a concrete setting, imagined possibilities are typically projected into a spatio-temporal limbo that is felt to be neither external nor internal to the imaginer. When I imagine how to row a boat (and even when I do so in sensory detail), the scene I summon up lacks the distinctive situatedness of something hallucinated. Even if I expressly attempt to project a state of affairs that is at some significant distance from myself—and perhaps even partly superimposed on an actual perceptual scene—what I imagine still lacks the sense of obdurate otherness that is found as a matter of course in hallucinated scenes. And I can always, by a further effort, overcome this imaginary distance and make myself one with the imaginatively projected situation—which I cannot do readily, if at all, in hallucinating the same situation.

4. *Involuntariness.* With rare exceptions, hallucinations arise without our express volition. This may happen in various circumstances—in psychopathological states or when hypnotized, asleep, drugged, and so on—but whatever the causes or conditions of hallucinations, they tend to emerge spontaneously and beyond our conscious control. Indeed, they often appear so rapidly and with so little warning that we are astounded or shocked that any such thing could happen. (Contrast this reaction with the characteristically *mild* surprise that occurs in imagining.) Furthermore our ability to control or terminate hallucinations once they have appeared is usually quite limited: witness the "voices" of the schizophrenic patient, auditory presences that mercilessly pursue and threaten.[26] Hallucinations may also recur with distressing and unpredictable frequency, as in Sartre's persisting hallucinations of crabs (occasioned by mescaline).[27] There is little, if anything, that the hallucinating subject can do to ward off these unwelcome *revenants*—in contrast with imaginative experience where the obsessive recurrence of an imagined object can be dealt with much more effectively. In fact, as imaginers, we are normally able to terminate, once and for all, a given imaginative appearance, and even if we cannot do this, we can alter the subsequent course of this appearance.

5. *Belief.* The involuntariness of hallucinatory experience reflects its predominant thetic activity—belief in the empirical reality of its content. Voltaire remarked that hallucinating "is not seeing in imagination: it is seeing in reality."[28] And "seeing in reality" entails believing that what one apprehends is present to one's senses as spatio-temporally existent. As Jean-Étienne Esquirol said in 1833, "A man who has the inner conviction of a sensation actually perceived while no object fitting for its excitation is at the threshold of his senses, such a man is in a condition of hallucinating."[29] Or as Freud put it more pithily, "Hallucination brings belief in reality with it" (1917, 230).

Hallucination involves belief in the empirically real precisely because of the vivid sensory quality of hallucinated content.[30] We adhere to the reality of what we hallucinate inasmuch as it appears to us not only as the sort of thing that *could be* perceived (this is true of many things we imagine) but as *actually* perceived. By "actually" is meant perceived *in the present* as an occupant of the very same spatio-temporal field in which one is situated oneself. In this way, the hallucinator's belief is to be distinguished from the sort of thetic activity that inheres in either memory or imagination. In contrast with mnemonic belief, hallucinatory belief does not bear on realities in their pastness (i.e., as having-been-present-in-my-past) but on realities that appear (or *appear* to appears) at the present moment. As contrasted with what happens in imagining, in hallucinating we place credence in the existence of *some* presently appearing object or event; we do not suspend committed belief altogether and entertain pure possibilities. If we include anticipation in a schema for comparing different types of thetic character, we arrive at the following diagrammatic results:

Type of act or activity	Thetic character and temporal mode (Empirical) reality			Possibility
	Present	Past	Future	Omnitemporal
Perception	X			
Hallucination	X			
Memory		X		
Anticipation			X	
Imagination				X

Does this mean, as the diagram suggests, that there is *no distinction* to be made between the belief-character of hallucination and that of perception? Here we are forced to recognize that there are in fact two forms of hallucinatory belief. The first is experientially indistinguishable from perceptual belief; occurring in what is called colloquially a "full-blown hallucination," it involves the same fully committed credence in empirical reality that characterizes ordinary perception. The second form of hallucinatory belief is less intensely committed in character; in this case, the hallucinator remains able to distinguish between what is hallucinated and what is actually perceived. The paradox is that the hallucinated content, even though distinguishable from what is genuinely perceived, is still regarded as real. The patient who does not confuse his recurrent hallucinations of a person dressed in a certain way and standing under his window with bona fide perceptions of just such a person actually standing under his window nevertheless maintains that both presences are real: "Yes, there is someone there, but it's someone else."[31] Qualitative distinctness does not preclude the belief that both forms of presence are empirically real, as we can also observe in many cases of "hearing voices": the hallucinated voices are experienced as real (encroaching on one's senses from the outside, occurring in the present, etc.) and at the same time as different from ordinary, authentically perceived human voices. Indeed, it may be this very difference that accounts for the frequently reported "eeriness" of numerous hallucinatory experiences. The implication, in any case, is that the thetic character of empirical reality possesses sufficient ambiguity or latitude to allow it to be the object of at least two different forms or modes of belief, one of which is common to perception and full-blown hallucination while the other is peculiar to a less intense type of hallucination.

No such overlap of belief-forms emerges when we compare hallucination or perception with imagination, which does not in any way involve belief in empirical reality. The imaginer remains content to posit pure possibilities. It is clear that the natural alliance between perceiving and hallucinating in this regard, and thus the basis for their mutual differentiation from imagining, is to be found in the fact that hallucination not only resembles perception but seems to provide a form of surrogate perceptual experience. This is why we are often tempted to term hallucinatory experience "quasi-perceptual," where the "quasi" indicates that the hallucinated content may in certain cases be taken as fully valid perceptual content. We might say that hallucination fashions a world *like* the perceptual world, and one that momentarily usurps its place, even though such a world is in fact no world at all. In this, the hallucinatory departs widely from the imaginer, whose mentated mini-worlds neither resemble the perceptual world nor replace it with something quasi-real.

III

Of the various psychical phenomena with which imagination may be compared, fantasy is no doubt the most ambiguous and difficult to define. "Fantasy" is a polysemous word which in ordinary parlance denotes a variety of acts ranging from near-hallucinatory and quite involving experiences, through reveries and daydreams, to mere "passing fancies."[32] Because of this equivocality, attempts at strict definition are in danger of effecting premature foreclosure. Consider, for example, one recent attempt: "Fantasy is defined as verbal reports of all mentation whose ideational products are not evaluated by the subject in terms of their usefulness in advancing some immediate goal extrinsic to the mentation itself" (Klinger 1971, 9– 10). Conspicuous in this statement is its entirely negative character; we are told what fantasy is *not*, not what it is. Moreover the single criterion mentioned—not evaluating results of mental activity in terms of usefulness—is so general as also to apply to imagining, to hallucination, and even to memory. Greater specificity is clearly called for.

When we try to become more specific, however, we notice that the ambiguity of fantasy is not only verbal. It is also, and more important, *phenomenal*. For human experience includes a whole series of phenomena that can be considered types of fantasy, from children's "theories" about the adult world to the Walter Mitty daydreams of adults themselves. Compounding the problem is the fact that these phenomena are not always readily isolatable from each other. They tend to overlap in such a way as to make strict separation extremely difficult: "There are many transitional forms. . . . Fantasying shades into remembering when it uses memories and when the inaccuracies of memory are fantasies. For corresponding reasons, fantasying shades into perceiving, anticipating, and planning (Schafer 1968, 37). Nevertheless, fantasy tends to ally itself more with certain mental activities than with others; it is not indifferently connectable with all such activities. In particular, it has a tendency to border on *hallucination*, on one hand, and on *imagination*, on the other. In the former case, a fantasy becomes increasingly involving, dramatic, and sensuously vivid. It draws the subject into its grip in such a way that he or she is on the verge of losing control of the experience, which may then become fully hallucinatory.[33] But there is a second possibility as well—namely the conversion of fantasy into imagination. Such a conversion typically occurs in daydreams or reveries, when what had been a full-fledged fantasy suddenly becomes an experience in which the autonomous action of the subject is much more prominent than in fantasy proper. The daydream or reverie ceases to be as engrossing as before and is experienced as something merely entertained (hence more easily controllable) by the now-imagining subject.

But here we must ask: What *is* fantasy if it is still distinguishable from hallucination and imagination? Even while admitting that fantasy is exceedingly difficult to pinpoint in its pure state (Sartre would call it "metastable"),[34] we may single out five distinctive characteristics.

1. *Narrative character.* Perhaps the single most stirring feature of fantasies is their tendency to tell a story. This feature is based on their sequential structure, which contrasts with the fragmentariness of most hallucinating and imagining. In fantasy, individual episodes are woven together to realize a more or less coherent story line, instead of being allowed to appear in isolation. A representative fantasy is given in the following autobiographical account of Jerome Singer's:

> Within the format of [my] fantasied football games, Poppy Ott emerged as the super-star, the shifty-hipped, clever broken-field runner and accurate passer. As time passed the overt motor representation of an imagined game was no longer socially feasible and I began to draw the game on paper in cartoon form. I would visualize an entire league series, draw significant highlights from each game, occasionally write out play-by-play accounts of the games, and keep statistics on the various achievements of my fantasy players in the same way that the newspapers do for running or passing averages. As I grew into adolescence, Poppy Ott, who was supposedly a few years older than I was, grew up too. He left Tutter to play professional football and, after so well-documented setbacks, emerged as the greatest football player of all time on a Boston professional team of my own creation. (1966, 19–20)[35]

Several significant aspects of this "Poppy Ott" fantasy should be noticed. First of all, it was initially inspired by Singer's boyhood reading of a series of children's books which featured Poppy Ott as one of the principal characters. Notably Singer did borrow the fictitious personage of Ott from these books, but also he placed Ott into fantasies which by their very form and structure continued the narrative mode of the original stories. It was as if the fantasies took over at the point where the stories left off. Second, in the early stages of his Ott fantasies, Singer depicted their content in dramatized actions, drawings, or in words. Only later did he turn to visualizing as the predominant mode in which to realize these fantasies. Moreover the fantasies were not unrelated to actual events in Singer's life; for example, they appeared especially frequently during the football season. In all of these ways—by dramatization, drawing, and writing, and by correlation with actual events—Singer drew on resources that reinforced the inner continuity, sequential character, and general credibility of his fantasy experiences. The result was that "the entire fantasy sequence settled into a fairly circumscribed pattern. In high school and even into adult life I would deal with situations that were monotonous or dull by resorting consciously to playing out a particular game in which Poppy Ott starred" (1966, 19–20).

No such "circumscribed pattern" characterizes imaginative experiences, which lack the fundamental consistency and coherency of fantasies of the sort Singer describes. Indeed, it is even questionable whether we can be said to imagine the *same* object or event again and again, and any sense of a perduring spatial or temporal "field" in which a narrated action could take place is lacking in imaginative presentations. Thus, without any basis for recurrency or spatio-temporal stability, it is very difficult to superimpose a narrative form on what we imagine. For such a form to "take," a certain continuity in content and manner of presentation is required. In the absence of such continuity, isolated episodes may appear, but they will not fit together to constitute anything like a story. The result is that imaginings are inherently nonnarrative in character; episodic at best (though often much more fleeting even than this), they disintegrate too quickly to possess a strictly narrative structure—"one glimpse and vanished" (Beckett 1965, 7).[36]

2. *Sense of participation.* The tales that are told in fantasies differ from explicitly literary tales in two important regards. First, there is not a comparable concern with *form* in the two cases. Literary tales are fashioned with an eye to their formal perfection, and part of our pleasure in coming to know them stems form our apprehending their well-crafted formal qualities. Fantasies are, as it were, *purely narrative*, stories spun solely for the sake of their content—a content that is typically, as Freud observed, either erotic or ambitious in tenor (1908, 147). At the same time they often give the impression of "taking their own course," that is, proceeding without the express direction of the fantasist.

Second, fantasied stories always involve the fantasist himself or herself as a participation in their narrated scenes. This fantasist (who is none other than "His Majesty the Ego")[37] represents himself as partaking in the unfolding action of the fantasy in either of two ways. On the one hand, he may do so straightforwardly by depicting himself as present *in person* in the fantasy, as one of its *dramatis personae*—though the exact nature of this presence varies considerably from fantasy to fantasy. On the other hand, the fantasist may participate in the fantasied action *by proxy*, either by identifying himself with one of its presented personages (e.g., Poppy Ott) or by designating one of these personages as his delegate or representative (e.g., as when the fantasist thinks to himself, "That's my type of man").

A further and closely related phenomenon is found in what psychoanalysts call "reflective self-representation," that is, a distinct sense of oneself as separate from the self that is represented (directly or indirectly) in the fantasied scenes. This peculiar self-consciousness is by no means constantly present—it tends to come and go—but it is always felt to be within reach: "the suspension of the reflective self representation is temporary or oscillating, or, in other terms, easily and effortlessly reversible" (Schafer 1968, 94).

These aspects of participation in fantasy may be contrasted with what happens in imagining and hallucinating, especially the latter. In hallucinating, the subject typically feels himself or herself to be the passive recipient or victim of external forces over which he or she has no control (hence their frequently frightening character). Only rarely does one represent oneself as *participating*, in person or by proxy, in a hallucinated scene. In fact one's sense of self-identify may be so weak that one feels that a dead or depersonalized self is being attacked by the threatening forces. The imaginer, on the other hand, normally retains a quite intact sense of self-identify. Indeed, his or her reflective self-representation may be even more pronounced than that of the fantasist, particularly during experiences of controlled imagining: "*I* am imagining this," one is implicitly saying to oneself at such moments. By the same token, and perhaps as a consequence of this secure self-consciousness, there is a tendency for the imaginer *not* to represent himself or herself as a participant in the imaginatively projected scene. This is not to deny that one may do so on occasion, especially when one imagines *how* it is to be in a certain imagined situations. Yet if imagining-how thereby requires one's participation, this is not the case with regard to simple visualizing or imagining *that* such-and-such obtains. These latter spread before the imaginer momentary scenes of which he or she is the mere witness, situated at their edge as it seems. In such instances one does not depict himself as a participant in the ongoing action.

3. *Waywardness.* By this term, I refer to the specific character of control that the fantasist experiences vis-à-vis his or her fantasy. In contrast with both fantasy and imagination, hallucination allows for very little conscious control, arising as an externally imposed and often overwhelming experience. It is true that certain hallucinations may be elicited at will, but once having emerged even these have a way of taking over the whole of one's awareness and of vanishing unpredictably and independently of one's volition. Fantasies are subject to considerably more control throughout. The fantasist can encourage their initial appearance (coax them into being, as it were), exercise varying degrees of influence upon their development, and draw them to a close by merely diverting his or her attention. But we should not exaggerate the controlled character of fantasy. As was remarked earlier, fantasying tends to take its own course, not to the wild and bizarre extent of hallucinating, but nonetheless to the point of appearing to generate its own content. It is in this sense *wayward*, seeming to have a will of is own and spinning itself out. The fantasist is usually content to assume a position of engrossed awareness so as to follow the unfolding narrative. This contrasts with what is found in imagining, where the factor of control is much more prominent. In almost every case, the imaginer can imagine precisely as, how, and when he or she wishes to. No comparable controllability of content manifests itself in fantasies, most of which arise and proceed spontaneously. The point is not that such fantasies *cannot* be controlled (as if so often the case in hallucinating) but that they are less frequently and thoroughly controlled than are imaginative experiences.

4. *Wish fulfillment.* In a much-quoted statement, Freud asserted that "a happy person never phantasies, only an unsatisfied one. The motive forces of phantasies are unsatisfied wishes, and every single phantasy is the fulfillment of a wish, a correction of unsatisfying reality" (1908, 146). We need not posit wishes as "motive forces" in order to agree with Freud. Fantasies are experienced as wish-fulfilling, whatever the exact status of wishes may be in the total system of the psyche. Thus "wish-fulfilling" as used here refers to an actually experienced trait of fantasies, not to their general function. Fantasies set forth situations that, by their very nature, represent the fulfillment of wishes. The sense of fulfillment is itself based on the fact that fantasies present relatively compete depictions of their own

content, and their narrative character aids immensely in presenting scenes that are complex enough (spatially, temporally, and in other ways) to be *scenes of satisfaction*.

The term "satisfaction" is important here. The primary affect attaching to fantasy experiences is that of pleasure. We find most fantasies pleasant to behold, and this is so even when the scenes they portray are sadistic or self-reproachful. It is no less enjoyable to witness the fulfillment of our own vengeful or self-critical thoughts than it is to project the fulfillment of altruistic or erotic impulses or thoughts enacted—but enacted precisely in fantasy. Where *actual* enactment might well bring consternation or horror, enactment in fantasy gives rise to pleasure. Much as in viewing movies, we know that the scene fantasies proffer, however terrifying they might be if they were in fact present, are by no means real ones. There is a "willing suspension of disbelief," but by the same token there is the assurance that what we witness is not to be believed as actually occurring.

The factor of wish-fulfillment brings fantasy closer to hallucination in one respect and to imagination in another. It is clear that fantasy and hallucination resemble each other to the extent that each projects entire scenes or situations; each thus provides a sufficient pictorial basis for representing the fulfillment of a wish by some particular action or set of actions. Imagining, in contrast, is often too scanty in its presentations to allow wish-fulfillment to be adequately represented. Nevertheless, in terms of affective quality, fantasy and imagination are closer to each other than either is to hallucination. Hallucination elicits fully and deeply felt emotions, often of an anxious or apprehensive nature, while the emotions associated with fantasying and imagining are comparatively tepid. Where a peculiarly self-indulgent pleasure is the main affect experienced in fantasying, a muted surprise or even an absence of overt emotion is characteristic of imagining.

5. *Belief.* As in the case of several other basic traits of fantasy, its thetic activity situates itself *between* the corresponding activities of hallucinating and imagining. On the one hand, this activity differs from the sort of committed belief found in hallucination, since fantasied content is not posited as real or as competing with the real. As Freud formulates it, "daydreaming is never confused with reality" (1900, 50)—as opposed to nocturnal dreaming, where the confusion occurs constantly. Nothing in what we fantasy induces us to consider it as actually taking place before us. Indeed, the more attune and open to fantasy we are, the more we rely upon a sure sense of

the difference between what we experience in fantasy and what we experience in hallucination or in ordinary perception.

On the other hand, the thetic character of fantasy is to be distinguished from that of imagination insofar as what we fantasy is not experienced as purely possible. Thanks to its narrative form, fantasied content evokes in us a special allegiance—a conviction that what we are witnessing is, if not empirically or externally real, at least real *in mente*. Such content has a peculiar ability to persuade us that the scenes we are fantasying exist by right—by *psychological* right—if not in fact. As a consequence we ascribe to them what Jung calls "*esse in anima*" (Jung 1947–75, *Collected Works VI*, 45) or what other psychoanalysts term variously "inner reality," "internal reality," and above all "psychical reality."[38] The scene being enacted in fantasy does not represent or even adumbrate what is empirically real or purely possible; it has a distinct form of psychological presence that calls forth neither the commitment of hallucination or perception nor the noncommittal attitude of imagining. In fact the resulting sense of the psychically real involves a turning away form the extra-psychically (i.e., materially or socially) real.[39]

Extra-psychical reality is replaced, not by a quasi-perceptual hallucinatory reality, but by a psychical reality that is of our own making.

A last remark is in order. It cannot be denied that important continuities and overlaps occur between the four acts that have been compared in this chapter: memory may furnish the framework and even the details of hallucinating, fantasying, and imagining; fantasy can collapse into hallucination or be taken up into imagination; hallucination can be instigated and modified by all of the other acts, just as it may significantly influence them in turn; and imagining may draw on each of the others for its specific content, while also (though infrequently) lending content to them. But any such mutual impinging must be distinguished from epistemological dependency. For each of these four acts can occur independently of the others and in their absence, and none serves as a necessary condition for the rest. Moreover each is eidetically differentiable from the others, possessing its own unique set of distinctive characteristics. Although resemblances exist among certain of these characteristics, distinctions are to be found even here: the controllability of fantasying and that of imagining, however similar, are not precisely the same; the positing activities of hallucination and of memory, though both bearing on empirical reality, do so in very different ways. We may conclude, therefore, that a descriptive analysis of memory, hallucination, and fantasy reveals these acts to be epistemologically and eidetically distinct not only from imagination but from each other as well.

Notes

1. The structure of imagining itself is described in detail in my *Imagining: A phenomenological Study* (1976). The same work also contains a comparison of imagination and perception (chapters 6 and 7) and a specification (in the Introduction) of the ways in which imagining, remembering, fantasying, and hallucinating have been inadequately distinguished from each other in Western psychology and philosophy.

2. See Aristotle, *Metaphysics* (980b: 24–30). See also Aristotle's explicit linking of memory and imagination in *De Memoria et Reminiscentia*: "Memory, even the memory of objects of thought, is not without an image. . . . And it is the objects of imagination that are remembered in their own right" (1972, 49).

3. Quoted from *Leviathan*, his italics. Note that "fancy" and "imagination" are interchangeable for Hobbes.

4. In Hobbes's proto-empiricist view, *all* mental acts stem from sensation: from it, "the rest are derived" (1968, 85). But memory and imagination are more directly derived from sensation than are other acts.

5. Also: memory "is nothing but the springing up again of reminiscences" (1968, 264). Such a view is not restricted to Hobbes or Vico. An eminent imagery researcher writes that "images are not merely imitations, *but memory fragments*, reconstructions, reinterpretations" (Horowitz, 1970, 4), my italics.

6. Note that McKellar supports his position by invoking the same argument as Aristotle or Hobbes: "No imagination image can occur that is not composed of elements derived from actual perceptual experience" (1957, 23).

7. On the same page, Hume suggests another criterion for distinguishing between ideas of memory and ideas of imagination. The "order and form" of the former must conform to their "original impressions," while no such conformity is required of the latter. But Hume comes to reject this criterion when he acknowledges that it is "impossible to recall the past impressions, in order to compare them without present ideas, and see whether their arrangement be exactly similar" (p. 85).

8. The situation in fact is more complex than this simple division implies. The generic term "memory" (active form: "remembering") subsumes spontaneous recall and labored recollection, but it also includes intermediate acts such as "reminiscing," which may be spontaneous *or* controlled.

9. As remembered, of course, my *act* of imagining possesses a determinate temporal position: I imagined x at time y, and this remains true indefinitely. But the *contents* of my act are neither positioned on an objective time-line nor located in a determinate spatial expanse. Rather, these contents exfoliate, at whim or at will, without regard to any precise point of origin in space or in time.

10. Freud also muses upon how "unexpectedly accurate memory can be" (p. 11) and is struck by the "hypermnesic" quality of dreams which reproduce earlier and long-forgotten situations (Freud 1900, 11–17).

11. On this point, see Brian Smith, *Memory* (1966, 108).

12. As William James says, "An object which is recollected, in the proper sense of that term, is one which has been absent from consciousness altogether, and now revives anew. It is brought back, recalled, fished up, so to speak, from a reservoir in which, with countless other objects it lay buried and lost from view" (1950, 646). Described thus, retentiveness cannot be restricted to specific skills we have learned; it applies to anything and everything that, having once been experienced, has now sedimented itself into our permanent stock of recallable material.

13. ... the "characteristic by which we distinguish the [memory] images we trust is the feeling of familiarity that accompanies them" (Russell 1921, 161).

14. For Smith's own reservations as to this thesis, see (1966, 42, 96).

15. "Memory is then the feeling of belief in a peculiar complex object.... The object of memory is only an object imagined in the past ... to which the emotion of belief adheres" (James 1950, 652).

16. Hume also writes: "To believe is ... to feel an intimate impression of the senses, or a repetition of that impression in the memory" (1966, 86). Aristotle agrees: "Belief will have as [its] object nothing else but that which, if it exists, is the object of the perception" (*De Anima*, 428a: 28–30).

17. See Husserl's *The Phenomenology of Internal Time-Consciousness* (1962), sections 16–28 and appendixes I and II. See also Husserl's *Ideas.* (1958), sections 43, 99–101, and 111. My two essays "Imagination and Repetition in Literature" (Casey 1976a) and "The Image/Sign Relation in Husserl and Freud" (Casey 1976b) discuss Husserl's classification in more detail than can be attempted here.

18. See, for example, Pierre Quercy, *L'Hallucination* (1930, 112 and 559), and Jean Lhermitte, *Les Hallucinations* (1951, 25). For a critique of this definition, see Erwin Straus "Phenomenology of Hallucinations," in Straus's text *Phenomenological Psychology* (1966, 277–289).

19. See also Freud (1900–1901, 544–46 and 598ff) and (1923, 20). These passages make it clear that although the formation of dream-images specifically involves the cathexis of memory traces, the memory that is thereby revived is of a former *perception*.

20. Especially page 230: "One might speak quite generally of a 'hallucinatory wishful psychosis,' and attribute it equally to dreams and amentia." On the dream as a prototype of neurotic symptoms, see *The Interpretation of Dreams* (Freud 1900, xxiii). On the relation between dreams and insanity, see ibid. (88–92).

21. For a comprehensive overview of such nonpathological paranormal experiences, see Horowitz, (1970) especially chapter 1.

22. I saw "actual" or *possible* because of the fact that many hallucinators do not believe that what they hallucinate is actually present before them. They assume what Lhermitte calls a "critical" attitude even as they are hallucinating (Lhermitte 1951, 26). Also see section 5 below.

23. Straus provides a detailed chart on page 285 on the projection that occurs in hysterical phobia and paranoia (1966, 223–24).

24. Such projection is then analogized to the projection that occurs in hysterical phobia and paranoia (pp. 223–24).

25. That there is a link between sensory vivacity and projectedness is suggested in Lord Brain's definition of hallucinations as "mental impressions of sensory vividness occurring without external stimulus, but appearing to be located outside the subject" (Brain 1962, 828).

26. As Straus observes, such voices are all the more insidious and uncontrollable for being disembodied: "eluding all limits and boundaries and not hindered by walls or distances, such voices are overwhelming and irresistible in their power. The patient is helpless!" (1966, 286). Evident here is the close link between the eternality of hallucinatory phenomena and their involuntariness.

27. For a brief account of Sartre's hallucinations, see M. Contat and M. Rybalka, *Les écrits de Sartre* (1970, 26). The technical term for hallucinatory persistence is "flashback" or "throwback."

28. Quoted by T. R. Sarbin and J. B. Juhasz (1967, 348).

29. Quoted from Esquirol's *Observations on the Illusions of the Insane* by Straus, in his chapter "Phenomenology of Hallucinations," (1966, 288–89).

30. As Straus observes, "sensory experiencing and experiencing the real one are one and the same" (1958, 162).

31. See Maurice Merleau-Ponty's discussion of this case in *Phenomenology of Perception* (1962, 334). Striking instances of hallucinatory voice are given in Joanne Greenberg, *I Never Promised You a Rose Garden* (1964) especially chapters 6–8. It is misleading to term either of these experiences a "pseudo-hallucination" (Horowitz 1970, 9). There is nothing *experientially* "pseudo" about such experiences; indeed, their sense of reality is such as to be able to cause considerable consternation. Not to be fully believable is not necessarily not to be believable at all.

32. Actually the ambiguity of "fantasy" is even more extensive than this. As Charles Rycroft has written, "At present the word is used to mean (I) a general mental activity, (ii) a particular, neurotic form of this activity, (iii) a state of mind raising from it and (iv) the fictive realm in which it occurs" (1968, 52).

33. As Schafer writes, "Although fantasying is recognized (or recognizable) for what it is by the subject, through regression it can succumb to the primary process and lose its index of being 'in the imagination'; in that case, it turns into a delusion or hallucination, and it is coped with by the subject as though it existed in the immediate outer world" (1968, 38).

34. The term "metastable" is used by Jean-Paul Sartre in *Being and Nothingness* (1975) to describe constantly changing and transitional modes of activity. See especially part I, chapter 2, and part II, chapter 2, of *Being and Nothingness*.

35. Singer records other examples on page 20. See also the instances of elaborate children's fantasies cited by Anna Freud in *The Ego and the Mechanisms of Defense* (1967, 73).

36. My claim concerning the narrative character of fantasies does not mean that all fantasies must be as intricate and quasi-literary as Singer's. The point is rather that there is a strong tendency toward a full narrative form—the stringing together of episodes into a single story—even if this form is realized only imperfectly on given occasions. As Schafer says, "[fantasy] has a narrative aspect. In some instances, however, its content is an isolated static representation, the remainder of the narrative being blocked from development, and, thus, only implied. In these instances, fantasy overlaps idle, odd, or obsessive thoughts. In other instances, the fantasy's narrative *organization* is minimally developed; then, fantasy and stream of consciousness overlap" (1968, 38).

37. We can immediately recognize His Majesty the Ego, the hero alike of every daydream and of every story" (Freud 1908, 150).

38. See C. G. Jung (1947–75, 6: 45). D. W. Winnicott writes, "Fantasy is part of the individual's effort to deal with inner reality" (1958, 130). Heinz Hartmann avers that fantasies "open internal reality" to the individual (1961, 373). Freud first proposed the use of the term "psychical realty" in *The Interpretation of Dreams*. (1900–1901, 613 and 620).

39. Thus Hartmann writes, "Fantasy always implies an initial turning away from a real situation" (1939, 373). And in Eugen Bleuler's classic description, "what is usually called fantasy disregards one or more aspects of reality, replacing them by arbitrary presuppositions; it is autistic" (1951, 416). But to turn away from or disregard empirical reality is not necessary to *deny* this reality, as Anna Freud implies when she writes that little Hans "denied reality by means of his fantasy" (1967, 73).

References

Aristotle. 1972. *Aristotle on Memory*, trans. by R. Sorabji. London: Duckworth.

Aristotle. *Metaphysics*. In R. McKeon, ed., *The Basic Works of Aristotle*. New York: Random House, 1941, p. 689.

Aristotle. *De Anima*. In R. McKeon, ed., *The Basic Works of Aristotle*. New York: Random House, 1941, p. 588.

Beckett, S. 1965. *Imagination Dead Imagine*. London: Calder and Boyars.

Bleuler, E. 1951. Autistic Thinking. In I. D. Rapaport, ed., *Organization and Pathology of Thought*. New York: Columbia University Press.

Brain, W. R. 1962. *Diseases of the Nervous System*. London: Oxford University Press.

Contat, M., and M. Rybalka, 1970. *Les Écrits de Sartre*. Paris: Gallimard.

Casey, E. 1976. *Imagining: A Phenomenological Study*. Bloomington: Indiana University Press.

Casey, E. 1976a. Imagination and repetition in literature. *Yale French Studies* 52 (Spring): 249–67.

Casey, E. 1976b. The image/sign relation in Husserl and Freud. *Review of Metaphysics* 30: 207–25.

Freud, A. [1936] 1967. *The Ego and the Mechanisms of Defense*. New York: International University Press.

Freud, S., and J. Breuer. [1893–95] 1955. *Studies on Hysteria*. Translated by J. Strachey. *Standard Edition, II*. London: Hogarth Press.

Freud, S. [1900] 1953. *The Interpretation of Dreams: First Part*. Translated by J. Strachey. *Standard Edition, IV*. London: Hogarth Press.

Freud, S. [1900–1901] 1953. *The Interpretation of Dreams: Second Part*. Translated by J. Strachey. *Standard Edition, V*. London: Hogarth Press.

Freud, S. [1908] 1959. Creative writers and day-dreaming. Translated by J. Strachey. *Standard Edition, IX*, London: Hogarth Press, pp. 141–153.

Freud, S. [1917] 1957. A metapsychological supplement to the theory of dreams. Translated by J. Strachey. *Standard Edition, XIV*. London: Hogarth Press, pp. 217–236.

Freud, S. [1918] 1955. From the history of an infantile neurosis. Translated by J. Strachey. *Standard Edition, XVII*. London: Hogarth Press, pp. 3–122.

Freud, S. [1923] 1961. The Ego and the Id. Translated by J. Strachey. *Standard Edition, XIX*. London: The Hogarth Press, pp. 3–68.

Greenberg, J. 1964. *I Never Promised You a Rose Garden*. New York: Signet.

Hartmann, H. 1961. *Ego Psychology and the Problem of Adaptation*. Translated by D. Rapaport. New York: International Universities Press.

Hobbes, T. 1968. *Leviathan*. Edited by C. B. Macpherson. London: Pelican.

Horowitz, M. J. 1970. *Image Formation and Cognition*. New York: Appleton-Century Crofts.

Hume, D. 1967. *A Treatise of Human Nature*. Edited by L. A. Selby-Bigge. Oxford: Clarendon Press.

Husserl, E. 1962. *The Phenomenology of Internal Time-Consciousness*, Translated by J. Churchill. Bloomington: Indiana University Press.

Husserl, E. 1958. *Ideas*. Translated by W. R. Boyce Gibson. London: Allen and Unwin.

James, W. 1950. *Principles of Psychology*. New York: Dover.

Jung, C. G. 1947–75. *Collected Works VI*. Princeton: Princeton University Press.

Klinger, E. 1971. *Structure and Functions of Fantasy*. New York: Wiley.

Lhermitte, J. 1951. *Les Hallucinations*. Paris: Doin.

McKellar, P. 1957. *Imagination and Thinking*. New York: Basic Books.

Merleau-Ponty, M. 1962. *Phenomenology of Perception*. Translated by C. Smith. New York: Humanities Press.

Quercy, P. 1930. *L'Hallucination*. Paris: Alcan.

Russell, B. 1921. *Analysis of Mind*. London: Allen and Unwin.

Rycroft, C. 1968. *Imagination and Reality*. London: Hogarth Press.

Sarbin, T. R., and J. B. Juhasz. 1967. The Historical background of the concept of hallucination. *Journal of the History of the Behavioral Sciences* 3: 348.

Sartre, J.-P. 1975. *Being and Nothingness.* Translated by H. Barnes. New York: Washington Square Press.

Schafer, R. 1968. *Aspects of Internalization.* New York: International University Press.

Singer, J. 1966. *Daydreaming.* New York: Random House.

Smith, B. 1966. *Memory.* London: Allen and Unwin.

Straus, E. 1966. Phenomenology of hallucinations. In *Phenomenological Psychology.* New York: Basic Books.

Straus, E. 1958. Anesthesiology and hallucination. In *Existence.* Edited by R. May et al. New York: Basic Books.

Vico, G. 1968. *The New Science.* Translated by T. G. Bergin and M. J. Fisch. Ithaca: Cornell University Press.

Winnicott, D. W. 1958. *Collected Papers.* New York: Basic Books.

5

The Texture of the Real: Merleau-Ponty on Imagination and Psychopathology

James Morley

Introduction

This chapter will show that Maurice Merleau-Ponty's thought radically recasts the relation between the real and the imaginary in a way that can illuminate our understanding of psychopathology. Though Merleau-Ponty is well known for his thesis of the primacy of perception and the introduction of 'embodiment' to philosophical discourse, he is less known for the theory of imagination contained within, and generated by, his understanding of perception. Specifically, I will elucidate Merleau-Ponty's appropriation of gestalt psychology, which allowed him to view the imaginary-real as an open-ended continuum. His pivotal concept of perceptual faith which foregrounds the fundamentally ontological character of the imaginary-real nexus will be explicated. It will be suggested that this concept of perceptual or ontological faith[1] provides a richer basis for understanding the spectrum between psychopathological and healthy-minded ways of life that is foregrounded in situations of pathological breakdown. A constituent component of this perceptual faith is what Merleau-Ponty calls a "tolerance for ambiguity," a fundamentally precon-ceptual acceptance of a world that can never be absolutely divided between imaginary and nonimaginary (subjective or objective) phenomena. This vital act of trust, while taken for granted in everyday life, provides a framework for elucidating not only *being* but also the nexus between *unwell* and *well-being*.

Overview of Merleau-Ponty and Imagination

The theme of imagination remained latent throughout most of Merleau-Ponty's early writings only to become more explicit toward the end of his life. In his mixed reviews of Jean-Paul Sartre's imagination research,[2] Merleau-Ponty objected to certain aspects of his friend's articulation of imagination and emotion. Though appreciative of Sartre's general phenomenological approach to psychology, Merleau-Ponty distanced himself from Sartre's claim that imagination is a "negation" of the real and that a "chasm" exists between these polar opposites—later developed by Sartre into his famous for-itself/in-itself dialectic. From this, one could speculate that Merleau-Ponty's early emphasis on the term "perception" may have been motivated by a wish to differentiate his own philosophical enterprise from that of Sartre's. In any case, Merleau-Ponty's thesis of the primacy of perception[3] could appear to stress the perceptual over the imaginary. But, when we distinguish his use of the term "perception" from the empiricist principle of 'experience' that originated from Locke, it is becomes evident that the thesis of the primacy of perception privileges neither the interior psychological self nor the external physical world; rather, it treats as paramount the 'relation' between the perceiving self and the perceived world.[4] Experience, as a relation mediated by the lived perceiving body, is understood to be pre-categorical to the classical metaphysical antonyms inherent to formal thought. This is what Merleau-Ponty meant in the thesis of the primacy of perception when he said that he wanted to bring rationality and the absolute "down to earth" (Merleau-Ponty 1964c, 13). This expanded understanding of perception recasts the imaginary-real relation. To elucidate this repositioning, I would like to review his phenomenological appropriation of the cardinal idea of gestalt psychology which so influenced the entire course of his intellectual life. This is *Prägnanz*.

The Gestalt Concept of *Prägnanz*

Merleau-Ponty's phenomenology bolstered gestalt psychology's critique of perceptual atomism with the ontological turn intrinsic to his phenomenology. In opposition to the materialist metaphysics, never fully rejected by gestaltists, existential phenomenology understands the existence of the world as inseparable from human experience. Gestalt psychology's insight into the perceptual process is thus taken up by Merleau-Ponty as an insight into the structure of *the world itself*. Whereas the gestaltists, and many cognitive psychologists in their wake, relegated perceptual phenomena to the domain of interiorized entities such as schemes or models that are projected *onto* the perceptual world, existential phenomenologists reject such "subjective objects" in favor of the world itself. Putting aside the ontological assumptions of a material world composed of mathematical quanta, phenomenology takes the insights of gestalt psychology more seriously then did the gestaltists themselves[5]—who remained in confusion over the issue of subjective/objective status of perceptual phenomena. The gestaltists successfully attacked atomism, but they forfeited their accomplishment by reverting to form/inside, matter/outside. Wholes cannot be reduced to their parts, nor can they be subsumed into the categories of *res extensia* or its inverse, the subjective *cogito*. Tragically misunderstanding the significance of their own discovery, the gestaltists overlooked the ontological implications of their most lasting contribution to psychology, this being the law of "good gestalt" or *Prägnanz*: that the unity or organization of a phenomenon will only be as coherent, or 'good', as the prevailing conditions permit (Kaffka 1935; Koehler 1947). This is also expressed as "matter always pregnant with form." The implications of this concept of pregnancy is that matter and form are secondary, or better, *fused* within the structure of the phenomenon itself. To use a metaphor: the water and mortar are not same as the hardened cement. In terms of figure and ground, material phenomena cannot be experienced apart from their forms. Hence all experience exists in the context of a focal theme whose comprehensibility emerges from the back-*ground* that encloses it. Matter is figural to form, and vice versa.

The figure-ground, or theme-horizon, structure provided the basis for gestalt psychology's critique of the perceptual atomism of the Helmholtzian constancy hypothesis, which asserted that there is a quantifiable correspondence between sensory data and perception. But, as Merleau-Ponty spends nearly one-third of the *Phenomenology of Perception* illustrating, experiments on perceptual illusions demonstrate that no such exact correspondence exists. He constantly shows how the perceptual field is of another order from that of the physical environment (as posited by the standpoint of natural science) because it is always already meaningfully organized. The concept of good gestalt allows psychologists to surpass the reductionist view that the perceptual world is composed of corpuscles, atoms, or binary quanta of sensation that strike the sensory organs of the physical body and are then organized by a nonphysical cognition process *apres coup* into meaningful perceptual wholes. In this view the translation process between the physical sensations and the meaningful interpretations of a 'mind' is never made clear, it is only a hypothesis. By contrast, the principle of

Prägnanz affirms that everyday perceptual phenomena are already meaningful at the moment of their emergence. *Prägnanz* bridges the distance
between internality and externality and, in its wake, the imaginary and the
real. Moving in the same direction, Merleau-Ponty closes this gap even
more tightly. Merleau-Ponty's appropriation of the findings of gestalt psychology leads readily into his treatment of the imaginary-real relation.

The Imaginary Fabric of the Real

The imagination was an implicit theme running through Merleau-Ponty's
earlier works and, in the end, proved to be central to the formulation of his
final ontology as laid out in *The Visible and the Invisible* (1968). The close
association of the imaginary and the perceptual that is a latent feature of his
early study of perception, becomes explicit in the final articulation of his
philosophy. The later recasting of his ontology involved a fuller articulation
and a more central positioning of the imagination that refutes the conventional assumption of the image as a "a weakened perception" or of the
imaginary as the polar opposite of the real.[6] Not only does this later view
place imagination on a par with perception, but it also alters its very nature
in a way that is a radical departure from previous metaphysical traditions,
both idealist and materialist. Its radicalism lies in the revelation, unique to
Merleau-Ponty that, like the pregnancy of the figure-ground dynamic, the
imaginary is already woven into the very *texture* of the perceptual world; he
directly refers to this correspondence between the imaginary and the real in
the preface to the *Phenomenology of Perception* when he writes of how "the
real is a closely woven fabric" (1962, x).

Perceptual Faith

Merleau-Ponty's philosophy of the imaginary only becomes evident thor-
ough an analysis of his conception of perceptual faith. In the *College de
France* lectures, he says:

The distinction between the real and the oneiric cannot be identical with the simple
distinction between consciousness filled with meaning and consciousness given up
to its own void. The two modalities impinge on one another. Our waking relations
with objects and others especially have an oneiric character as a matter of principle:
others are present to us in the way that dreams are, the way myths are, and this is
enough to question the cleavage between the real and the imaginary. (1970, 48)

In this quote, the oneiric comprehends not only what we think of conventionally as imaginary but also our intersubjective relations. Merleau-Ponty's striking observation that "others are present to us in the way dreams are, the way myths are," asserts that our intersubjective relations have an imaginary aspect that links them to our experience of dreaming. Our knowledge of other minds, like our phantasms, is not objectively (factually or materially) verifiable, but we *believe* in others as we *believe* our dreams and fantasies while we are experiencing them. Seeing is believing. In this regard our relations with others have an oneiric imaginary character, but such relations are nonetheless very much part of ordinary perception. If others, who are real, are nonetheless present to us in the manner of dreams and myths, this itself is sufficient to undermine any attempt to dichotomize the real and the imaginary. The imaginary is a dimension of the spectrum of experience, from active instrumental reasoning across to passive sleeping. Underlying both the imaginary and perception is the principle of perceptual or *ontological* faith.

Throughout the *Phenomenology* (1962, 297) Merleau-Ponty, developing Husserl's concept of *urdoxic* positing, used the words "confidence," "faith," and "belief" to understand the ground of both perception and imagination. The distinction between imagination and perception is that this quality of faith is more explicit in the case of imagination, namely dreams and fantasies. This is one reason why he so often devotes his analyses to discussions of illusions, psychopathology, and child development. It is obvious to us that our illusions, dreams, fantasies, and myths are sustained by belief, whereas the role of faith in waking perception is only exposed through reflection and interrogation.

Merleau-Ponty opens *The Visible and Invisible* by explicating the foundations of what he calls "perceptual faith." Perceptual faith is faith in the reality of the perceived world:

We see the things themselves, the world is what we see: formulae of this kind express a faith common to the natural man and the philosopher—the moment he opens his eyes; they refer to a deep-seated set of mute "opinions" implicated in our lives. But what is strange about this faith is that if we seek to articulate it into theses or statements, if we ask ourselves what is this *we*, what *seeing* is, and what *thing* or *world* is, we enter into a labyrinth of difficulties and contradictions. (1968, 3)

What Merleau-Ponty is interrogating here is the basis of our fundamental assumptions about reality. He recalls Saint Augustine's famous observation about time: we all know what time is until we try to articulate this knowledge. So too, Merleau-Ponty contends that the reality of the perceived world, treated as knowledge by the naive everyday "natural" person, is actually no more than a matter of faith, or as he puts it, "opinion." It is this perceptual faith of the natural attitude that is the presupposition upon which natural science itself is founded.

The Imaginary-Real: A Tightly Woven Fabric

It is in order to establish the fragility of perception that Merleau-Ponty re-examines the relation between the real and the imaginary. Our deep-seated faith about the fact of material existence goes hand in hand with an assumed distinction between the real and the imaginary, yet the very fact of dreaming itself calls into question the reality status of waking perception. In dreaming, we spontaneously lose our reference marks in relation to the so-called real or perceptual world. Therefore in the opening of *The Visible and the Invisible* Merleau-Ponty argues,

> ... if we can lose our reference marks *unbeknown to ourselves* we are never sure of *having* them when we think we have them; if we can withdraw from the world of perception without knowing it, nothing proves to us that we are ever in it, nor that the observable is ever entirely observable, nor that it is made of another fabric than the dream. Then, the difference between perception and dream not being absolute, one is justified in counting them both among "our experiences," and it is above[7] perception itself that we must seek the guarantee and the sense of its ontological function. (1968, 6)

It is important to emphasize here that Merleau-Ponty is not considering the world to be synonymous with a *mere* dream, in the manner in which Plato distrusted the senses or the *Vedas* teach of waking reality as illusion or *maya*. The world is there, Merleau-Ponty would say, but its "guarantee" and "ontological function" lie in a broader context then that indicated by perception alone in that both perception and imagination are interwoven through the common dehiscence of experience.

The recollection of a dream is unsettling to the newly woken subject because, during the course of the dream, its reality was sustained with the same perceptual faith that is given to the waking world. It is not only the content of the dream, such as violent or erotic wishes, that is unnerving to the newly awakened subject but it is the inability to escape the reality of the perceptual faith that the dreamer had previously given to the dream that is so disorienting on waking. The dream has a power as a reality in its own right. Our dream experiences often reveal condensed existential truths before which the mundane world can seem very dry. This is because in everyday life, as amply illustrated by Kierkegaard and Heidegger, we can defer the anxieties of our human condition by throwing ourselves into the fragile respite (of *das man*) that is offered to us by the unreflective perceptual faith. But to go too far in this direction would be to give the imaginary a higher status then that of the perceptual, thus merely reversing the conventional error made by the naive natural attitude.[8] Then again, there are those rare lucid dreams in which we are aware of ourselves as dreamers, but it is equally rare to find ourselves as lucid perceivers thus aware of ourselves as engaged in the perceptual faith. It is, I believe, just this sort of lucidity that Merleau-Ponty sought from his new ontology. Rejecting the convention of treating the real as more true then the imaginary, Merleau-Ponty asks the thinker to be equally lucid in both theaters, insisting that the lucidity in one presupposes a lucidity in the other.

Psychopathology as the Breakdown of Perceptual Faith

While the perceptual faith is not an explicit decision, in the moral sense of the word, it is, nonetheless, an implicit act without which there would not be that "sense of reality" required to pursue life with a minimum of relaxation and wholesome well-being.[9] Psychopathology is an instance where this faith in the reality of the perceptual world becomes precarious. It is a common misunderstanding to think that psychotic patients believe in the reality of their hallucinations. Nor is it clear that victims of hallucinations are entirely unable to distinguish the perceptual (real) from the hallucinatory (imaginary) (Straus 1966; Frith and Donne 1988). What is catastrophic for victims of hallucinations is their incapacity to feel confidence in *both* the perceptual and the imaginary. Such episodes, characterized by R. D. Laing (1962) as *ontological insecurity*, invoke a suspicion of the reality of any self or any world—real or imaginary. The fact that pathological subjects cannot fully believe their experiences is precisely why they are so painfully unlivable. Moreover it is this agitated anxious uncertainty that leads to the pathological project of absolute certainty. For example, a paranoid delusional system is preferable to the ambiguity of not having absolute possession of the other persons's thoughts. The delusion of persecution, like all delusions, eliminates the ambiguity at the heart of intersubjectivity and makes life more livable for the paranoid. For such unfortunate people, exile into an unambiguously threatening world is safer than the open-endedness of the social world—which is one of vulnerability and trust. Victims find abusers, compulsives perpetually repeat, ritualized sexual paraphilias are preferable to the uncertainty and risks of flesh-and-blood love relations. Murder resolves any doubt about a lover's fidelity.

Psychopathologists and their patients cannot take for granted the perceptual faith of the natural attitude; instead, they have come to see perceptual faith as a developmental achievement that allows one to live in the amorphous everyday world with an unreflective ease. This is a pre-reflective somatic 'trust' that the world is real. The very fact of our being able to live out our life-projects, hopes, and relations with others is a testimony to this fundamental *faith* in the existence of the world—a faith unavailable to those whose lives are restricted by severe psychopathology. As with intimate personal relations, where we can never have exact certainty of the quality of other people's fidelity to us, so is it the case with the reality of the world. Through socialization, most of us learn to forget, defer, or suspend our doubts as we move on to continually recommit ourselves to the perceptual world and our relations with one another. Through the examples of our childhood caretakers we come to consent to the fragile uncertainty of the world, take our chances, and surrender to the givens of the ambiguous open-ended situation before us.

In psychopathological conditions, surrender to the perceptual faith is problematic. Psychotic experience is, in contrast to the relaxed stance of mundane experience, an extremely agitated hyper-vigilant standpoint symptomatic of *ontological doubt*. This is manifested in an incessant probing for the foundations of the real in a way that sadly parodies certain forms of philosophical and aesthetic reflection. As has been so well demonstrated in the work of Louis Sass (1991), this hyper-rationality or disembodied distance from the world is available to our understanding through surrealist, abstract expressionist, and modernist art generally where the perceptual and the imaginary are deliberately, even playfully, blurred. It must be kept in mind, however, that, for the artist, this blurring is an aesthetic inquiry performed with the purpose of exploring the boundary of the real and the imaginary; in short, it is a methodically provisional uncertainty. The artist or philosopher rarely loses his ability to return to the "security" granted by the perceptual faith.[10] So, while the aesthetic act is a play with boundaries, pathological loss of boundaries is brought on by nature-nurture dynamics beyond the person's control. This is a distinction that is too glibly neglected by authors who excessively valorize or romanticize psychopathology. Be this as it may, I would next like to ask how we come, in light of developmental psychology, to take for granted our "sense" of the reality of the world.

The Developmental Account of Perceptual Faith

Merleau-Ponty supports his analysis of the perceptual faith and its breakdown in psychopathology through the insights offered by developmental psychology. In the Sorbonne lectures he reviews Piaget's (1954) descriptions of how the infant develops a sense of reality through its relations with objects. Directly after birth the infant shows a withdrawal of interest in any object that is removed from its view. The object ceases to exist for the infant once it disappears from direct perception. This changes at roughly six months when the child begins to behave toward objects as though they will continue their existence despite their unavailability to the senses. Hence, instead of falling out of existence, the object will only fall out of sight; disappearance is transformed from a problem of existence to one of spatial location. Here the child has achieved what Piaget calls "object constancy," which has profound consequences regarding its emotional relations with its adult caretakers. Commenting on Piaget's study throughout his Sorbonne lectures (1964a), and even as late as his final working notes (1968), Merleau-Ponty points out that this ontogenetic phenomenon describes the birth of *both the imaginary and the real, namely that they are interwoven from the first moment of their conception, always already threaded together through their divergence.* It is this divergence that is the texture of the "tightly woven fabric of the real."[11] The divergence is not a merely cognitive act, something Piaget's "dogmatic rationalism" misses (1964a, 202; 1968, 204), but, as described above, it is an affective or global assent to belief in the spatiotemporal permanence of the self, world, and others. Indeed, there is no good reason to believe in the reality of the things. The infant's future "mental health" or psychosocial well-being rests on its being able to come to trust that its caretakers will return from absence and fulfill its needs (Ainsworth 1979; Bowlby 1988). Later researchers have found that "object permanence" is inextricably bound to "social attachment" (Chazin 1981). The developmental issue of infancy, better described by the psychoanalyst Erik Erikson (1963), is to develop a mutual affective investment with the caregiver. This is a much more broad phenomenon than the merely cognitive schemes referred to by Piaget. Instead, this mutuality is a postural disposition toward the world that transforms early infantile experience into a coherent and sensible reality. Erikson calls this a sense of "basic trust" in a manner not unlike Merleau-Ponty's description of perceptual faith. As the epigenetic ground to psychological development, any failure to experience and take up basic trust toward the world would lead, Erikson suggests, to the pathological withdrawal from the social order with, of course, demoralizing consequences. This parallels the psychotic position described earlier where reality (real or imaginary) is experienced through an unbearably anxious doubt. Through the active exploration of the world and the reliability of its caretakers, the infant develops a reasonable or "good enough" faith—never an absolute certainty—that the mother or object will return. Eventually the reality of the world becomes a sort of habit, which like most opinions, we come to take for granted.

Health, Tolerance of Ambiguity, and Psychopathology

Our ability to take the imaginary-real for granted can be further distinguished from pathological experience through Merleau-Ponty's reading of Else Frenkel-Brunswik's study of psychological rigidity in his Sorbonne lectures. As one of several postwar studies of the psychological dimension of Fascism, Frenkel-Brunswik used ideas from the Rorscharch diagnostic tradition to uncover how authoritarian attitudes were symptomatic of deeper more enduring personality traits. Hermann Rorschach (1929)—who, incidentally, understood his test as a study of perception, not imagination—found that nonpathological subjects could see many contrasting, even contradictory, images in the same inkblot card. Furthermore they could explain what exact parts of the blot provoked their images thus revealing an attentiveness to the perceptual as well as the imaginary. Ordinary subjects found no contradictions in their uneventful transitions from personal image to inkblot card. They lived the relationship in a crisscrossed, interchangeable or, in Merleau-Ponty's terms: *chiasmatic* manner. In other words, the perceptual and imaginary were experienced as already convergent or intersected with one another. As with ordinary daydreaming, subjects could weave into and out of their fantasies as polyglots can change languages, yet never confusing one with the other. Rorschach suggested that this fluency across orders of reality, the imaginary and the real, is emblematic of normative psychological well-being or, in William James' famous expression:

"healthy mindedness." Nonclinical participants viewed the world with what Frenkel-Brunswik called a "tolerance for ambiguity." She found this flexibility to be particularly lacking in psychologically rigid authoritarian personalities. Merleau-Ponty emphasizes in the Sorbonne lectures that this study is not bound to any political ideology—right or left. One can be rigidly liberal as much as one can be rigidly conservative. The opposing extremist ideologies are different manifestations of the common symptom shared with psychopathological conditions: *perceptual inflexibility anxiously demanding absolute certainty.* While one could debate the plausibility of linking psychopathology to ideology, what is clear is that this research supported Merleau-Ponty's own ontological thesis that our human home-world[12] is characterized by a pre-categorical ambiguity sustained by the perceptual faith. This is a belief or affective assent to the existence of the world despite its ambiguous perpetually incomplete, open-ended nature. In light of Merleau-Ponty's thesis, nonpathological experience would be revelatory of an openness to just this pre-categorical domain, whereas the pathological demand for imaginary or perceptual certainty would be a turning from, and refusal of, this domain. Particular psychopathological syndromes exemplify this issue.

In an earlier section, psychotic experience was understood in terms of an intolerance of the uncertainties of perceptual faith. The current discussion, with its emphasis on a tolerance of the ambiguous link between the real and the imaginary exemplified by ordinary experience, offers an interpretive framework for understanding other forms of psychopathology as well. For example, paranoids are infamously incapable of interpersonal trust. Obsessives strive for an imaginary control that perpetually eludes them. Compulsives ritually repeat to unsuccessfully satisfy unending imaginary doubts.

Mania and depression are especially illustrative. In each condition we are witness to an *intolerance* of such ambiguity. In mania, the imaginary runs amok and overwhelms the real, uprooting the patient from any anchoring in the realities and limitations of everyday life. Manic optimism is a refusal to perceive the boundaries and limitations of imaginary possibilities imposed by the facticities of the real world. Thus mania is a flooding of the imaginary into the real. In depression, by contrast, the imaginary, with its reach into a potentially hopeful future, is in a condition of dessication and collapse, leaving the patient weighed down in a burdensomely boring present and a future that is only a repetition of the past—with no prospect

of release. Depressive gloom is characterized by a pessimism, a refusal to
allow the imaginary to animate the real—to see one's self and world
through hopeful possibilities. All such syndromes can be characterized as a
striving for some absolute ontological certainty in a manner that makes one
unable to function on the most rudimentary levels of social life. Such is the
pathological incapacity to tolerate the imaginary-perceptual ambiguity that
characteristic of ordinary human experience.[13]

Conclusion

Disputes over the relation between the imaginary and the real, or about
whether truth resides in subject or object, in our "inner" experience or
in our experience of the "outer" world, could be misleading for psychiatry
in its attempts to *understand* psychopathology. By according the "index of
reality" (1970, 41) to both the imaginary and the perceptual, showing that
an absolute distinction between them is not only impossible but is in fact a
defining characteristic of psychopathology itself, Merleau-Ponty offers psychiatry a potentially useful framework for addressing the spectrum between
"healthy mindedness" and psychopathology. Medical psychiatry may overlook this point because natural science, according to Merleau-Ponty, presupposes the perceptual faith, but it does not elucidate it. The medical
model is founded upon a faith in the truth of the perceptual world, but it
does not reflect upon it, nor in any way acknowledge that this truth is
actually a matter of faith. By interrogating this faith, Merleau-Ponty does
not question the validity of scientific endeavour, and he rightly acknowledges the limits of phenomenology, but he does question the ontological
premises upon which the natural scientific endeavour is based and, most
especially, its claim to an absolute monopoly on truth or 'reality'. The real is
an inclination, an assent to belief. It is, Merleau-Ponty says, an opinion, an
opinion that is fragile because it is so easily usurped by new opinions—as
the history of science so well demonstrates. Staring into a Rorschach card,
one's perception of a cloud shifts from a blob of white, to a face, to a cotton
ball, and so on; each perception is true as it emerges, but its truth is fragile,
precisely because it is so absolutely and completely substitutable by another
perception. Via *Prägnanz*, the coherence of any experience is only as good
as prevailing conditions permit. In the same way, it is not the imaginary or
perceptual that hold an absolute ontological status, but it is the perpetual
circuit between the two and the act of faith out of which these two aspects

of being arise that allow for the lucidity of the world. Both are grounded in a pre-categorical zero point "at the joints, where the multiple entries of the world cross" (1968, 260), perhaps best described by Merleau-Ponty, in his last published paper, as "the imaginary texture of the real" (1964c, 165).

Notes

I wish to express my thanks and appreciation to my friend & colleague James Phillips for reviewing an earlier draft of this chapter and offering many important and insightful suggestions.

1. I prefer the term "ontological" faith for the following reasons. The phrase "perceptual faith" was used within the context of *The Visible and the Invisible* (1968) which is an unpublished text left incomplete at the moment of Merleau-Ponty's death. This leaves open the question of the author's final intentions. Furthermore the use of the word "perceptual" seems to contradict other statements he makes throughout his writings in regard to Husserl's more technical expression: "urdoxic positing." This is a belief that is a priori to any possible experience—imaginary or perceptual. Hence the term "perceptual faith" is unfortunately contradictory. Taking *The Visible and Invisible* as a whole, I believe that the term "ontological faith" better expresses Merleau-Ponty's intentions as it is more consistent with his final thesis that like the visible and the invisible, imagination and perception are inherently interwoven and sustained by a faith that is foundational to both modes of experience. This is a *pre*-perceptual faith, likewise a pre-imaginary faith, best described through the more general term: ontological faith. Having expressed these reservations, I will maintain the term "perceptual faith" for the sake of clarity and consistency within this chapter.

2. See Merleau-Ponty's review of Sartre's book *L'Imagination* (1937, 9–10). This is Merleau-Ponty's first published reference to Sartre's theory of imagination. He continues to critique Sartre's approach to imagination throughout the course of his writings.

3. Summarized by Merleau-Ponty as: "The perceived world is the always presupposed foundation of all rationality, all value, and all existence," in *The Primacy of Perception* (1964c, 13).

4. "Perception" is a term over which Merleau-Ponty expressed misgivings in the working notes of *The Visible and the Invisible* (1968). In this text he strove to work outside the entire nomenclature of consciousness, perception, and subjectivity as these terms were laden with historically dualistic sedimentations that detracted from his overall philosophical project. For example, he writes: "The problems posed in the Ph.P. [*Phenomenology of Perception*] are insoluble because I start there from the 'consciousness'– 'object' distinction ..." (1968, 200). In other words, these terms presuppose dualism. He strives to rearticulate "perception as *divergence (écart)* ..." (Ibid., 201) or *dehiscence* (opening). Explicitly: "Moreover, we also do not allow ourselves to introduce into our description concepts used from reflection, whether psychological or transcendental: they are more often than not only correlatives or counterparts to the *objective* world. We must, at the beginning, eschew such notions as 'acts of consciousness' 'states of consciousnes' 'matter' 'form' and even 'image' and 'perception'. We exclude the term perception to the whole extent that it already implies a cutting up of what is lived in to

discontinuous acts ... (Ibid., 157–158). Clearly, Merleau-Ponty felt restrained by his earlier psychological terminology as his latter thought focused on the ontological foundations to these psychological categories.

5. The gestalt psychologists remained in confusion over the issue of subjective/objective status of perceptual phenomena. While they successfully exposed the impossibility of perceptual atomism, they forfeited their accomplishment by reverting to the naturalistic equation of form with subjectivity and matter with objectivity. See Gurwitsch (1966), Dillon (1971, 1988), and Richer (1979), who comment on these mixed ontological commitments.

6. In his *Sorbonne Lectures* Merleau-Ponty points out that the image as "not just an inner or psychic 'thing,' but instead a global conviction" (1964b, 194).

7. In the original French the passage reads: "et c'est au-dessus de la perception elle-meme' (1968, 20).

8. As in the case of archaic thought, romanticism, and popular religious cults.

9. In his classic text *The Variety of Religious Experiences* (1902) William James uses the expression "healthy mindedness" to describe the attitude of pluralistic religious optimism. He contrasts this fundamental belief in the goodness of the universe and its ambiguous "higher power" with what he calls the religion of the self-loathing or "morbid" mindedness which is dominated by a harsh, judgmental, monotheistic deity. James's understanding of this healthy pluralistic faith corresponds somewhat with the notion of tolerance of the imaginary-real ambiguity which I am trying to develop in this essay.

10. Jung is attributed to have said that James Joyce dove gracefully into the depths of the unconscious, whereas his (Joyces's) schizophrenic daughter drowned in it.

11. This seems to echo Kant's concept of synthetic imagination. Kant writes of the "pure transcendental synthesis of imagination as conditioning the very possibility of experience" (1929, 120). This is the moment of contact between sense experience and its abstract representation which can never be broken down into one or the other. Merleau-Ponty cites this aspect of Kant's thought in his "primacy of perception" thesis (1964c, 18–19).

12. In his latter thought, Heidegger emphasizes the concept of *Heimat* (homeland) in a way that could be of relevance here. In a recent doctoral dissertation by Fredrik Svenaeus (1999), the phenomenon of 'homelikeness' is characterized as a basis for a phenomenology of well-being and health.

13. The concepts of 'ego autonomy' and 'rigid character' in recent psychodynamic theory (Shapiro 1981) seems to approach psychopathology in a way that would support the idea of mental health as a tolerance of the ambiguity between the imaginary and the real.

References

Aanstoos, C. 1987. The psychology of computer models and the question of the imagination. In E. L. Murray, ed., *Imagination and Phenomenological Psychology*. Pittsburgh: Duquesne University Press.

Ainsworth, M. D. S. 1979. Infant-mother attachment. *American Psychologist* 34: 932–37.

Bowlby, J. 1988. *A Secure Base: Parent-Child Attachment and Healthy Human Development.* New York: Basic Books.

Chazin, S. E. 1981. Development of object permanence as a correlate of dimensions of maternal care. *Developmental Psychology* 17: 79–81.

Dillon, M. 1988. *Merleau-Ponty's Ontology.* Bloomington: Indiana University Press.

Dillon, M. 1971. Gestalt Theory and Merleau-Ponty's Conception of Intentionality. *Man and World* 4.

Gurwitsch, A. 1966. *Studies in Phenomenology and Psychology.* Evanston: Northwestern University Press.

Erikson, E. 1963. *Childhood and Society.* New York: Norton.

Exner, J. E. 1978. *The Rorschach: A Comprehensive System,* vol. 1. New York: Wiley.

Frith, C. D., and D. J. Donne, 1988. Towards a neuropsychology of schizophrenia. *British Journal of Psychiatry* 153: 437–33.

James William. 1902. *The Varieties of Religious Experience.* New York: Longmans Green.

Kant, E. 1929. *The Critique of Pure Reason.* Translated by N. Kemp Smith. London: Macmillan.

Koehler, W. 1947. *Gestalt Psychology.* New York: Liverwright.

Koffka, K. 1935. *Principles of Gestalt Psychology.* London: Routledge and Kegan Paul.

Merleau-Ponty, M. 1937. L'Imagination. *Journal de Psychologie Normale et Pathologique* 33: 9–10.

Merleau-Ponty, M. [1945] 1962. *Phenomenology of Perception.* Translated by Colin Smith. London: Routledge and Kegan Paul. Originally published as *Phenomenologie de la Perception.* Paris: Editions Gallimard, 1945.

Merleau-Ponty, M. 1964a. Structure et conflicts de la conscience enfantine. *Bulletin de Psychologie* 18: 171–202.

Merleau-Ponty, M. 1964b. Maurice Merleau-Ponty à la Sorbonne: Résumé de ses cours établi par des étudiants et approuvé par lui-meme. *Bulletin de Psychologie* 18: 109–308.

Merleau-Ponty, M. 1964c. Eye and mind. In *The Primacy of Perception.* Edited by J. Edie and C. Dallery. Translated by W. Cobb. Evanston: Northwestern University Press. Originally published as *L'Oeil et l'espirt.* Paris: Éditions Gallimard, 1964.

Merleau-Ponty, M. 1968. *The Visible and the Invisible.* Edited by C. Lefort. Translated by A. Lingis. Evanston: Northwestern University Press. Originally published as *Le Visible et L'invisible.* Paris: Éditions Gallimard, 1964.

Merleau-Ponty, M. [1968] 1970. *Themes from the Lectures at the College de France 1952– 1960,* Evanston: Northwestern University Press. Originally published as *Résumés des Cours, Collège de France 1952–1960.* Paris: Éditions Gallimard, 1968.

Piaget, J. 1953. *The Construction of Reality in the Child.* New York: Basic Books.

Richer, Paul. 1979. The concepts of subjectivity and objectivity in Gestalt psychology. *Journal of Phenomenological Psychology* 14, No 2.

Rorschach, H. 1942. *Psychodiagnostics: A Diagnostic Test Based on Perception*. New York: Grune and Stratton.

Sass, Louis. 1991. *Madness and Modernism*. New York: Basic Books.

Shapiro, David. 1981. *Autonomy and Rigid Character*. New York: Basic Books.

Straus, Erwin. 1966. Phenomenology of hallucinations. In *Phenomenological Psychology*. New York: Basic Books.

Svenaeus, Fredrik. 1999. The heurenutics of medicine and the phenomenology of health. Ph.D. dissertation. *Linköping University Studies in Arts and Science*.

Wertz, F. 1993. Cognitive psychology: A phenomenological critique. *Journal of Theoretical and Philosophical Psychology* 13: 2–24.

II

Pathologic Imagination and Psychodynamic Thought

6

The Creative Role of Fantasy in Adaptation

Ethel Spector Person

Lovers and madmen have such seething brains,
Such shaping fantasies, that apprehend
More than cool reason ever comprehends.
The lunatic, the lover, and the poet
Are of imagination all compacted. . . .
A MidSummer Night's Dream (act V)

While fantasies are sometimes hard to access, most of us—about 96 percent according to a number of different researchers in the United States—nonetheless report having had daydreams or reveries at one time or another (Singer 1996, 57). The psychologist Silvan Tomkins's response to this finding makes an important point: "If daydreaming is a trivial activity, then most Americans are wasting some part of every day. If it is a pathological activity, then most Americans are sick. If it represents a sublimated drive gratification, then most Americans are either underfed, underwatered, or undersexed."[1]

If fantasy is not just an atavistic carryover from an earlier stage of our development—the mental equivalent of the superfluous appendix—what functions does it serve? Vital ones it appears, since many psychoanalysts have observed that an inability to fantasize is just as pathological as an excessive immersion in fantasy. Acquiring the capacity to fantasize (or to tap into the fantasy inherent in novels, movies, and other cultural materials) is a developmental achievement, without which one's life is bloodless, passionless, and sometimes lacking in hope and forward momentum as well.

Fantasy is situated within the context of imagination. Imagination, which depends on the ability to create and manipulate symbols, is the mental capacity to think of possibilities beyond the evidence of immediate sense perceptions. Imagination allows us to contemplate alternatives to the real world of people, places, and things, to the time-bound events of the past and the present.

Imagination is one of humankind's major adaptive tools. Without it, there could be no picturing of mental alternatives to current discomfort or deprivation, no planning of a future course of action, no creative rethinking of the past to make it pertinent to the present and future. Using the imagination to scan trial actions and conjure up a range of responses, and thus to predict the immediate and long-term future, is essential to both scientific thinking and fantasy thinking, and one of their common characteristics. Still there are significant differences. Fantasizing is a unique kind of imagined thought that serves a psychological or emotional purpose rather than a primarily pragmatic one.[2]

The Hiddenness of Our Fantasies

Ever since the first psychoanalytic patient, Anna O., described her own daydreaming as a private theater, fantasy has often been called a theater of the mind, not a bad description considering that fantasies generally have a main character (most often the implied agent of action), a goal, an action, an object of the action, and a setting.[3] The fantasizer plays three roles, as the author of the fantasy script, as a player in the drama—often the star of it—and as the audience for whom the fantasy is devised.

The theatrical metaphor notwithstanding, fantasy is much more often private than public. The hiddenness of our fantasy lives is protean. Its most obvious form is secrecy. We consider our fantasies deeply personal, we choose whether or not to share them, and generally regard them jealously. But the degree to which we keep these meaning at a remove from our own self-knowledge may surprise us. Relying on fantasies as old friends and considering their meaning transparent, we may be unaware that we actually know little about them and do not appreciate their meaning, their importance in our lives, or their wellsprings. Conscious fantasies, then, are private property, personal secrets carefully concealed. Even in this age of psychological and sexual freedom, they are seldom explicitly shared.

Why are we willing, even eager, to share our dreams but determined to hoard and hide our fantasies? One reason is that we feel more responsible for daydreams than for nightdreams. Nightdreams come unbidden, but conscious fantasy, because we conjure it up and are aware of manipulating it to suit ourselves, implicates us very directly. In some ways fantasies seem more revealing of the self—its appetites or obscure, quirky desires—than dreams or even the most intimate narratives of a lived life. One feels shame in exposing certain fantasies to the outside glare, no matter how gratifying they are within the protective landscape of the mind. A particular fantasy, it is feared, would reveal grandiose or obscene ambitions, infantile needs, otherwise well-disguised impulses to aggression, kinky sexual appetites, or worst or all, some grotesque wish or need of which we ourselves are unaware. Consequently conscious fantasy is not generally dwelt upon in everyday conversation.

Nor does conscious fantasy form a large portion of clinical work with the exception of sexual fantasies or fantasies about the therapist, which are called "transference fantasies." In part, patients may fail to report their fantasies spontaneously, regarding them as too embarrassing, too revealing, or, alternatively, as irrelevant. Or they may fear that speaking their fantasies out loud may rob them of their power to soothe, to confer pleasure.

Just as important to the relative absence of conscious fantasy in the psychoanalytic dialogue is the fact that psychoanalysts have been more interested in uncovering unconscious fantasy and its role in pathology than in deciphering daydreams. The reasons for this bias go back to the very beginnings of psychoanalysis.

While Freud discovered the importance of fantasy in our lives, the way he came upon it led him to emphasize its role in psychopathology rather than in health. He got his first inkling of the power of fantasy through studying hysterical patients. His original theory was that early life sexual trauma was the culprit in his patients' sexual neurosis, and he interpreted their hysterical symptoms as symbolic representations of their sealed-off traumatic memories.[4]

Soon after, however, Freud abandoned the seduction theory to argue instead that his patients' apparent "memories" of having been seduced were, in fact, fantasies—derivatives of unconscious childhood wishes rather than distorted memories of real experiences.[5] Thus Freud arrived at a totally new theory, proposing that his women patients' seduction fantasies were invoked to disguise their own sexual wishes and thereby to avoid guilt. No longer did Freud believe that hysterics suffered from terrible buried memories; instead, he believed they suffered from intense conflicts connected to childhood fantasies that emerged out of their own infantile sexual desires.[6]

Freud's one-hundred-and-eighty-degree turn in theorizing the etiology of hysteria marked the beginning of his conceptualization of *psychical reality* as distinct from *external, material reality.*[7] Thus Freud moved fantasy out of the realm of the purely imaginary into the world of reality, but reality of a specific kind—psychical reality.[8]

Freud's insight into hysteria led him to theorize the underlying causes of many other disruptive mental phenomena as well. All of them, he believed, shared a source in the forbidden wishes of early childhood, and all of them shared a function, serving as defenses against the forbidden, the unbearable. Being unbearable, these wishes had been buried—a process Freud later termed "repression." But once buried, they still craved expression, which took the form of symbolic representation and gratification in hysteria and hysterical paralysis, and also in phobias, obsessions, delusions, hallucinations, and so forth.[9]

Freud's reformulation of hysteria was essential to the birth of psychoanalytic thinking, grounding it in an appreciation of innate desires and the fantasies they give rise to and particularly emphasizing *unconscious* fantasy.[10] But because Freud first focused on fantasy in the context of pathology, his emphasis from then on concerned its role in symptom formation. In fact the search for the unconscious fantasy material that fuels neurotic symptoms is at the heart of classical psychoanalysis.

Although psychoanalysts appreciate the role of unconscious fantasy in character and behavior, in clothing and self-decoration, indeed in everything that constitutes what we think of as our very essence, many analysts, following Freud's lead, still focus primarily on the negative role of fantasy. Thus the psychoanalytic exploration of fantasy has centered more on its connection to symptoms, less on its creative-adaptive functions, and more on unconscious fantasy than on daydreams, daydreams being viewed primarily as substitute gratification, a retreat from the external world.

But Freud did give us some key insights into the adaptive aspects of fantasy. For example, he was aware early on that the writer makes use of daydreams in his fiction, and that fantasy themes disseminated through stories are key to the construction of a culture's myths. Even so, he never emphasized the essential role of daydreams in individual adaptation or group cohesion. In fact, fantasy plays a major role in guiding the choices and adaptations we make and the relationships we form. Fantasies are among the most powerful of the catalysts that infuse and organize our lives, dictating romantic, familial and professional goals, fueling behaviors, engendering plans for the future.

Two Models of Daydreaming

Fortunately, Freud proposed two different models for understanding the function of conscious fantasy, one in which he related daydreams to dreams (in *The Interpretation of Dreams*) and a second one in which he connected fantasy to children's play (in "Creative Writers and Day-Dreaming"). Each of these models has an important place in understanding different functions of conscious fantasy, but their focus and implications diverge.[11]

Freud's dream model primarily described fantasy as substitute wish-fulfillment for repressed wishes. To the degree that fantasy substitutes for action, its impact on the lived life is minimal. But Freud's play model of fantasy posits several other major functions for fantasy (Freud, "Creative Writers and Day-Dreaming" and "Formulations on the Two Principles of Mental Functioning").

Fantasy, like play, is often invoked to master unpleasant feelings and to plot future dreams.[12] Various childhood games are pleasurable because they help the child deal with uncomfortable feelings including dependency and powerlessness, for example, as in the invocation of the Fort Da game to master separation anxiety.[13] Such games permit the young child to feel more in control, to reverse passivity into activity, helplessness into mastery. Gradually such childhood games evolve into the fantasy playlets or make-believe games that focus on role playing.

These more advanced pretend or make-believe games have a developmental function: not only are they invoked as a mode of mastery in response to emotional disequilibriums, but they can also serve as rehearsals for future adaptations insofar as they project the child's goals and an image of what the child wants to be. Freud saw that one of the primary motives in make-believe was the wish to be "big"—and one certainly observes children spending a lot of time trying on adult roles, playing at being "Mommy" or "Daddy" or Firefighter of Nurse.[14]

At some point in childhood, fantasy subsumes the functions of play. As the research psychologist Eric Klinger puts it, both "play and fantasy reflect current focal concerns of the individual—unresolved current problems, unfinished tasks, role conflicts, and prominent affective responses, as well as the challenges of identity and commitment posed by the individual's social relationships" (1971, 49).

Whereas Freud's dream model focuses on the source of daydreams in the infantile past, his play model emphasizes how current events and hopes for the future trigger daydreams and how daydreams, in turn, play a role in modifying the present and shaping the future. Combining Freud's dream model and his play model, let me expand the working definition of conscious fantasy: it is a daydream that surfaces in the stream of consciousness, a narrative compounded of emotion, thought, internal dialogue, and (predominately visual) sensory impressions. Sometimes highly schematic and abbreviated, sometimes minutely articulated and detailed, it is shaped by the imagination to fulfill a psychological function. On the simplest level, fantasy provides substitute gratification for what is lacking in life, releasing tension or dispelling frustration. It sometimes functions as a "safe-house" in which feelings and impulses, otherwise viewed as unacceptable, are discharged. But it serves multiple other functions as well. Daydreaming often signals recognition of an emotional reality previously denied. Fantasy may be invoked to provide a feeling of safety or to stabilize self-esteem. Fantasy may be directed to the promotion of sexual arousal or self-soothing. It may also be invoked to solve old problems, revising past defeats and wounds, or to aid in the working through of trauma.

Thus fantasizing, despite its wishful imaginative core, plays a very real role in our lives, or rather, many roles. Perhaps most important of all, daydreaming lends solace in sorrow and pain. Fantasizing a happier future may permit us to bear an untenable present rather than be overwhelmed by depression and feelings of hopelessness. Therefore fantasy's chief benefit may be that it allows the fantasizer to hope, to trust in the future, even in a seemingly hopeless situation. The unhappy or abused child who can imagine more loving parents, happier times, a different world, may grow up relatively unscathed, the good life still within the realm of imaginative possibilities and thus an actual possibility.

Moreover fantasy may help make that tomorrow possible, insofar as our expectations and hopes for what is yet to come, much of which is encoded in fantasy, fuel our behavior and thinking in the present. Thus, in addition to creating a general ambiance of hope, fantasy may lay a practical foundation for it.

A Classification of Fantasies

Different kinds of fantasies carry out these different functions. Classifying fantasies according to their function, the nature of the occasion (or trigger) that prompts them, and their duration, I have found it useful to distinguish among transient fantasies, repeating fantasies, and generative fantasies.

Transient daydreams, by definition fleeting, are contingent; they surface in response to a particular external stress, problem, or situation. Envious on the occasion of someone else receiving a coveted prize, a man may conjure up winning the lottery, being offered a prestigious job, or going to bed with his rival's wife. The man mobilizes the daydream to restore, at least momentarily, his deflated narcissism. Like dreams, such fleeting mental products may be hard to remember. But they still serve the immediate function of restoring a lost equilibrium (whether due to stress, anxiety, or the loss of pride) through positing a remedy.

Fleeting fantasies also serve as a regulator for strong affect. Thus a fleeting fantasy may be invoked to contain anxiety or other dysphoric feelings. Affect-driven fantasies include the murderous fantasies so often evoked by rejection and the fantasies of impoverishment fueled by depression.[15] We may say of these fantasies that their content appears to be affect-driven rather than wish-driven.

Fleeting daydreams, evanescent though they may be, are adaptive and revealing and extremely useful in deciphering what we are currently feeling in our relationships, and they are particularly useful in the therapy setting where they constitute a primary route of recognizing the tenor of the transference. Transference fantasies may be preformed, arise in reaction to something current in the therapy, or encode expectations of cure.[16]

Quite different are *repeating fantasies*; these are of a durable, repetitive nature and may recur unchanged from childhood through adult life or, alternately, reappear in slightly edited re-editions, sometimes even after long periods of banishment.[17] A daydream that is repeated unchanged or with only slight modifications from adolescence or even latency into adulthood becomes a familiar friend, one whose benefits such as self-soothing or sexual arousal are cherished. Repeating fantasies are stimulated not so much by contingent events as by ever-recurring hungers. Masturbatory fantasies, for example, are often life-long aids to sexual arousal and performance, invoked at frequent and predictable intervals. Many of these enduring fantasies are what are called "organizing" fantasies—that is, they play an essential role on a day-to-day basis in solving those central unconscious conflicts and problems of early life that continue to exert an influence in the present. Sometimes it is easy to see that a whole life revolves around

one of these organizing fantasies. For example, consider a man whose intimate life revolves around the wish (need) to beat out a competitor, based
on an underlying fantasy of vanquishing a rival brother or father, itself the
product of an unresolved infantile conflict.[18]

In contrast, *generative fantasies* are generally future-oriented and are
invoked in response to future desire and intentionality. Thinking about
one's future is inevitably chockablock with fantasy, some of it well-formed
and highly articulated, some of it mere snippets of imagery. Here we
encounter family romance fantasies, fantasies of love and marriage, of
pregnancy and parenting, of work, achievement, and ambition. For example, a young woman intermittently fantasizes getting married, visualizing
the ceremony, the dress and the veil, with changing representations of the
groom depending on whom she is interested in at the moment (a fantasy
brilliantly depicted in the film *Muriel's Wedding*). Such fantasies appear
at varying intervals from adolescence up until the time that she actually
marries. While stable over time, this fantasy does not have the tenacity of a
life-long repeating fantasy.

In scripting the future, our focus is different at various stages of
development. In early adolescence, our hopes for what we may become
(what we often call the ego ideal) take the form of grandiose fantasies of
mastery and mighty deeds. But at every stage of life, fantasy can act as a
rehearsal for future action, a storyline that can be incorporated into a life
plan, a template for behaviors that are either literal translations (enactments)
or symbolic expressions of the fantasy's narrative content. Generative fantasy
provides the major locus (much of it preconscious) for imaginative dress
rehearsals and trial-actions, thus a route to understanding the fantasizer's
hopes, dreams, and plans for the future.

While there are major differences between life-long repeating fantasies
and future-linked generative reveries, they also overlap, bleed into one
another. At the extremes of the continuum, repeating fantasies have a more
primitive, dreamlike quality, while the generative fantasies are often more
practical and realistic, indicating possible future scenarios, generally (but
not invariably) experienced as desirable. Repeating fantasy appears closer to
primal unconscious fantasy, with relatively little ongoing input from the
outside world, while reverie or generative fantasy appears closer to the more
logically articulated thinking processes of waking life. Repeating fantasy,
formed early in life, is more drive-instigated and more often uses body
metaphors to express itself. Reverie, or generative fantasy, while ultimately

shaped by unconscious fantasy as all fantasy is, is further from it, more responsive to current issues of mastery and narcissistic regulation, to the lineaments of ambition, power, and future possibility.

Because generative fantasy is cast in a more realistically articulated form, it is more susceptible to external influence, that is, it is more changeable in response to cues from the surrounding culture, and to changes in that culture. But both generative and repetitive fantasies may be enacted, and both play significant roles in the course our lives take.[19]

Not only unconscious wishes and feelings, but the fantasizer's current life situation, longings, conflicts, and hopes shape and infuse daydreams. The following daydreams, all reported by the same woman, but from different stages of her life, suggest how daydreams are triggered by one's immediate discontents and emerging needs, and how the resulting wish-fulfilling fantasies are balm to those specific disequilibriums, sometimes pointing the way to new adaptations. The construction in these daydreams ranges from the relatively transparent to a very simple kind of symbolic transformation to a fairly complex symbolic structure, the range having to do in part with the age at which the woman had the fantasy.

Daydream Number One

Circumstances Surrounding the Fantasy My brother was born when I was three and one-half. After that I did not play with dolls, only stuffed animals.

I had sometime long before entering first grade wanted a dog—a dog to walk in the woods, a dog to curl up with me beside the fireplace, a dog for me to feed and brush. My mother was afraid of dogs, my baby brother allergic to all life forms, and the nanny had had enough on the farm where she was born. Only I longed, and wished on each star and every birthday candle, for a dog . . . I would not play with dolls. I only played with stuffed animals. My play, of course, was maternal. I wanted to be a mother dog.

The Fantasy By the time I was seven I despaired of receiving my dog. One day I was in music class. I was asked to refrain from singing and simply move my lips. I am tone-deaf and must have been singing out of tune with the others. I was bored. Music always bored me. I imagined a black-and-white dog: a dog with one ear down and one ear up who appeared in the middle of the circle we were sitting in and ran to me. I scooped him up into my lap and imagined holding, petting, kissing him. He became mine. At first I only played with him in music class, then other times. I knew it was a game. But it was a game I loved. I can't remember the name I gave him or exactly what we did together, but the dog was mine.

Fantasy Number Two
Circumstances Surrounding the Fantasy I had always planned to be a writer. From age five on I knew it was what I would do. I read in order to write. I looked at everything in order to write about it.

I was born on Easter Sunday and had a religious Southern Baptist nanny until I was fourteen.

Sometime around the age of thirteen, my mother took me to see the film of Laura Hobson's *Gentlemen's Agreement*. The Holocaust pictures had already been in *Life* magazine. As I was leaving the film, which is about the cruelties of anti-Semitism, I decided I would someday end prejudice and poverty and inequity in the world.

The Fantasy From the time I saw the movie until the time I went to college, I would daydream about how I could save the world from nuclear disaster, hunger, disease, injustice through writing a major book—a kind of modern *Uncle Tom's Cabin*. This "I will save the world fantasy" was shockingly out of keeping with my general sense of reality and ordinary life. But I didn't even notice how grandiose and peculiar it was.

Fantasy Number Three
Circumstances Surrounding the Fantasy My father was an athlete and, in particular, a swimmer. He had supported himself through college by working as a lifeguard at a Catskill hotel.

When I was about four, he insisted that I dive into the water. Although I was frightened, he insisted. I dove, but then vomited out of fear. I was then embarrassed. I never quite got over my fear of diving; however, I became a champion swimmer, long distance, perfect form, and so forth. I was always ahead of my age group at camp.

Also by high school age, I knew about the Greek gods, and the story of Persephone was particularly interesting to me.

The Fantasy My high school was on the East River. To and from school, I could walk on the esplanade past Gracie Mansion. I would lean over the edge of the rail and watch the water. I imagined that a dark and terrible god who lived in the water would pull me in and drown me, take me to his kingdom under the water and make me his slave. There were many small variations of this story: he would love me, he would hate me. He would simply drown me, and I would die. The fantasy was frightening and interesting. I also thought about jumping into the water. He would pull me down under, and so forth.

When I was upset, I would go to the river and stare at the water, contemplating, waiting for the god to appear. I knew it was a fantasy, but it somehow drained my emotion away.

In these daydreams, and in fact in all daydreams, it is not only the narrative that gives us a glimpse into the daydream's coded meaning, but the fantasy's context, its effect on the daydreamer, and its meaning to the daydreamer. The dog fantasy serves to establish a make-believe bond between girl and imaginary dog that in some way substitutes for the bond she lost when she was displaced in her mother's affections by the birth of her brother. The fantasizer also takes the maternal role, but in relationship to a dog, not to a baby, thus repudiating the mother-child bond on one level, reduplicating it on another (with reversal of roles). She invokes the fantasy at a particular moment, in a singing class in which she feels inadequate and rejected (she's been told not to sing) and is therefore in need of affection, of feeling connected.

The save-the-world fantasy is a typical daydream of ego enhancement, embracing two poles—the wish to feel important and the wish to feel virtuous. There is a suggestion in the background material (the reference to being born on Easter Sunday) that there may be an unconscious identification with a religious savior.[20] Feeling important is also a balm to being ignored or abandoned.

In the River God fantasy, it is readily apparent that the fantasizer's somewhat problematic relationship with her father has become linked to unconscious Oedipal longings and is sexualized in her daydreams, though symbolically—the sexual version ("he would love me") alternating with a self-punitive, perhaps masochistic, variation ("he would simply drown me, and I would die"). As this fantasy reveals, the nature of the pleasure attached to fantasy is sometimes ambiguous.

All fantasies, simple though they appear, generally conceal a wish, defenses against the wish, a latent self-identification (in the example cited above, with the Christ figure), an experimentation with new relationships, or a modification or reversal of old ones. Each makes use of past experience or stories that the fantasizer has been exposed to as part of the narrative structure.

Insofar as fantasies always push toward direct or indirect actualization, each also has implications for the future life of the fantasizer. The woman just described got her dog, achieved a very successful literary career in addition to being involved in socially conscious activities, and although she first married a man who metaphorically tried to drown her, the second time around she married someone who loves her devotedly. By their very nature, fantasies (except for those that are fixated, neurotic as it were, or fantastic in their construction) are capable of evolution, of moving in a direction that allows for—indeed paves the way for—some measure of gratification in the real world. Fantasy is shaped not just by the past but by hopes for the future. And it is shaped by the stories and fantasies to which we are exposed.

Shared Fantasies

Fantasies are mediators between the inner and outer worlds; they are fueled by both the fantasizer's biological emotional needs as shaped by his or her personal history, and by circumstance. But the storylines of fantasy cast a wider net; they borrow their narrative content from the cultural surround. Not only do fantasies serve multiple functions in individual adaptation, but they are part of interpersonal and social cohesion as well. Some fantasies are communal at inception: that is, they borrow narrative content, consciously or unconsciously, from the fantasy content of significant others—of families and small groups.

Some fantasies are literally shared—that is, one person communicates a fantasy to another, or two or more people jointly create it. Sometimes that sharing is conscious, as when someone tells his fantasy to someone else; at other times a fantasy is telegraphed out of awareness—preconsciously. In any intimate relationship, one individual's fantasy life inevitably impacts or intersects the other's, thus becoming an integral part of their bond. The interaction of the fantasy system colors, or even decisively shapes, the relationship.

Shared fantasies are not unusual; they form part of the very ground of human relationships. We imbue all our significant relationships with fantasy, and intimate relationships provide the ideal medium in which shared fantasies can proliferate. Sharing fantasies intensifies the emotional and psychological connections between people. In fact the deepest emotional ties generally occur between people who have *congruent* or *complementary* fantasies whether explicitly shared or communicated through subliminal cues.

In the *congruent fantasy*, two people have the same wishes and impulses and construct a daydream as a joint venture, creating what Hans Sachs calls a "community of two." And shared fantasies can form the basis of communities of three or four, or more. The implicit bonding between the fantasizers is grounded in appreciation of the shared wish; the sharing of the fantasy relieves the unpleasant feeling of guilt, shame, and anxiety that often accompany wishes. Congruent fantasies include joint revenge fantasies, death and rebirth fantasies (frequently seen in suicide pacts), and comrade-in-arms fantasies. Or two people may form a bond based on antisocial Bonnie and Clyde fantasies of us-against-the-world fantasies.

In the *complementary fantasy* two individuals adopt (and sometimes act out) reciprocal roles—slave and master, student and mentor, rescuer and rescued, wild child and restraining parent, lover and beloved, and so on. A man whose underlying fantasy is based on the wish to be dominated may be drawn romantically only to powerful women who in turn need to act the dominant role. In a complementary fantasy, the fantasizers may stick with their respective roles, or they may be flexible, shuttling back and forth between the two (as when children negotiate, "Now I get to be the mother and you be the baby, because I was the baby yesterday").

Culturally Transmitted Fantasies

Although Freud acknowledged the impact of external circumstances on fantasy, only recently has there been a major paradigm shift in both psychology and psychoanalysis to a specific focus on an important aspect of communal life in the way our minds are formed. As the psychologist Jerome Bruner puts it:

When we enter human life, it is as if we walk on stage into a play whose enactment is already in progress—a play whose somewhat open plot determines what part we may play and toward what denouements we may be heading. Others on stage already have a sense of what the play is about, enough of a sense to make negotiation with a newcomer possible. (Bruner 1990, 34)

Part of that negotiation concerns the newcomer's ability to create fantasies that are compatible with those of others in his or her world. The boundaries between our inner and outer worlds are porous, and they remain so long past childhood, indeed throughout life.

Individuals are integrated into the mores and customs of the culture at least in part through shared fantasies and the myths, art and popular culture that embody them. Our cultural narratives provide storylines that the fantasizer may not be able to create independently but can adopt as an umbrella for many different wishes or needs. Thus fantasy can be seen to play an integral role at the intrapsychic level, at the interpersonal level, and in our very socialization.

As children mature, fantasy envelopes or narratives permeate their environment, not only through their immediate contact with relatives, friends, and peers but also through their exposure to fairy tales, novels, films, television, pop versions of history, and other cultural sources. They are exposed to, and participate in, the same conscious and preconscious fantasies as others in the world around them and become acculturated to that world, just as in their early years participation in shared fantasy and fantasy play link them to the worlds of the family and the nursery school. Some of that culture-based fantasy reflects mainstream values, but some of it, particularly when the culture is in flux, subtly subverts those values. Thus, depending on the specifics of time and circumstances, fantasy can play either a conservative or an evolutionary role.

Culturally mediated fantasy comes to us not just passively, through our families and through culturewide myths, but through our active exploration of cultural materials. Each of us processes the raw materials of the culture to see what we can cobble together for use in scripting our own wishes and needs, our preconscious and unconscious fantasies. We might call the material we choose from the culture at large *borrowed fantasy* or *shared cultural fantasy*, to distinguish it from the *shared fantasy* communicated explicitly or subliminally in exchanges with people we know. Our ability to borrow fantasy is thus analogous to the power of our distance receptors, hearing and sight, in that it gives us access to experiences beyond our immediate surroundings. Sharing fantasy interpersonally, on the other hand, is more like using the senses of taste, touch, and smell in our contacts with the surrounding environment.

The scope of possibilities that we can imagine always depends on our exposure to the world in which we live, whether that exposure is as a participant or as an observer. In constructing our personal daydreams, we employ—both in and out of awareness—what we know of our real selves and what we fantasize as our possible selves. Studying the lives of people we know (whose inner world we imagine), reading and watching fictional depictions, and assessing cultural icons, we gauge the culture's range of our alternatives and select those that suit us, which we then modify through our own creative synthesis.[21]

As we concoct our fantasies, choosing from menus that contain selections from art as well as from life, we can make identifications not just with fictional characters or with real-life people but with cultural icons who are both. For those of us who are conformists by bent, fearful of straying beyond the range mainstream culture endorses or tolerates, those icons who are innovators and rebels, a Madam Curie, a Jackie Robinson, an Oscar Wilde, are particularly liberating, helping us to conceive of possibilities beyond our customary limits.

What we borrow draws heavily on fictional stories, and we have considerable testimony about its impact on us. Carlos Fuentes puts it graphically: "You are what you eat. You are also the comics you peruse as a child" (1990, 4). Referring to her convent education, Eilene Simpson observes: "As girls who are read fairy tales daydream about becoming princesses, we who are read the lives of the saints daydreamed of becoming saints" (1987, 30–31). Because who would know better than writers themselves, novels contain numerous depictions of fictional characters being influenced by what they read and living out their most treasured stories: Cervantes's *Don Quixote* is acting out the tales of medieval chivalry consumed in his youth; Emma in Gustave Flaubert's *Madame Bovary* believes in the romances she reads and acts on them, to her detriment (Fuentes 1990, 17). Writers understand that fantasy, like art, is a two-way street, the flow of information and sensation shuttling ceaselessly back and forth between the internal and external worlds we inhabit.

Borrowed fantasies provide material for vicarious wish-fulfillment and for scripting individual fantasies. But what we borrow does not always stay in the realm of fantasy and may affect the real world. As we observe fantasies enacted by others, we are freer to act out comparable fantasies of our own. Moreover, as we discover that some of our peers share some of our fantasized identifications, we can use that commonality to foster intimate ties. We use our mutual identifications to join in groups, where our ties are based on our idealization of, and corresponding imaginative identification with, the same icon, leader, or hero (Stimpson 1987, 30–31). Such groups may promote the enactment of the shared fantasy.

The psychoanalyst Jacob Arlow illustrates a culturewide myth, and the acting out of that myth, with the case of a little girl in a religious society who is socialized to imitate the ideal qualities of purity, virtue, and love associated with the Madonna (what might be construed as the myth of—or the ideal of—pure and saintly womanhood). To take hold and flourish, to be disseminated throughout a culture, such myths have to work on a number of different levels, providing channels for multiple and sometimes conflicting needs and longings. Thus, as the child's identification with the Madonna socializes her, enabling her to fulfill her society's expectations, it also gives her a culturally sanctioned mode of gratifying an unconscious, unacceptable, incestuous wish, as can be infered from the passion with which many nuns give themselves as brides of Christ. (Arlow 1951).

Our myths primarily have an acculturating effect; that is, they act to preserve the status quo. However, under extraordinary circumstances, they may also lead to profound cultural change. From time to time we are the beneficiaries of a great creative artist or innovator who pushes the envelope, introducing into the culture the possibility of significant change. Change of that magnitude cannot be accounted for, however, by any great man theory of history that characterizes it as the consequence of one person acting in solitude. Jacob Arlow describes the true prophet as one "who correctly divines and expresses the emergent but still inarticulate dreams and aspirations of his people, " the "midwife of humanity's dreams" (Arlow, 397).

Our myths undergo a sea change, and sometimes radical change, as the outcome of a shift in "collective imagining,"[22] the product of almost imperceptible imaginative changes that occur among many people simultaneously, in response to altered circumstances and a changing milieu. The coalescence of these changes into one overarching insight is the province of the artist/creator. The result may be scripts geared not just to anxiety-free or guilt-free indulgence of fantasy or to acculturation, but to authentically new modes of gratification, hence to social transformation.

Notes

This chapter has been adapted from my book *By Force of Fantasy: How We Make Our Lives* (Person 1996).

1. Sylvan Tompkins, from the Foreword to Singer (1966, p. xii).

2. The distinction between directed thinking, on the one hand, and dreaming and fantasizing, on the other, was first made by Carl Jung in "Concerning the Two Kinds of Thinking," a paper that appeared as chapter one in his *Psychology of the Unconscious* ([1916] 1957). Nonetheless, there is a continuum between goal-directed abstract thinking and daydreaming, rather than a sharp divide.

3. Laplanche and Pontalis describe the function of fantasy as providing a setting for desire. They refer to this as a "mise èn scene" of desire. See Jean Laplanche and Jean-Bertrand Pontalis (1973).

4. Writing in 1896, in *The Aetiology of Hysteria*, Freud put forward the thesis "that at the bottom of every case of hysteria there are *one or more occurrences of premature sexual experience*, occurrences which belong to the earliest years of childhood, but which can be reproduced through the work of psycho-analysis in spite of the intervening decades. I believe that this is an important finding, the discovery of a *caput Nili* in neuropathology" (Freud 1896, 203). One simple example of a troublesome (if not classically traumatic) memory that served as the source of a symbolic symptom is to be found in Freud's case of Frau Cäcilie M. whose presenting complaint was a severe facial neuralgia. In a conversation with her husband, Frau Cäcilie M. felt one of his remarks as a stinging insult. Recounting the impact of that insult in session, "suddenly she put her hand to her cheek, gave a loud cry of pain and said: 'it was like a slap in the face.'" Freud's interpretation was that the patient felt as though she had been slapped in the face and the symptom symbolically represented that slap. Although a metaphoric transformation of the traumatic memory took place, there was no wish-fulfillment involved (Breuer and Freud 1893–95, 178).

5. As early as 1897, in a letter to Wilhelm Fliess, Freud had said that his discovery of the role of fantasy in hysterical illness caused him to understand that fantasy occupied as large a role in mental life as any external reality. (Freud 1954, 215).

6. By 1908 Freud had concluded that it was fantasies that fueled hysterical symptoms, stating that "every hysterical attack which I have been able to investigate up to the present has proved to be an involuntary irruption of daydreams...." The quote continues: "Our observations no longer leave any room for doubt that such fantasies may be unconscious just as well as conscious; and as soon as the latter become unconscious they may also become pathogenic.... In favorable circumstances, the subject can still capture an unconscious fantasy of this sort in consciousness" (Freud 1908, 160).

7. The assumption that material reality cannot be totally apprehended has bedeviled clinical attempts to distinguish pathogenic trauma from repressed fantasy. Freud's formulation, crucial though it is, had the unhappy result of drawing attention away from the role of traumatic events in patients' symptoms, and away from the different ways fantasies and memories are sometimes stored. In Freud's revised view, the patient's creation of seduction fantasies for herself was "of scarcely less importance for [her] neurosis than if [she] had really experienced what the phantasies contained. The phantasies possess *psychical* as contrasted with *material* reality, and we gradually learn to understand that in the world of the neurosis it is psychical reality which is the decisive kind" (Freud 1916, 368).

8. Freud's motives for changing his mind have been attacked from two different sides. Some have criticized Freud for basing his original seduction theory on inadequate data;

they question whether Freud's patients actually reported scenes of seduction or whether these scenes were reconstructed by Freud in the course of analysis. Schimek, for example, says: "The majority of [Freud's] female patients did not report conscious memories of seduction, but merely memories, thoughts and symptoms that Freud *interpreted* as the disguised and indirect manifestation of an infantile sexual trauma. In other words, we are dealing with inferred, unconscious repressed memories of seduction that are related to the patient's conscious production, much as the latent is to the manifest content of a dream." The opposite camp criticizes Freud for the revision of his original theory, arguing that Freud retracted his findings not on the basis of new observations or insights, but out of fear of the disapproval of his community. Leaving aside the question of whether or not Freud's seduction data were reported directly by his patients or reconstructed by him, it does seems clear that Freud genuinely came to doubt that sexual trauma was the primary etiologic agent in hysteria. Several different considerations caused Freud to change his mind, among them the fact that hysteria was so common at the time that if its causes were inevitably related to early-life seduction, he would have to implicate as seducers many fathers (or other male relatives) who seemed to him to be of impeccable respectability and decency. Doubting this to be plausible, he began to look for a different explanation to account for what he now took to be seduction fantasies, to try to understand what could have initiated them and why they were so prevalent. See Schimek (1975, 846).

9. Freud's new formulation had the negative impact of drawing attention away from the impact of trauma, memories, and early relationships on our subsequent adaptations. But as incorrect in certain respects as this formulation turned out to be—particularly from today's perspective, when the importance accorded real life events has been restored—it did prepare the way for Freud's profound insights into the key role of fantasies in our lives.

10. Freud's abandonment of the seduction theory opened up the way to his discovery of infantile sexual activity, viewed as innate and subject to a preordained developmental sequence, culminating in the development and resolution of the Oedipus complex. But this reversal in Freud's thinking skewed the field toward an almost exclusive focus on the role of the developing stages of sexuality and their accompanying wishes and fantasies both in the formation of neurosis and in healthy adaptation.

11. In studying dreams, Freud first worked out the relationships among daydreams, night dreams, and unconscious fantasy, and between wish-fulfillment and fantasy. For Freud, the wisdom of language had established the fundamental connection that existed between the dreams of daytime—fantasies—and of nighttime. Except for the fact that they occur during waking life rather than during sleep, daydreams, he believed, were like nighttime dreams, since both had their source in the wishes buried in unconscious fantasy and both served as vehicles for wish-fulfillment. (Recent findings of research psychologists, who are generally uninterested in unconscious fantasy in the Freudian sense, lend support to the view that daydreaming and nightdreaming form part of a single and continuous flow.) Several different observations help to make this point: In any given individual, daydreaming and nightdreaming share the same style and are triggered by the same kinds of external—sometimes internal—stimuli. They share some of the same imagery, and they both appear to peak at 90-minute cycles. As the research psychologist Eric Klinger puts it, daydreaming and nightdreaming "make up a single

continuum of human consciousness in which one continually shades into the other—much as each day the varied world of daytime shades into the equally variable world of night" (1971).

12. Drawing a parallel between play and fantasy, Freud proposed that both issued from the same motives, insofar as both offer a vehicle for the imaginary fulfillment of wishes and both provide a high pleasure yield. Play and fantasy are similar in yet another way. Neither the child at play nor the adult fantasizing has obscured his basic reality. In both instances, awareness of external reality and the ability to enjoy the make-believe or fantasy exist simultaneously. But in order to reap the pleasures of make-believe, one momentarily suspends one's immersion in reality. (To the degree that the sense of reality is eroded, and the fantasy believed to be real, one has entered into the domain of delusion.)

13. Whereas theorists prior to Freud had viewed play as a preparation for practicing useful skills, Freud hypothesized that one of its primary purposes was to work through anxiety and other current emotional stresses. He saw both play and fantasy as being invoked as solutions to current problems in the child's emotional world. For example, observing a year-and-a-half-old boy engaged in a game of a disappearing spool (the Fort Da game), Freud wrote a charming account of play invoked for purposes of mastering separation anxiety. Throwing away the spool is the boy's attempt to transform an event in which he experienced himself as passive (his mother's occasional and to him inexplicable disappearances) into one in which he was active (*he* was the one who did the abandoning or casting out). The game is pleasurable because it symbolically represents control over the mother's whereabouts, reassuring the child that he can at will effect the reappearance of that which he longs for so passionately.

14. Play and fantasy both address similar wishes and problems, and both draw on unconscious fantasy. According to Klinger, play and fantasy share a common origin and are undifferentiated until about three years of age, after which they develop along parallel lines up until about puberty. At puberty, as play becomes less important, fantasy activities become more important. Shame is not the only factor in this changeover. With the child's increasing capacity for narrative, fantasy becomes an ever more viable substitute.

15. Prescribing medication for anxiety and depression often triggers affect-driven fantasies. Take the case of an anxiety patient. Paradoxically, it is sometimes difficult to medicate an anxious patient, because the anxiety may lock onto fears about the medication. Thus the patient may fail to comply because of an unspoken, unanalyzed fantasy. For example, one of my patients, who is reluctant to take any medication despite her raging anxiety, fantasizes that the druggist will incorrectly fill her prescription and inadvertently give her something that will kill her; alternately, she imagines that the medicine will some years from now be found to cause cancer. On occasion, she toys with the fantasy that the medicine will so lower her inhibitions, that she will act with reckless abandon.

16. Transference fantasies often arise in response to incidental changes in the therapeutic frame, and breaks in the frame are inevitable over the course of time. Take a simple example. I am on the phone with an emergency call and, as a result, buzz my next patient in a few seconds after he or she rings the bell. Different patients respond with different flash fantasies that are clues to understanding their underlying concerns. One

man believes I have purposely set up an experiment to see how he will respond, and tells me of a psychology professor at Harvard who habitually asked applicants to open a window he had nailed shut in order to see how they would react to stress. One woman thinks I have forgotten the appointment and have abandoned her. Another is sure the fault is hers; she has the wrong day or time. One man has the flash fantasy that I have been murdered, another that the crime is still in progress, that he will break down the door, kill the assailants, and rescue me.

17. Fleeting and repeating fantasies are what some analysts have referred to as daydreams and conscious fantasies, respectively. For example, Peter Neubauer refers to repeating, organizing fantasies as "conscious fantasies," to distinguish them from fleeting fantasies, and so do many other psychoanalysts. But the problem is that the term "conscious fantasy" in this restricted sense gets confused with the term "conscious fantasy" which is used to differentiate the whole class of conscious fantasies from unconscious fantasies. I have chosen to use the term "repeating" fantasy in order to distinguish it from conscious fantasy in the larger sense. Peter Neubauer presented this distinction at a presentation entitled "The Clinical Value of the Dream" at a Panel of the American Psychoanalytic Association on December 19, 1993.

18. One sometimes discerns that a childhood fantasy and its derivatives pervade the whole trajectory of a life. Mr. Jason, now in his midsixties, recalls the passionate family romance of his childhood and identifies derivatives of that fantasy in many areas of his adult life. As a young boy of about six, he came to believe that he was the son of Maharajah. Unhappy with his parents and their virtual adoration of his older brother, he lay awake at night, crying and praying for his true father to rescue him. Why he chose Indian royalty is unknown to him, but he is dark and may even be said to have a slightly Asian look. The Maharajah fantasy receded, replaced at age 11 by a related preoccupying fantasy. Feeling more and more an outsider in his own family, enraged to the point of rebelliousness, he imaginatively identified (in the opening years of World War II, when his father was in the service) with the Japanese enemy—their values, their lifestyle, and their hostility to Americans. As an adult this man appears the very paragon of equanimity, partly because he has managed to sublimate his childhood anger and rebelliousness constructively. Derivatives of his earlier fantasies survive in his profound intellectual and aesthetic interest in Japan. He has traveled there extensively, learned Japanese, has embraced one of the Asian religions, and is sexually attracted to Asians. He appears to compensate for a feeling of a lack of nurture as a child by passionate nurturing of his lovers, commonly the flip side of fantasies of being rescued and nurtured.

19. While repeating fantasy is best understood using Freud's dream model, and generative fantasy and fleeting fantasy using his play model, all fantasies are multilayered. Therefore they always conceal preconscious and unconscious material. But by focusing almost exclusively on the unconscious meaning and infantile origins of fantasy, we lose insight into its adaptive, creative potential in charting new paths.

20. A conscious or unconscious identification with famous people on whose birthday or other significant anniversaries we happen to be born is not at all uncommon.

21. The language of possible selves and alternate selves runs through psychological literature. I first became aware that this was the precise language to convey an important aspect of fantasy through the very title of Jerome Bruner's *Actual Minds, Possible Worlds* (1986).

22. *Collective imagining* is the term used by Lynn Hunt to describe what she calls the "political unconscious" in her book, *The Family Romance in the French Revolution* (1992). She borrows that term from Frederic Jameson, who elaborated it in *The Political Unconscious: Narrative as a Socially Symbolic Act* (1981). It is similar to my term cultural unconscious which I coined in 1988 in my paper "Romantic Love: At the Intersection of the Psyche and the Cultural Unconscious" (1991). Others have independently used the same term, probably because it so vividly captures a quality of unconscious that thus far has not been explicitly addressed. Jacqueline Rose uses the term in a throwaway line in the Introduction to her *Haunting of Sylvia Plath* (1993). She writes of Plath's use of fascistic and Holocaust imagery, "it . . . appears like the return of the repressed—a fragment of the cultural unconscious that will not go away" (p. 8). And Edith Kurzweil refers to the cultural unconscious affecting psychoanalytic theories in different geographical areas in her book *The Freudians: A Comparative Perspective* (1989).

References

Arlow, J. 1951. The consecration of the prophet. *Psychoanalytic Quarterly* 20: 374–97.

Bruner, J. 1986. *Actual Minds, Possible Worlds.* Cambridge, Mass: Harvard University Press.

Bruner, J. 1990. *Acts of Meaning.* Cambridge: Harvard University Press.

Freud, S. [1896] 1962. The aetiology of hysteria. Translated by J. Strachey. *Standard Edition, III.* London: Hogarth Press, pp. 189–221.

Freud, S. [1887–1902] 1954. *Origins of Psychoanalysis: Letters to Wilhelm Fliess, Drafts and Notes: 1887–1902.* Edited by M. Bonaparte, A. Freud, and E. Kris. New York: Basic Books.

Freud, S. [1907] 1959. Creative writers and day-dreaming. Translated by J. Strachey. *Standard Edition, IX.* London: Hogarth Press, pp. 141–53.

Freud, S. [1908] 1959. On hysterical phantasies and their relation to bisexuality. Translated by J. Strachey. *Standard Edition, IX.* London: Hogarth Press, pp. 157–66.

Freud, S. [1911] 1958. Formulations on the two principles of mental functioning. Translated by J. Strachey. *Standard Edition, XII.* London: Hogarth Press, pp. 215–26.

Freud, S. [1916] 1963. *Introductory Lectures on Psycho-Analysis.* Translated by J. Strachey. *Standard Edition, XVI.* London: Hogarth Press.

Freud, S. [1921] 1955. Group psychology and the analysis of the ego. Translated by J. Strachey. *Standard Edition, XVIII.* London: Hogarth Press, pp. 69–143.

Freud, S., and J. Breuer. [1893–95] 1955. *Studies on Hysteria.* Translated by J. Strachey. *Standard Edition, II.* London: Hogarth Press.

Fuentes, C. 1990. *Myeslf with Others.* New York: The Noonday Press.

Hunt, L. 1992. *The Family Romance in the French Revolution.* Berkeley: University of California Press.

Jameson, F. 1981. *The Political Unconscious: Narrative as a Socially Symbolic Act.* Ithaca: Cornell University Press.

Jung, C. [1916] 1957. *Psychology of the Unconscious.* New York: Dodd, Mead.

Klinger, E. 1971. *The Structure and Functions of Fantasy.* New York: Wiley.

Kurzweil, E. 1989. *The Freudians: A Comparative Perspective.* New Haven: Yale University Press.

Laplanche, J., and J.-B. Pontalis. 1973. *The Language of Psycho-Analysis.* Translated by D. Nicholson-Smith. New York: Norton.

Neubauer, P. B. 1993. The clinical use of the daydream. Unpublished manuscript presented at the panel "Clinical Value and Utilization of the Daydream," Scientific Meetings of the American Psychoanalytic Association, New York City, December 19, 1993.

Person, E. 1996. *By Force of Fantasy: How We Make our Lives.* New York: Basic Books.

Person, E. 1991. Romantic love: At the intersection of the psyche and the cultural unconscious. *Journal of the American Psychoanalytic Association* 39: 383–411.

Rose, J. 1993. *The Haunting of Sylvia Plath.* Cambridge: Harvard University Press.

Schimek, J. 1975. The interpretations of the past: Childhood trauma, psychical reality, and historical truth. *Journal of the American Psychoanalytic Association* 23: 845–65.

Singer, J. 1966. *Daydreaming: An Introduction to the Experimental Study of Inner Experience.* New York: Random House.

Stimpson, I. 1987. *Orphans: Real and Imagined.* New York: New American Library.

7

The Madonna Imago: A New Interpretation of Its Pathology

M. C. Dillon

I

The essence of the Oedipus complex lies in the plausible assumption that Mother is the first love object. This is a mistake. Mother is not a love object because infantile experience is not articulated along the axes of self-other, inner-outer, subject-object. The infant's perspective is unaware of itself as a perspective. Indeed, that unawareness of itself as a perspective is what defines infantile consciousness, whether it lives through a newborn or an adult body. Mother is a separate object only from the standpoint of an adult observer; for the infant, Mother is a global presence whose being is not yet distinct from the infant's own being. *Différance* has not yet come into play; it is only a portent existing in the demand of the transcendent world to have its articulations acknowledged.

Infantile amnesia limits phenomenological investigation of the quality of early experience. One can only observe the behavior of infants and speculate. These speculations, in turn, are corrupted by projection of adult qualities where it is exactly the departures from the quality of adult experience that we seek to understand. Freud regularly refers to the infant as an ego or subject when, according to his own theorizing, the ego is relatively late in developing. He classifies the instincts associated with self-preservation and survival as ego-instincts and treats them as primordial. This dualism of self and other governs Freud's thought throughout; it confounds his understanding of love and obscures otherwise compelling insights.

Freud characterizes the earliest phases of life as primary narcissism remaining unmindful that the metaphor he has chosen is that of reflection, specifically reflection that presupposes the self-alienation of recognizing oneself in an external object. The very idea of narcissism depends upon a separation of subject and object that allows the subject to find herself in an object—an external reflection—yet this separation is an achievement that lies before the infant, something about her de facto condition that she will have to learn through painful experience. Separation involves the coming to awareness of having a perspective, a process that begins at birth, reaches a height of intensity at adolescence, and starts to regress with senility, never having reached completion.

According to Freud, the teleology of pleasure-seeking is driven by the goal of reenactment and repetition: one seeks to return to earlier occasions of pleasure to recapitulate them. The earliest intentional behavior he attributes to infants is the turning of the head to recapture the vision of the mother's breast that will position her nipple in reach of the infant's mouth. This model of explanation predelineates the Oedipal structure of adult love: one seeks to recapitulate with adult partners the quality of pleasure imprinted in infancy. With Mother, one has the unique and never-to-be-repeated experience of the confluence of ego instincts and sex instincts: the goals of primary narcissism, pleasure and survival, are coincidentally fulfilled by Mother's warmth and nutrition, the pleasures of her soft, enveloping body and her breast. Mother is thus the primal love object, the paradigm that governs our erotic striving, the memory we seek to retrieve through latter-day surrogates. The quality of her love, present in the past obscured by infantile amnesia but operative in the ceaseless proliferation of associations and derivatives going on in the unconscious, is what we seek to make present again.

This is a tragic view of love, tragic because doomed to failure, and doomed to failure because success cannot be conceived much less achieved. Could one, *per impossibile*, find the perfect surrogate, she would be prohibited by the law of exogamy, a law psychologically enforced by impotence or frigidity. But, of course, the perfect surrogate cannot be found: no woman can be primordial Mother. Even one's own biological mother would fall short of this expectation, just because she is now, despite her eminence and privilege, a person among persons, and no longer the polymorphous global presence Mother is to the infant. The quest for the primal love object is blocked by stronger forces than the incest taboo; it is stymied by the very process of maturation that brings it about: to have reached the phallic stage is already to have passed beyond the possibility of living through the primordial identification with Mother. Every attempt to repeat this experience is regressive in the double sense of violating the reality principle and longing to revert to infantility.

Unbridled sex instincts, Freud tells us, are sadistic: not sadistic in the sense of seeking to inflict pain on the sex object, but sadistic in the attempt to dominate and control.[1] Whence, then, arise the tender emotions associated with mature forms of sexual expression? What motivates the transformation of narrowly sexual aims into love? Freud defines love in several ways at different points along the course of his own developing thought: love is aim-inhibited repetition; love is "the relation of the ego to its sources of pleasure" (1966, 99); love is "primarily narcissistic, is then transferred to those objects which have been incorporated in the ego, . . . and expresses the motor striving of the ego after these objects as sources of pleasure" (102); love is subsumed under eros, the life instinct that seeks higher forms of organization through binding and unification. The problem of accounting for the genesis of the tender emotions of love from the sheer pleasure-seeking of sex instincts may be subsumed under the greater problematic of sublimation, the channeling of raw instinct into culturally higher forms. As Ricoeur points out, sublimation presupposes a vision of ends, a teleology drawn by final causes, which Freud's energy-based economics is at a loss to explain.[2] Tender emotions: this paltry phrase names the difference between rape and love. Eros manifests itself in all the strategies of manipulating the other in order to achieve one's own frisson, attempts to dominate, suborn, and deceive; efforts to purchase, possess, and use. Eros also motivates acts of generosity, self-sacrifice, and loyalty; moments of valor, creativity, and deep pathos. Every account of love from Plato to the present aims at understanding the nature, genesis, and portent of these tender emotions, be that understanding couched as a reduction to unconscious biological causes or, at the other extreme, as an elevation to supernatural heights of a mystical principle of cosmic unification. Freud embraces the gamut: Mother is the source of love, and her title is as celestial as it is biological; she cannot be conceived apart from the confluence of nature and nurture.

But how is she to be conceived? Specifically, how does she evoke the tender emotions that bind testosterone to *poiesis*?

I have argued that Freud's explanatory paradigm, based as it is on an economy of dualism, goes astray in two ways: it fails to understand the syncretic quality of infantile experience by presupposing a self-other separation, which has to be overcome through mediations across an ontological fissure, and it compounds this failure by conceiving these mediations as driven by a retrospective mechanism of repetition and reenactment which leaves the telic and creative aspects of desire, named as sublimation, strictly unaccountable.

II

To understand love is necessarily to understand its antithesis—if, that is, love and hate are opposites, a binary system constructed around the fulcrum of a negation. For Freud, the fulcrum is the dualism between the external world and the internal organism. Hate originates in the exogenous domain of worldly stimuli that generate pain by building tension and give rise to flight, movement away, repulsion, or, in the extreme, aggression and attempts to destroy. Love's origin lies in narcissistic organ-pleasure, release of libido from endogenous sources, which attracts us to ourselves and motivates us to repeat the motions through which we please ourselves. Mediating across the negation that separates outer from inner is Mother, the object of a primordial identification. At his best, Freud describes this identification in terms of the logic of syncretism and indistinction of perspectives, but his metapsychological commitments to an explanatory paradigm based on dualistic economical principles change the logic of syncretism into the logic of mediation: Mother becomes the external object that must first be introjected through transference of narcissistic investments or cathexes, and subsequently alienated through the mechanism of repression based on enforcement of the law of exogamy through the castration complex.

Departing now from Freud, I would venture the hypothesis that the enigma of the tender emotions is illumined by the structure of identification or, better, syncretism. In primordial indistinction, self and Mother merge, and polymorphous infantile sensuality permeates the continuum wherein self–Mother–world overlap. The organism's project of survival is not lived as self-interest, as the term ego instinct suggests, but rather is diffused throughout the syncretic continuum as a global telos. Even on the part of the adult Mother, it would be mistaken to regard the project of the infant's survival as a mediation between self-interest and altruism; it is closer to the model of symbiosis wherein the interests of the two organisms merge into ambiguity and indistinction.

This community of interest, lived through rather than reflected upon, subtends the existential value of golden rule morality and constitutes a founding moment of ethics. The thematic attribution of interests or desires like unto one's own to others, coupled with the pathos of respect for the self-interests of a self who is not oneself, forms the basis for ethical consciousness. Ethical consciousness is reflective, a relatively late acquisition that presupposes development of perspectival awareness or recognition of community across discrete individual bodies and their separate interests. The origin of this reflective awareness cannot be explained by appeal to analogy—which always begs the question of the ground of the identification it seeks to explain—because the analogy is itself founded upon the pathos of syncretism.

Here, in my view, is the elusive truth of the Oedipal structure, a truth obscured by the two mistakes mentioned above and the symbolism that perpetuates those mistakes by concretizing Mother into an individualized imago. Mother is not Jocasta, not Mary, not Madonna: Mother is a diffuse and enveloping global presence from which individual personae emerge through a process of differentiation and psychophysical maturation.

Here, also, is the elusive truth of Freud's controversial thesis of infantile sexuality. The infant—Mother—world syncretism is sensual. It is incipient sexuality: its sexual moment is present as a vague portent, but is not thematic. Sexuality proper requires a passage through the psychophysical changes of puberty, and it is mistaken to read the resultant structures of thematic desire backward into infancy. It is equally mistaken to regard infant and Mother as dwelling in asexual intimacy. They dwell in a sensuous domain permeated with the primal qualities of pleasure and pain: milk and feces flow and ebb; bodies intertwine, separate and come together again in a primal dance configured by uneasy desire driven by the mobile dialectic of primary and secondary processes. The pleasures of the nipple presuppose the pains of hunger, engorged breasts, and cellular level awareness of becoming, transience, approaching end.

Mother and infant must lose each other for the infant to find its self and Mother to retrieve her self; they must separate from each other in order to survive as mortal individuals. The germ of differentiation drives the entire process of child-bearing and informs the symbols of organic becoming, the symbols through which we conceive life–death–life, love–hate–love.

III

How shall I pursue love if I am not capable of recognizing it? How shall I find my love if I am not capable of recognizing her? Freud tells us that our inchoate knowledge of love and its object is primordial and tragic: in the mode of self-deceptive repression we betray through denial what we cannot consciously acknowledge, that our desire is forlorn, destined to wistful mourning and neurotic displacement, barred from realization by biological necessity and the imperatives of culture. The tragedy is mitigated by re-nunciation, redirection, resignation, in a word, sublimation. Socrates, Christ, and Buddha: world-historic symbols of the transcendence of eros in the direction of pure spirituality. Transcendence is possible by virtue of transference. Desire must be mobile, free to move from object to object, able to attach itself to different kinds of objects, capable of transforming itself as it ascends through the chakras, the stages of the cross, the levels of the divided line.

What is the magnet that attracts eros and draws it through phases of self-transcendence toward higher levels of self-realization? The appeal to which Socrates and his kindred archetypes responded is the finality of peace, the stilling of desire. The best among us move from union with Mother's flesh to union with Father's spirit. From nonself to self to nonself again. The goal is release: release from desire, release from flesh, release from *samsara*. Success or failure is determined by ethical categories: *arete* and *sophrosyne*, redemption from sin, reduction of karmaic debt. Oedipus goes willingly to his death, having paid the debt of his desire, illumined by its end, guided alone by his inner eye—leaving his sons to recapitulate the agony of his passion and pride, chaste Antigone alone being capable of discerning the inner truth of the death of the flesh.

This narrative is vindicated exclusively by the appeal of an after world founded upon the psychodynamics of fear and *ressentiment*. That is to say, it cannot be vindicated. Where does this leave love?

There is another appeal. This is the appeal of a fleshly other to be recognized in her otherness, and to be affirmed in the reversibility of flesh and the merging of its desire.

IV

How shall I pursue love if I am not capable of recognizing it? How shall I find my love if I am not capable of recognizing her? If I recognize love in

the mode of nostalgia for an immediate and unconditional fulfillment of all
my desires, then I am in vain pursuit of a past that truly was never present,
and my longing to recapitulate that infantile quality of experience is genuinely regressive. It is recognizable in my tantrums when my rights of absolute and exclusive possession are threatened, and equally recognizable in my
boredom with the object possessed and secure. Yet we are properly guided
by reminiscence: it need not lead us into nostalgia or preconfigure desire as
a compulsion to repeat.

Gestation is separation. It is division and formation of new unities. The
passages of individual maturation are inevitably marked with the pain of
transition. Mother expels me from her body, weans me from her breast,
spurns the gift of my feces, and rejects me as a suitor. She educates me to
self-sufficiency by withholding her nurture. She forces me to attenuate my
demands and accommodate her own. She turns me toward the world, and
leads the way out of the bower, distributing her care to my father, siblings,
and other members of the community whose needs, demands, and offerings
rival my own. She prepares me to balance immediate sensuous gratification
with deliberate calculation and negotiation. As she withdraws from me, she
becomes more distinctly herself and less an extension of my barely formulated wishes. Mother is an emergent agonist, the vehicle of the introduction of negativity—disappointment, refusal, retribution—into a world
in which it had been no more than a heavy portent. Mother punishes me,
uses violent means to enforce a will contrary to my own, thus enabling me
to recognize my will as my own.

It is Mother who socializes me. Although she may invoke the name of
the father, she does so for her own purposes, mediating the law through her
own desire, which alone gives consistency to the pattern of exceptions. The
period of latency is ill-named by Freud—who also stresses the hypothesis
of repression beyond credibility with the figures of castration. This is the
period of initiation to the world, the third term of the syncretic triad that
now defines itself and establishes its own autonomy with its peculiar systems
of impartial rewards and punishments, pleasures and pains. Infantile desire is
not so much repressed as it is articulated, thematized, and distributed among
objects and persons, each bearing its own implacable logic of demands and
offerings that feeds back into the differentiation of desire.

Puberty extends infantile sensuality into thematic sexuality which, in
turn, introduces a new quality of reflection and alienation. Secondary sexual
characteristics are public. They define the changeling as sexual in the eyes of

a world in which sexuality has been demonized and imbued with shame. Shame is a disease of reflection: the adolescent learns to see herself through the alienated perspective of those who know her secret and regard it with an admixture of scorn and greasy prurience. This is when the narcissus flowers: challenged from the outside by the look of the other and undermined from within by the unwelcome changes distorting her familiar body, the identity of the changeling becomes her mania. Public and private personae develop and collide: she locks her door and grooms herself for and against scoptophilic appreciation and intrusion. Above all, she forms intense bonds around the axes of identification and betrayal. She acquires a perspective aware of itself as such, threatened and attracted by difference, longing for affirmation across the distance of otherness. She wants a friendly mirror in which to find herself. She wants friendly flesh through which to feel herself, to explore and exploit the powers and pleasures newly afforded her. She does not want to be hurt or violated or betrayed or defiled. Neither does he.

Do they want Mother? They do not want their mothers, the concrete maternal figures with proper names who overflow with admonishment and sanctions. But they do want community, intersection of perspectives, a space where pathos is secure against the hostile and threatening other. Recognition of this space in the social topography of adolescence is guided by reminiscence. I can sense the resonances of community, recognize the perspective that intersects here and now with my own, experience the outside of my inside because I have dwelled in such a place in a previous lifetime. If I have not enjoyed the warmth of syncretism—or, rather, to the extent that I have not—I am lost, and the quest to find myself in the eyes of another, at best overwhelming, is undermined from within.

We do want Mother, need Mother. More accurately, we need the enabling that Motherdom has or has not nurtured within us in a prehistory faded beyond recall, but lingering on in the qualitative penumbra of our daylight hours. We need to be able to recognize love when it is present in ourselves and others, to discern within ourselves and others the marks of genuine pathos. This is the etiology of what Freud called the tender emotions. It is the horizon of care that binds community. It is the foundation of ethical consciousness, our primordial directedness toward reciprocity. It is also the engine of vengeance.

But . . . is this not a formula for nostalgia, compulsion to repeat, and regression to infantile modes of being-with? Is this not the source of

demand, the insatiable quest for unconditional nurture, unqualified affection, undistracted attention? It can be and, perhaps often is, but it need not
be. The distinction needed here is provided by Freud in the array of concepts centering around fixation and unfinished business. Gestation is separation, and regression takes place when there has been no departure. The
issue is maturation, adjustment to the challenges and claims of otherness,
acquisition of the reality principle as a way of living. What may be unfinished is the process of weaning, and the fixation is a refusal to relinquish the
simple pleasures of infancy and take on the complex pleasure-pain of loving
others differentiated from oneself. Ethical consciousness is not only the
recognition of genuine care, it also involves reciprocation, even initiation,
of care.

The uninterpreted half of the Oedipus story is Jocasta's abandonment
of her son for the sake of her own self-interest, an act as extreme, excessive,
and destructive as her welcome of the young, limping, regal champion into
her bed. In both cases she should have known better. The good Mother is
absent from this scene. Oedipus was not weaned with care, and he reca-
pitulates the excesses of his infancy in his manhood. Oedipus is vindicated
by his gentle transition out of his body into death, not because it is a passage
to pure spirituality, but because it is emblematic of his growing ability
to deal appropriately with the transcendent reality revealed through his
relentless quest for truth. The truth of Oedipus does not lie in the story of a
universal longing for Mother; it resides in the story of a noble and painful
recovery from a wretched childhood. In my reading, the story of Mary's
son is tragedy unmitigated by self-transcendence: the infant of the Virgin,
the product of immaculate conception, dies into assimilation by the Father
never having known woman, never having reciprocated the touch of that
other. Infinite, disembodied wisdom treated this pre-adolescent androgyne
as badly as Socrates treated Alcibiades, and for the same reason: denial of
embodiment as ground of morality. It is this denial that constitutes the
wretched childhood of Western civilization.

V

What of the sexual dimension of ethical consciousness and care? The first
thing to be said is that sexuality is intrinsically charged with value: desire
essentially informs good and bad. The classical denial reaffirms the truth.
"All is fair in love and war." Fairness is at issue from the start. The statement

is true for infantile consciousness, the consciousness that saturates our history of both love and war. It simply condenses the thesis of infantile sadism, the will to master the frisson-producing presence, a pervasive will oblivious to otherness and separate perspectives informed by pathos it has not yet learned to perceive.

Thematic sexuality is a differentiation of infantile sensuality that does not exist for itself before puberty. When, during adolescence, it does emerge with the evolution of reflection, shame, and the capacity for cataclysmic organ-pleasure, it emerges into a context permeated with the Hegelian quest for recognition and identity; it is configured, one way or another, as much by that context as by the somatic context established by the flow of hormones and the intense pleasure potential of the maturing genitals.

Freud argued that, during puberty, polymorphous pleasures consolidate in the genitals and unify under the telos of reproduction. I think he was led astray by unexamined presuppositions derived from theistic natural law theory but was nonetheless in touch with a fundamental truth, namely that it is definitive of consciousness to unify its themes while attending away from the horizons that encompass and inform them. My thesis is that the thematic genitally focused sexuality that emerges at adolescence emerges within a horizon structured by the quest for affirmative recognition of identity, a quest that supervenes and encompasses any latent impetus toward reproduction (or contribution to the gene pool) as well as overt pleasure-seeking—in a word, sexual desire. When sexuality emerges as such, it is incorporated within the project of love which has been gestating from the start: it is not mere coincidence that, through mutual reinforcement, the two entelechies converge, actualize, and peak at the same time.

Let me conclude with a thought about the dark side of sexlove and its relation to ethical consciousness. Ethical consciousness is pathos for the other. The proper metaphor is reversibility rather than unification: reversibility preserves identity and difference but allows for transference, reciprocity, and corporeal empathy. I can feel your pleasures and pains through the reversibility of flesh, feel them at the level of fleshly sentience rather than infer them analogically. I am attuned to this from the start by the imprinting of the primordial syncretic experience. I am vulnerable to your pathos: my identity feeds on it and nurtures it. I can open myself to this experience or erect defenses against it. These options are not exclusive: the fact that we are encased in separate gloves of skin that simultaneously keep us apart and allow us to touch each other opens a continuum of modes of intercorporeity—of proximity and distance, vulnerability and defense, cathexis and anti-cathexis, openness and closure—bounded by the limiting points of unification and oblivious indifference.

Mother taught me sensuous intimacy and pleasure. Mother taught me rejection and pain. The world reinforced these lessons. Freud was correct in holding that hate is an externalization of pain. Beyond that, however, hate is the externalization of bad: it is the projection of moral negativity upon a proximal other. I neither hate nor love across the distance of utter ignorance of the other's existence. The intensity of love and hate is directly proportional to degree of intimacy, and intimacy always portends both. The child who throws a tantrum in the supermarket and screams its hatred of Mother for all the world to hear is at the same time proclaiming its love. Astute mothers hear it that way. And astute mothers also hear the proclamation of love following the gift of the brightly wrapped candy bar desperately sought as a genuine, but highly conditioned, expression of sentiment: denial might have evoked rage. Infants are like that.

And so are infantile adults. It was William Congreve who wrote at the turn of the eighteenth century that

Heav'n has no rage, like love to hatred turn'd,
Nor Hell a fury, like a woman scorn'd.[3]

At the end of the twentieth century, O. J. Simpson and Sol Wachtler lifted Congreve's sexist bias. The general truth is that vulnerability produces lability. The defenses dropped in the glorious moment of declaration that ends the pain of isolation do not dissolve but recede like a virus to sally forth renewed when my own true love betrays my faith, just as my best friend did in high school. The more she was ensconced in my world, the more pervasive her scent in the furniture of my life, the more her absence radiates from my field of presence, the more I lament her passage through my days. The retrospective anti-cathexis is intensified by shock and surprise, as Freud discovered, and in the erotic domain it takes the form of an iterated compulsion to blame.

When erstwhile lovers, embittered by betrayal, come together to negotiate possession of children and communal property, the items on the table quickly become fetishes for lost self-esteem. I can relinquish the pleasures of her body when her eyes harden and mirror disgust where *lust* once beamed, but I cannot forsake the self I once sought in those eyes. The project of retrieval is determined by moral categories: I want, above all, to have been good and right and decent. I want it all to have been her fault.

If, as Freud suggested, my penis is my alter ego, the fetish of my identity, then to sheath another where I came into my own, is to cut me off from myself. It is not from my father that my fears of castration are born, he just foreshadows my own inevitable demise: that is the truth of the phallic plays recapitulated in the myth of Cronos and Ouranos. It is, rather, she I fear.

As Hillary Clinton knows, with her man's women spread all over front pages and centerfolds, self-esteem does not consolidate exclusively in the penis or its symbolic extension. Castration is a false concretion, another residue of Freud's penchant to condense a horizon within an overdetermined symbolic theme. The fact is that when we love, we love with our whole selves, that love regularly survives the wilting of the penis, that the phallic alter-ego is properly a transient phenomenon of adolescence, in short, that it is not loss of a body part that we fear when we give ourselves over to love: it is the threat to the totality of our being, the real threat of ontological rejection, that produces hatred and its derivatives (jealousy, deceit, battery, spite, etc.).

The possibility of rejection gives meaning to acceptance as the possibility of negation valorizes affirmation. The promise to love is a wistful reminder that desire and its demise transcend volition; it is an incantation against the precarious nature of love, an appeal to magic to secure our love against the vagaries of fate. As our sleeping bodies monitor the world with the goal of prolonging sleep against disturbance ambivalently coupled with vigilance to awaken to danger, so do our loving bodies monitor each other's behavior with a vigilance that cannot be suspended. Freud's own logic forced him to concede that ego and sex instincts cannot be conceived in isolation from each other: the reality principle forces mature lovers to acknowledge and compensate for the conditions beyond their control that govern their erotic fate. This is the difference between infantile syncretism and the mature love of separate identities whose affinities reinforce each other by virtue, not in spite, of the separation that grants them individuality.

Freud was uneasy about asserting an isomorphism between the capacity of an instinct to reverse into its opposite apparent in the vicissitudes of sadism–masochism and scoptophilia–exhibitionism, on the one hand, and love–hate, on the other. The binary terms—activity-passivity, self-other, inner-outer—which seem to map so cleanly onto the first two pairs of opposites, do not accommodate the love-hate indifference structure so easily. The reason for this should now be apparent: in love, the self-other relation is not a binary relation of mutual exclusion.[4] Alterity operates in the gestation of the self defining itself through the intimate alienation of reflection. And that alterity is derivative upon the alterity of the other's look that sets the process of reflection and self-identification in motion.

The self that is generated through the reflective process is mediated through the other's desire, to be sure, but that is only half the story—and to leap from that half-truth to the Lacanian conclusion that all sense of individual selfhood is *méconnaissance* is itself a mystified understanding. The other half of the truth is that the self of the other's desire never entirely fits me. I may be drawn to fulfill the other's desire, may work at that project in varying degrees of deliberation and conscious awareness, but that very effort presupposes an awareness of difference between the self I sense myself to be and the self that I would have to be to fulfill the other's desire. The foundation of both the selves in question is my body, and its malleability to desire has limits.[5] I may reject the persona projected upon me by the other's desire. The pathos of ethical consciousness, incipient in the syncretic phase and problematized during adolescence, demands mutual recognition in a dialectical process which, unlike Hegel's, involves a positivity grounded in our bodies and the world we inhabit. Mother's elbow, from some angles, may resemble her breast, but it will not give milk. And I must eventually learn that the gift of my feces may smell like shit to mom.

Mother prepares us for mature love; she does not beckon us back to oceanic engulfment. We do not seek to find her in a mate, just because she never was the model of an individual mate. By the time she becomes an individual, she is no longer primordial Mother. For the developing individual, each new love is truly the first love. One never knows whether he or she will be our last love, but that is always our hope.

Notes

1. This attempt is originally oblivious of pain caused to the other, hence not motivated by the attempt to cause it.

2. Paul Ricoeur (1970, 489–90): "All the procedures or mechanisms that are set into operation by the constitution of the higher agency, whether they be called idealization, identification, or sublimation, remain unintelligible in the framework of an economics.... Freudianism lacks a suitable theoretical instrument to render intelligible the absolutely primal dialectic between desire and the other than desire."

3. *The Mourning Bride*, III, viii.

4. Nor, for that matter, is the self–other relation a binary opposition in the first two pairs of opposites, but this is a separate issue that requires its own unique treatment.

5. With all due respect (and much respect is due) to Mitchell and Rose in *Feminine Sexuality* (1982), Mother's desire is not definitive of the infant's emergent sense of self as every flesh and blood mother knows. Mother is a powerful influence, but the infant's body has a mind of its own.

References

Freud, S. 1963. Instincts and Their Vicissitudes. Translated by Cecil M. Baines. In Philip Rieff, ed., *General Psychological Theory*. New York: Macmillan.

Lacan, J. 1982. *Feminine Sexuality: Jacques Lacan and the École Freudienne*. Edited by J. Mitchell and J. Rose, translated by J. Rose. New York: Norton.

Ricoeur, P. 1970. *Freud and Philosophy: An Essay on Interpretation*. Translated by D. Savage. New Haven: Yale University Press.

8

The Impossibility of Female Mourning

Jennifer Hansen

No woman is a genius: women are a decorative sex.

They never have anything to say, but they say it charmingly.

They represent the triumph of matter over mind, just as men represent the triumph of mind over morals.

—Oscar Wilde, from *The Picture of Dorian Gray*

This sentiment wittily expressed by Oscar Wilde is one religiously held by most philosophers canonized in the Western tradition. Spanning from Plato to Nietzsche, a period that the philosopher Martin Heidegger refers to as Platonism (Heidegger 1972), one can find innumerable examples of these men circumscribing women solely within the function of procreation. Woman is the matter from which men come to be and subsequently dominate in their divinely purposed role as rulers over the less intellectually endowed creatures. Woman is helpless to her hormones. She contributes little to the great works of culture, though her frippery may inspire men to master her allure by depicting her in art. Beyond her slight contributions as a decorative sex, woman seems to do more damage than she is worth.

Moreover psychologists such as Sigmund Freud argue that woman, as mother, will eventually devastate her son; she will leave him for another man: the father. Freud called this psychodrama played out early in the little boy's sexual life the Oedipus complex. As by now is well known, at the threat of losing his most prized cultural possession, the phallus, the son must renounce his profound sexual attachment to his mother. The renunciation of woman, as mother, must be mastered; it must be mourned. Mourning, for the son, is psychic matricide.[1] And it is precisely his mind, his intellectual powers, that allow the son to carry out this matricide. Indeed, his mind does triumph over his morals.

Though Freud focuses explicitly on the mechanism of psychic matricide that enables the little boy to become a man and take up his rightful place as an independent authority in culture, his writings reflect the philosophical tradition he inherits. Culture begins through sacrifice. And the work of many contemporary feminists is beginning to reveal that the necessary and sufficient sacrifice is woman (see Irigaray 1985, 1993; Oliver 1995; Le Doeuff 1990; Lloyd 1984; Brennan 1992). As Freud puts it, by unburdening themselves of their attraction to the mother, men are free to create. Creation may lead to genius. And the necessary mechanism for creativity is sublimation, which is a desexualization of the ego and the redirection of libidinal energy toward other things (Freud 1960, 44–47).

If, however, men cannot mourn their mothers, they fall into melancholia. And melancholia, according to Freud, cannot be mastered. In mourning, "reality testing has shown that the loved object no longer exists, and it proceeds to demand that all libido shall be withdrawn from its attachments to that object" (Freud 1957, 244). Hence, in mourning the matricide is successfully carried out. But in melancholia the love object becomes introjected into the self, thereby keeping the self tied up energetically with the object—with the mother. Unconscious struggles of love and hate ensue leading to the "profoundly painful dejection, cessation of interest in the outside world, loss of capacity to love, inhibition of all activity, and a lowering of the self-regarding feelings to a degree that finds utterance in self-reproaches and self-revilings, and culminates in a delusional expectation of punishment." So far I have only been talking of the son, but what of the daughter? If culture so reviles women, and the daughter must also kill off her attachment to the mother, then what hope lies for a woman's healthy mourning of her mother that would allow for her entrance into culture? What could possibly motivate the daughter to kill off that which she is, especially if she too must take her turn as mother?[2] It appears that the daughter is unlikely to ever break her attachment to her own mother. And, following on what I have said about Freud above, it seems that the daughter's fate is melancholia. Even if she finds the motivation to separate from her mother, she lacks the ability to desexualize her libido. Woman cannot sublimate; hence she is melancholic.

Julia Kristeva's book, *Black Sun: Depression and Melancholia*, surprisingly does not offer another reading of melancholia. Although many champion Kristeva as one of France's most important feminists, her prognosis for female melancholics is not good. In fact, with the exception of Kristeva's bold claim to "cure" depression, most of the essential insights of her book echo the misogyny of Platonism. As I will show in this chapter, women are left behind in Kristeva's book though she mentions their greater likelihood to suffer depression.[3] While Kristeva claims that great men of artistic genius show the rest of us how to conquer depression through creating art, she does not include women in this "us."

Before turning to Kristeva's writings on how one "cures" melancholia, I will first situate her work within the romantic writings of Friedrich Nietzsche and Freud. Both Freud and Nietzsche, important influences to Kristeva's work, reveal the conflicts in human self-consciousness. These conflicts illustrate the inherent suffering in human existence, a suffering for which art is a narcotic-like cure. Art soothes suffering and makes life bearable. Second, I will present Kristeva's argument that the production of artwork brings about a powerful catharsis rather than the mere narcosis that Freud and Nietzsche offer us. For Kristeva, art production is not an anti-depressant but is a "counterdepressant." Third, I will show that Kristeva does not believe that women have access to this counterdepressant.

Dissatisfied with Kristeva's analysis of depression and its fidelity to a misogynistic tradition, I propose new directions for "curing" depression besides the age-old wisdom of creating beauty from suffering or the recent fad of antidepressants. I suggest that we need to rethink the underlying ontology of intersubjectivity and specifically the ontology of female identity in order for our culture to seriously address the fact that women are depressed. Women's melancholia, which I am specifically interested in here, is a political issue calling for a cultural reimagining of *eros*, desire, and intersubjectivity if it is to be successfully averted.

Portraits of Pain, Opiates, and Morality

In his important work *Civilization and Its Discontents*, Freud claims that "life, as we find it, is too hard for us; it brings us too many pains, disappointments and impossible tasks. In order to bear it we cannot dispense with palliative measures" (Freud 1961, 22). Freud asserts this with such insouciance that the reader almost accepts this prognosis. Our illusions may rescue us from the horror of the reality in which we live. Our bodies suffer from physical and mental ailments, we contend with natural disasters and predators, and we negotiate the difficulties ensuing from the hell that is other people. Clearly, suffering is inherent to life, and no one appreciates this more than the melancholic essayist, philosopher, or the psychologist. So we turn to the philosophers and psychologists for help.

Freud speculates that we humans are thoroughly ruled by the pleasure principle. We strive for the experience of extreme pleasure coupled with an avoidance of pain. Viewing, or better yet creating art, may aid us in the avoidance of pain. In his portrait of the human being, art becomes understood as a psychological event. Art is measured and judged according to how well it produces the effect of happiness in its release of pain. Yet art does little to secure extreme pleasure. Freud postulates that the pleasure principle necessarily engenders suffering. To experience intense pleasure, we would need to be rid of the limitations of our body, natural dangers and disasters, potential predators, and, above all, our moral codes. Extreme pleasure comes from the complete abandonment of our ego-structure as well as by overcoming our physical limitations. Extreme pleasure lies in a realm with no limits, which is an experience fundamentally closed off to us, though its very possibility haunts us. One would come closest to understanding this pure expression of pleasure in the image of the Dionysian festivals of the ancient Greek world where the full expression of erotic drives became possible for the duration of the festival. Our moral codes no longer allow such debauchery and licentiousness, and thus life now becomes a frustration of pleasure.

Our super-ego, the part of our psychic structure that issues moral prohibitions, forces us to moderate our claims. It comes to be by our psychic apparatus projecting a surface that confronts limits such as the treachery of nature, the competition and threat that comes from other human beings, and the morbidity of our bodies. The super-ego translates these physical limitations as moral limitations; the surface projected by the psychic apparatus is molded by our external surroundings. In this confined space, we strive to secure a trifle of happiness that sadly becomes transient.

However, the artist or his spectator, for Freud, finds some relief in the illusions forged by the artist's imagination. The tortured artist turns away from the suffering caused by the external world into a private and internal world of imagination. Illusions, according to Freud, are "expressly exempted from the demands of reality-testing and [are] set apart for the purpose of fulfilling wishes which were difficult to carry out" (Freud 1961, 27). Art brings joy both to the artist and the spectator, but in an impotent way. Freud observes that "[art's] intensity is mild as compared with that derived from the sating of crude and primary instinctual impulses; it does not convulse our physical being" (Freud 1961, 26–27). Nonetheless, Freud counsels against us dismissing too quickly art as a means to moderate our claims to pleasure. Those who are sensitive and receptive to art "cannot set too high a value on it as a source of pleasure and consolation in life" (Freud 1961, 28). However, Freud also cautions against an overzealous attitude toward art's palliative effects. While art brings valuable relief to suffering and thus some happiness, Freud warns that "the mild narcosis induced in us by art can do no more than bring about a transient withdrawal from the pressure of vital needs, and it is not strong enough to make us forget real misery." Thus the production of art in the service of enjoying life functions as a mild narcotic, soothing for a short time our primal pain due to the frustration of the pleasure principle. However, the pleasure principle ineluctably returns in full force. Thus art is a mediocre treatment for suffering.

No one more passionately investigates the redemptive effects of art than Nietzsche does. In his *Birth of Tragedy*, he relays the wisdom of Silenus from Sophocles' *Oedipus at Colonus*:

Oh, wretched ephemeral race, children of chance and misery, why do you compel me to tell you what it would be most expedient for you not to hear? What is best of all is utterly beyond your reach: not to be born, not to *be*, to be *nothing*. But the second best for you—is to die soon. (Nietzsche 1967, 42)

Nietzsche, like Freud, portrays a wretchedness and deep suffering at the core of existence. And this suffering arises from the *principium individuationis*—the term denoting the fact that humans exist as solitary individuals with boundaries separating us from the other. The two motives underlying art which Nietzsche terms the Apollinian and Dionysian, grant different modes of relief.

Illusions and dreams spring out of the Apollinian drive. Concerning the Apollinian drive, which becomes embodied in the Greek god Apollo, Nietzsche writes that "this deep consciousness of nature, healing and helping in sleep and dreams, is at the same time the symbolical analogue of the soothsaying faculty and of the arts generally, which make life possible and worth living" (p. 35). Apollo and his dream illusions reveal to us, in an idealized manner, the truth of the suffering emanating from the *principium individuationis*. Nietzsche sees Apollo as the apotheosis of this principle disclosing the Greek yearning for a metaphysical primal unity embodied in the beautiful dreamy illusions of the Apollinian impulse. Apollo "shows us how necessary is the entire world of suffering, that by means of it the individual may be impelled to realize the redeeming vision, and then, sunk in contemplation of it, sit quietly in his tossing bark amid the waves" (p. 46). The apotheosis of the principle of individuation becomes represented in the Delphic maxims "know thyself" and "nothing in excess." Nietzsche recasts this as self-knowledge and moderation, two principles that thoroughly rule the Apollinian impulse. The dream world of appearance is a world where-in we contemplate ideal and beautiful forms. Nature and the individual self appear in harmony and peace with each other. These beautiful images justify life, claims Nietzsche, but what is more important to note is that these Apollinian images rest upon the substratum of Silenus's wisdom—the desire of self-abnegation. The Apollinian impulse is permeated by the Dionysian.

The Dionysian impulse expresses itself in festivals. Nietzsche reports: "In nearly every case these festivals centered in extravagant sexual licen-tiousness, whose waves overwhelmed all family life and its venerable tradi-tions; the most savage natural instincts were unleashed, including that horrible mixture of sensuality and cruelty ..." (p. 39). In these festivals individuals shed the boundaries of their personhood in a wave of self-forgetfulness. Nietzsche explains, "under the charm of the Dionysian not only is the union between man and man reaffirmed, but nature which has become alienated and hostile, or subjugated, celebrates once more her rec-onciliation with her lost son, man" (p. 37). Boundaries blur among indi-viduals who then melt into a primordial broth of universal harmony. As with the Apollinian impulse, this phenomenon also points toward a pri-mordial unity—a wholeness where selves and nature are no longer distinct. The Dionysian impulse of excess comes into strife with the Apollinian impulse of moderation, yet their strife rests in the work of art. Nietzsche argues:

The muses of the arts of "illusion" paled before an art that, in its intoxication, spoke the truth. The wisdom of Silenus cried "Woe! Woe!" to the serene Olympians. The individual, with all his restraint and proportion, succumbed to the self-oblivion of the Dionysian states, forgetting the precepts of Apollo. *Excess* revealed itself as truth. Contradiction, the bliss born of pain, spoke out from the very heart of nature. And so, wherever the Dionysian prevailed, the Apollinian was checked and destroyed. (pp. 46–47)

The Apollinian view of self-knowledge and moderation, satisfied in the contemplation of beautiful illusions, rests upon this other powerful impulse of self-abnegation revealing its truth of excess. The excess of the Dionysian destroys the moderation of the Apollinian, yet the sensuality and cruelty disclosed by Dionysian gets taken up once again in Apollinian idealized forms. The strife between the two impulses generates art. Thus the Apollinian serenely depicts the wisdom revealed from the excess of the Dionysian impulse.

He later supplements this cosmological scheme in *The Gay Science* wherein he claims that "throughout the entire range of art we demand first of all the conquest of the subjective, redemption from the 'ego,' and the silencing of the individual will and desire ..." (Nietzsche 1974, 48). Nietzsche claims that the artist opens up him/herself in order to become a site that expresses the primordial pain and contradiction at the heart of existence. The artist "is no longer an artist, he has become a work of art: in these paroxysms of intoxication the artistic power of all nature reveals itself in the highest gratification of the primordial unity" (p. 37). Art redeems and justifies existence; art makes the suffering and pain possible to endure. Nietzsche ponders whether the Greek's "*craving for beauty*, for festivals, pleasures, new cults was rooted in some deficiency, privation, melancholy, pain?" (Nietzsche 1967, 21). The Dionysian impulse is a "narcotic draught" of self-forgetfulness—a forgetfulness of pain. The outcome of such a silencing of individual will and desire is that art transforms subjective suffering into what is beautiful and enjoyable once it is writ large and taken away from the individual. As a musician,

[The artist] finds sounds for those secret and uncanny midnights of the soul in which cause and effect appear "out of nothing." More happily than anyone else, he draws from the very bottom of human happiness—as it were, from its drained cup, where the bitterest and most repulsive drops have merged in the end, for better or for worse, with the sweetest. He knows how souls drag themselves along when they can no longer leap and fly, nor even walk; his is the shy glance of concealed pain, of understanding without comfort, of farewells without confessions. As the Orpheus of all secret misery he is greater than anyone, and he has incorporated in art some things that had previously seemed to be inexpressible and even unworthy of art, as if words could only frighten them away, not grasp them.... (Nietzsche 1974, 143)

The musician dredges the "drained cup" of human happiness to express *his* deep melancholy *impersonally*. Such an act diffuses not only his subjective pain, but it sweetens it into an object of an *all too human* recognition. Melancholy music brings relief to its listeners in the recognition that someone has expressed the mood that weighs upon them. Nietzsche confesses "[m]y melancholy wants to rest in the hiding places and abysses of *perfection*: that is why I need music" (p. 325). Music is a need; it's an opiate that transforms melancholy into perfection. Stressing the psychological necessity of art, Nietzsche assures that "as an aesthetic phenomenon existence is still bearable for us, and art furnishes us with eyes and hands and above all the good conscience to be able to turn ourselves into such a phenomenon" (pp. 163–64). Thus art is a sedative for Nietzsche, ameliorating the pain of melancholy by transforming it through either Apollinian illusion or Dionysian music; pain begets redemptive beauty and perfection.

Both Freud and Nietzsche attribute this suffering and pain, engulfing us so ineluctably, to our moral codes. We require "redemption" or "palliative measures." It seems that with our technological advances we conquered much of the adversity that comes from nature and the inadequacies of our body. However, the suffering that issues from the fact that we are being-with-others, that we are intersubjective beings, eludes the advances of our modern technological age. Freud notes that civilization is built upon individual instinctual frustrations: we "sublimate," if we are men, our sexual erotic desires into cultural ideals and moral systems. All morality, an insight that Nietzsche was well aware of in his *Genealogy of Morals*, depends on an internalization and consequent sublimation of energy-seeking expression. Nietzsche argues:

All instincts that do not discharge themselves outwardly turn inward—this is what I call the internalization of man.... The entire inner world, originally as thin as if it were stretched between two membranes, expanded and extended itself, acquired depth, breadth, and height, in the same measure as outward discharge was inhibited. Those fearful bulwarks with which the political organization protected itself against the old instincts of freedom—punishments belong among these bulwarks—brought about that all those instincts of wild, free, prowling man, turned backward against man himself. Hostility, cruelty, joy in persecuting, in attacking, in change, in destruction—all this turned against the possessors of such instincts: that is the origin of the "bad conscience." (Nietzsche 1989, 84–85)

This internalization sets up what becomes the bad conscience for Nietzsche and the super-ego for Freud. The necessity of living together in communities turns individuals against themselves, humans internalize moral codes and begin to forbid the self from expressing its true desire. The need to internalize instincts, according to both Freud and Nietzsche, arises from the fact that constitutive to human beings is aggression. Nietzsche sees the release of this aggression, which is always intertwined with sensuality and eros, in Dionysian festivals. Freud describes this erection of the super-ego:

His aggressiveness is introjected, internalized; it is, in point of fact, sent back to where it came from—that is, it is directed toward his own ego. There it is taken over by a portion of the ego, which sets itself over against the rest of the ego as super-ego, and which now, in the form of "conscience," is ready to put into action against the ego the same harsh aggressiveness that the ego would have liked to satisfy upon other, extraneous individuals. (Freud 1961, 70)

Both Nietzsche's hostile bad conscience and Freud's aggressive super-ego create the fissures in selfhood—these moral agencies chastise the self for falling away from the cultural ideals. Thus our pain derives from within, from the cultural necessity to internalize instinctual aggression and erotic desire in order to live with others. The super-ego restricts and punishes our desires.

Love, Melancholia, and Art Therapy

Pain comes about not only from this internal struggle of the divided self, but decidedly from our intersubjective relations. Freud remarks that "we are never so defenceless against suffering as when we love, never so helplessly unhappy as when we have lost our loved object or its love" (Freud 1961, 29). Both the pain of individual existence, which plays itself out as a battle between our separation from some original wholeness, and our need to maintain this separation (unless we wish not to exist) harm us. The secondary source of pain, intersubjective relations, is a repetition of the primary pain. In our relations with others, most specifically in erotic relations, we are searching for that person who will return us to a state of wholeness where all our needs are met. Jacques Lacan argues, "[T]hat which is thus alienated in needs constitutes an *Urverdrangung* [primal repression], an inability, it is supposed to be articulated in demand, but it re-appears in . . . man as desire" (1977, 286). Humans, according to Freud, Nietzsche, and Lacan, come into existence through an initial traumatic separation from the originary wholeness (the mother)—a lost state haunting us during our lifetime quest to achieve some measure of happiness given that this original state of bliss has been lost. This loss transmutates into desire, which motivates the search for something or someone that/who will meet all our needs without us needing to demand this from others. The loss of a subsequent love object evokes an *anamnesis* of the primary loss.

Desire on all these models can never be satisfied; desire is for a return to a perfection that we cannot live in our earthly flesh. This is the same desire of which the neo-Platonists, such as Plotinus and Marsilio Ficino, promised would free the gifted man from his imprisonment in the flesh so that he may return to his perfect God. And it is also in this tradition that God is ineffable to those who mourn the loss of their union with Him. Similarly Kristeva asserts, "their sadness would be rather the most archaic expression of an unsymbolizable, unnamable narcissistic wound, so precocious that no outside agent (subject or agent) can be used as a referent. For such narcissistic depressed persons, sadness is really the sole object. . . ." (Kristeva 1989, 12) This primary loss—this fall from grace—instigates the search for substitute objects, yet no love is capable of mending such an "unnamable narcissistic wound." Kristeva ventures:

Conscious of our being doomed to lose our loves, we grieve perhaps even more when we glimpse in our lover the shadow of a long lost former loved one. Depression is the hidden face of Narcissus . . . we shall see the shadow cast on the fragile self, hardly dissociated from the other, precisely by the loss of that essential other. The shadow of despair. (p. 5)

No earthly love will repair the loss of the original heavenly "essential other." It is from Plato's Diotima first that Western man learns the inadequacy of earthly love. Diotima asks:

[I]f it were given to man to gaze on beauty's very self—unsullied, unalloyed, and freed from the mortal taint that haunts the frailer loveliness of the flesh and blood— if, I say, it were given to man to see the heavenly beauty face to face, would you call his . . . an unenviable life, whose eyes had been opened to the vision, and had gazed upon it in true contemplation until it had become his own forever? (*Symposium*, 563e, 1–7)

Platonism's comprehension of eros—a longing that impels its weary sufferers to transcend their earthly states—gets taken up in a psychoanalytic theory as a feverish search to return to the blissful state of primary narcissism. And it is this kind of perpetual dissatisfaction with earthly love, mortal existence, that makes the fulfillment of desire unattainable.

However, sublimation is the salve of the distress plaguing the melancholic desperately seeking reunion with perfection. The inheritance of the super-ego in the post-Oedipal identification with the Law of the Father provides subjects with somewhat sturdy armor. Sublimation guards against the devastating effects of unrequited love because in this process the bereft lover channels his erotic impulses into something higher. However, according to psychoanalytic theory, sublimation only functions with those who have stable super-egos. Without a stable super-ego, we become susceptible to suffering from unrequited love. The female, according to Freud, becomes the highest at risk, if not the only subject at risk, due to her inability to sublimate. Without the ability to sublimate, unrequited love drives its victim back into melancholia. This time melancholia issues from an unconscious loss of something that we thought we gained from the other. Women, who cannot sublimate and transform their erotic desire into something productive, have two options: (1) either cathect as needed onto new love objects (as I've already established very risky solution) to reclaim a primary wholeness that one once felt as an infant provided for by the mother or (2) repress desire. Traditionally, according to psychoanalysts, women took both of these routes with devastating effects. Without the ability to sublimate, desire is deathly.

Kristeva attempts to give a name to the primary object of loss—and the very loss of this object is precisely what leaves us divided against ourselves forever in search for something to reintegrate us. To name this object is impossible because the subject's relationship to it occurs at a point in his/her development before the acquisition of language. That is, the subject's relationship to this powerful, all-fulfilling primary object predates the consciousness of an outside; no comprehension of a differentiation between the subject and its cherished object exists. She chooses to name it the Thing. It is not, properly speaking, an object that exists in a space-time continuum, but rather it is something prior to objectification. It is the mother, but before the mother becomes an object that can be named. Language objectifies things—it allows us to describe them in a way that is, according to Kristeva, devoid of affect. Kristeva elucidates the phenomena of this unconscious search the melancholic carries out:

Ever since that archaic attachment the depressed person has the impression of having been deprived of an unnamable, supreme good, of something unrepresentable, that perhaps only devouring might represent, or an invocation might point out, but no word could signify. Consequently, for such a person, no erotic object could replace that irreplaceable perception of a place or preobject confining the libido or severing the bonds of desire. Knowingly disinherited of the Thing, the depressed person wanders in pursuit of continuously disappointing adventures with loves; or else retreats, disconsolate and aphasic, alone with the unnamed Thing. (Kristeva 1989, 13)

As stated above, one is able to overcome the dictatorship of the erotic Thing only if one successfully achieves a primary identification with the Law of the Father in which lies the cultural moral code and language. Kristeva claims that "primary identification initiates a compensation for the Thing and at the same time secures the subject to another dimension...." Ostensibly this other dimension is the social dimension, the realm of civilization where one learns to sublimate and therefore modify desire to support cultural bonds. The melancholic is one whose primary identification proves to be very fragile, and thus her moral agent is less efficacious in regulating desire. The melancholic is left with this loss that cannot be recuperated. Kristeva claims that melancholia "lays claim upon us to the extent of having us lose all interest in words, actions and even life itself" (p. 3). Melancholia is a sadness that defys articulation because it finds no relief in the arbitrariness of the symbolic discourse.

However, Kristeva reveals another side to this melancholia—a side that generates new and innovative forms in the imagination. She places herself in a long tradition beginning with Aristotle's remarks in the *Problemata*, wherein Aristotle asks, "Why is it that all those who have become eminent in philosophy or politics or poetry or the arts are clearly melancholics ...?" (Aristotle 1927, 953a10–13).[4] Situating herself within this same romantic tradition of melancholy, Kristeva pronounces:

My pain is the hidden side of my philosophy, its mute sister. In the same way, Montaigne's statement "To philosophize is to learn how to die" is inconceivable without the melancholy combination of sorrow and hatred—which came to a head in Heidegger's care and the disclosure of our "being-for-death." (p. 4)

Melancholia carves out a depth and breadth to the self and often motivates self-reflection and self-understanding.[5] In the unconscious, melancholia "establishes its archeology, generates its representations and its knowledge" (p. 8). The generation of imaginative forms, provoked by the loss of the unnamable Thing, is the ego's attempt to master and recuperate this loss. These forms evade symbolic articulation (the mere naming of things) and are therefore not meaningful within the social economy. Instead, the semiotic, which is what Kristeva sees as the prelinguistic organization of affect revealing itself in musical ruptures, rhythm, silences, or elisions, nourishes the imagination. This semiotic organization of affect generates a "new language" that culture calls the "work of art."

Productions of the imagination work against the melancholic's tendency to regress to a relation with the Thing. The melancholic, in her desperate search for an earlier wholeness disavows the symbolic and social realm. This disavowal grants the melancholic enough distance from culture to enable her to perceive an arbitrariness in the socially constructed meanings embedded in moral codes of conduct and language. A sign interrupts the melancholic's connection to the mother, for it separates a signifier from the referent; to speak of my mother in signs, in language, means to see her as distinct. No word will adequately refer to an affective state that has been killed off—so all words are equally arbitrary to the melancholic. The disavowal reveals a strong tendency to remain, partially, in the place of the ineffable Thing.

Furthermore the melancholic must combat her super-ego, which Freud claims is a receptacle of the *thanatos* drive. The melancholic must combat, in the face of recognizing the loss of the primary narcissistic state, the allure of the death drive attempting to return the fragile ego to an inanimate state. Freud terms this tendency on the part of the super-ego, the nirvana principle that seeks relief from the prohibitions and limitations of the super-ego after falling away from primary narcissism. The death drive motivates the Dionysian outbursts that Nietzsche depicts. Freud argues:

> In all renunciations and limitations imposed on the ego a periodical infringement of the prohibition is the rule; this is shown by the institution of festivals, which in origin are nothing less nor more than excesses provided by law and which owe their cheerful character to the release which they bring. The Saturnalia of the Romans and our modern carnival agree in this essential feature with the festivals of primitive people, which usually end in debaucheries of every kind and the transgression of what are at other times the most sacred commandments. But the ego ideal comprises the sum of all the limitations in which the ego has to acquiesce, and for that reason the abrogation of the ideal would necessarily be a magnificent festival for the ego, which might then once again feel satisfied with itself. (Freud 1959b, 81)

In his essay "The 'Uncanny,'" Freud expands upon the role that *thanatos* plays in creativity. In this work he argues that works of art portray, in an imaginary arena—free from reality-testing—uncanny experiences. Freud claims that the experience of uncanniness involves "something which is familiar and old—established in the mind and which has become alienated from it only through the process of repression ... something which ought to have remained hidden but has come to light" (Freud 1955, 241). The strongest source of this uncanny and anxious feeling is the fear of death. One is able to "safely," that is, free from criticism from the stern super-ego, diffuse the expression of repressed content through imaginative productions. In his essay "Creative Writers and Daydreaming," Freud argues that "... our actual enjoyment of an imaginative work proceeds from a liberation of tensions in our minds. It may even be that not a little of this effect is due to the writer's enabling us thenceforward to enjoy our own daydreams without self-reproach or shame" (Freud 1989, 443). In creating art, the artist wrests himself from repression—which ushered in his depression—so that he may express the content of his depression free from the harsh judgment of the super-ego. On the one hand, the artist procures a respite from the debilitating sadness of his fundamental loss, and on the other hand, he staves off the allure of the nirvana principle. Thus works of art allow the melancholic to achieve a level of mastery over the death drive in addition to an evasion of the symbolic.

Above, I demonstrated that for both Freud and Nietzsche the work of art induces a numbing narcosis. The beholder of the work of art or the artist experiences an anesthetization that relieves them from the primordial pain of existence—a pain that Freud and Kristeva attempt to decipher through exploring melancholia. Yet Kristeva sees the work of imaginative production as not merely numbing painful affect but effectively countering it. The work of art acts not as an "antidepressant" that dulls affect but as a "counterdepressant" that cures. Kristeva explains:

[A]esthetic and particularly literary creation, and also religious discourse in its imaginary, fictional essence, set forth a device whose prosodic economy, interaction of characters, and implicit symbolism constitute a very faithful semiological representation of the subject's battle with symbolic collapses. (p. 24)

This device of representing the melancholic's battle is not, according to Kristeva, an elaboration of the pain in order to wrest it from its repression in the unconscious. Such an elaboration attempts to "dissolve" the symptom through a "talking-cure," which is inappropriate for a subject who battles with symbolic collapse. Instead of attempting to dissolve the symptom:

[T]he literary (and religious) representation possesses a real and imaginary effectiveness that comes closer to catharsis than to elaboration; it is a therapeutic device used in all societies throughout the ages. If psychoanalysts think they are more efficacious, notably through strengthening the subject's cognitive possibilities, they also owe it to themselves to enrich their practice by paying greater attention to these sublimatory solutions to our crises, in order to be lucid counterdepressants rather than neutralizing antidepressants. (Kristeva 1989, 24–25)

Sublimating the erotic desire to return back to the unnamable Thing, in order to create art, allows for a catharsis unknown to Freud and Nietzsche who hoped only for a temporary numbing of pain.

Kristeva campaigns indirectly against the current approach to treating melancholia by administering antidepressants. She exposes the shortcomings of such medication, claiming "lithium interrupts the diversity process and holds the subject within a word's semantic field, ties him to a significance, and perhaps stabilizes him around an object-referent" (p. 59). The numbing of affect brought on by antidepressants disrupts the generation of polyvalent semiotic forms in the imagination and forces the depressed person to hold onto some symbolic signifier or referent. The work of art, for Kristeva, is compared to a resurrection for the artist—through the new language of the polyvalent semiotic, the artist is brought back from the depressed dead. "The work of art," says Kristeva,

> insures the rebirth of its author and its reader or viewer is one that succeeds in integrating the artificial language it puts forward (new style, new composition, surprising imagination) and the unnamed agitations of an omnipotent self that ordinary social and linguistic usage always leave somewhat orphaned or plunged in mourning. (p. 51)

Due to the subject's denial of the "normal" process of negation, the self becomes omnipotent in an attempt to recreate the blissful state of primary narcissism. Negation, according to Freud, opens the subject up to judgment, forcing him or her to distinguish between imagination and reality. Freud explains, "what is not real, what is merely imagined or subjective, is only internal; while on the other hand what is real is also present externally. When this stage is reached, the pleasure principle is no longer taken into account" (Freud 1959a, 183). The inner/outer distinction made possible by negation stagnates creativity for Kristeva and forces the subject out of his/ her attachment to the maternal Thing. Only through a denial of this negation, as in the case of fetishism, is there a solution to pain. Fetishism allows for an inward retreat in fantasy and imagination—precisely what negation disallows. And the catharsis springs from the creative or semiotic articulation of the Thing.

Yet this catharsis requires that the subject can sublimate, so while her "treatment" of melancholia is allegedly more effective than Freud and Nietzsche, she relies on the traditional valorization of sublimation. Kristeva asserts, "sublimation alone withstands death. The beautiful object that can bewitch us into its world seems to us more worthy of adoption that any loved or hated cause for wound or sorrow. Depression recognizes this and agrees to live within and for that object, but such an adoption of the sublime is no longer libidinal. . . . Beauty is an artifice; it is imaginary" (p. 100). The artist turns suffering and pain into something beautiful. This ability, to transform pain into beauty, arises out of the fact that the depressed person is "a dweller in the imaginary realm."

Following the classic Kantian distinction, the imaginary realm is not a place for Kristeva but a time. In the humanist tradition, notably in the

works of Ficino, the melancholic falls under the influence of the planet
Saturn, which is the Roman transliteration of the Greek god Kronos. From
this historical fact, one can glean that there is a temporality to melancholia.
And because imagination, aided by sublimation, propels the melancholic
out of his state, it too has its own temporal structure. Melancholia is nos-
talgic, while imagination is hopeful. Freud writes, "the relation of fantasy to
time is in general very important . . . it hovers . . . between three times—the
three moments of time which our ideation involves" (Freud 1989, 439).
Imagination unites past, present, and future by allowing something from
one's past that was repressed be awakened by a present trauma, to help
create a future possibility by wish-fulfillment.[6] Yet in Kristeva's view the
future is a possibility that is closed off to the melancholic. She writes:
"massive, weighty, doubtless traumatic because laden with too much sorrow or too much joy, a moment blocks the horizon of depressive temporality or rather removes any horizon, any perspective" (p. 60). The failure
to project oneself towards a future—toward an open horizon of possibilities
that have yet to be imagined—leaves the melancholic, and most likely
the female melancholic, wedded to the past. "Riveted to the past," muses
Kristeva, "regressing to the paradise or inferno of an unsurpassable experience, melancholy persons manifest a strange memory: everything has gone
by, they seem to say, but I am faithful to those bygone days, I am nailed
down to them, no revolution is possible, there is no future. . . ." It is women
who cannot enjoy the relief of wish-fulfillment satisfied by ideations produced from sublimating "for the loss of the object seems beyond remedy for
a woman and its mourning more difficult, if not impossible" (p. 86). So for
women, according to Kristeva, there is no future, and more disturbingly,
there is no revolution. The melancholic woman, born under the planet
Saturn, dedicates herself to a past time and refuses the future.

Is There a Feminine Artist?

Given the effectiveness of art production in the battle over depression—
given the possibility of revolution given to those who can sublimate—what
possible prognosis is there for women? Kristeva equates depressed speech
with the semiotic, which she also sees as the maternal tongue or women's
speech. She argues, "being caught in woman's speech is not merely a matter
of chance that could be explained by the greater frequency of feminine
depressions—a sociologically proven fact. This may also reveal an aspect of

feminine sexuality: its addiction to the maternal Thing and its lesser aptitude for restorative perversion," namely mechanisms such as sublimation (p. 71). In Kristeva's analysis of artists, only one is a woman—are we to suppose that the others are of a feminine disposition? For Kristeva sublimation is a valuable activity. For example, she writes "sublimation ... is the sole 'container' seemingly able to secure an uncertain but adequate hold over the Thing" (p. 14). In a recent interview Kristeva revisited Freud's remarks in *The Ego and the Id* concerning how the death drive, *thanatos*, is freed in sublimation. She adds to his view the following:

[I]f the death wish is freed in the sublimation the question is where does it go? And we have eventually two answers. The first, is that it goes back to the ego and can destroy the ego, thus giving rise to depression. Or the death wish can attack the organs of the ego, the body itself and give rise to different somatic illnesses. On the other hand, this remaining death wish that is freed in the sublimation can attack the others, the different links of the self in connection with society or the paternal, maternal and other objects. This kind of death wish freed explains maybe why the subject in the state of sublimation has also been thought of as having a dissident position in social links, a sort of anarchistic position that makes him or her uneasy in any kind of link. It has the potentiality of revolutionary or marginal critical position in the field. (Kristeva 1999)

Freud argues in *Civilization and Its Discontents*, that "the work of civilization has become increasingly the business of men, it confronts them with ever more difficult tasks and compels them to carry out instinctual sublimations of which women are little capable" (Freud 1961, 50). For Freud, sublimation is not a repression of the erotic drive but a means by which the unconscious transforms the erotic drive into a more suitable drive—one that doesn't violate societal taboos and disrupt civilization. Yet Kristeva disagrees, or finds evidence within Freud's writings that suggests that sublimation may have revolutionary potential—a revolutionary potential denied to women for she does not combat Freud's view toward women and sublimation. Kristeva's position on women and their ability to sublimate is as follows:

Now what about women? I do think Freud was wrong when he thought that women were incapable of sublimation because the maternal function is of course an essential function in the female destiny, but what happens in maternity is precisely the fact that it is invested in the sublimatory mood or in the same time the child itself and the maternal language that the women gives to the child so the sublimation process continues during motherhood and concerns as well the investments of the language by the mother insofar as she gives this language to the child and allows him or her access to language. Also, the mother invests, in a sublimatory way, the child itself. Everybody talks about the eroticization of the child's body by the parents and we know the seduction that can be a situation of exciting the acquisition of thinking and language, but the seduction may also be very harmful for the development of the psyche of the child. What happens with the maternal position is that the mother inhibits seduction and eroticism and invests the child in a different way than eroticism invests the object which means that—well, we don't have a particular word that describes this inhibited way of investment of the child, but we can say it is a sort of sublimation which gives way to tenderness, different sensory relationships between child and mother, etc.—so the sublimatory work continues during motherhood. And if we don't have such sublimatory functions the simple fact of upbringing a child of educating him or her is impossible. (Kristeva 1999, 135)

The prognosis that Kristeva may give is that women would be less depressed if culture actually conferred value on maternity. The woman as mother does sublimate her erotic drives, and maybe if this activity would be raised to the status of great art in culture, then the women might find their own "counterdepressant" to depression within the traditional labor of child-rearing.

Yet, as stated above, beyond a woman's lesser ability to sublimate, she is more depressed because she is the least likely to completely abandon her attachment to the mother. Freud argues: "In girls the motive for the destruction of the Oedipus complex is lacking. . . . Thus the Oedipus complex escapes the fate which it meets with in boys: it may either be slowly abandoned or got rid of by repression . . ." (Freud 1959c, 196). If the feminine character's only defense against her erotic drive is repression, then she is denied any direct expression of it. Freud links repression to the extreme hypothesis that women are intellectually inferior. In *The Enigma of Woman*, Sarah Kofman thinks through the consequences of Freud's position on repression and women. Kofman evinces that:

[W]oman has a lesser sexual life, she is in an atrophied condition, as it were, owing to "civilization." Because of her education and cultural repression, woman speaks less freely about her sexuality than man does. Society makes modesty or "shame" woman's fundamental virtue, require her to adopt a "reserved" way of speaking. . . . Freud's whole effort consists precisely, through analysis, in attempting to pull women out of their reserve by giving them the right, even the obligation, to speak. (Kofman 1985, 39–40)

Kofman sees Freud's project as one that will give the female a voice, and if we understand this voice from Kristeva's standpoint, it is a voice in the symbolic. Repression, as we know, "leaves symptoms behind it" to become "dissolved" through the "talking cure" (Freud 1959b, 154). As the patient

begins to unburden her unconscious during the analytic session, she mirac-
ulously translates the repressed erotic drive into the symbolic—but this kind
of speech is not aesthetic. Symbolic speech has none of the poetic elements
of Kristeva's semiotic. Furthermore the very foundation of culture may
crumble as the female analysand elaborates her repressed content in the
symbolic discourse, for she finds herself face to face with her own sexuality
and desire. And, as Freud warned in *Civilization and Its Discontents*, women's
unbridled sexuality threatens to break down the bonds of culture. Thus it
seems that for women the return of the repressed circumvents the imagination and erupts into the social code.[7] Might there be a way that women
might still express their repressed content in an artful manner?

On this question, Freud's writings are anything but hopeful. Freud
presents a psychoanalytic account for the lack of female cultural contributions. Freud isolates two kinds of wishes that motivate imaginative production or fantasies: ambitious and erotic. Ambitious wishes are those "which
serve to elevate the subject's personality" (Freud 1989, 439). Ambitious
wishes are relegated to men, which makes sense, for men would be motivated to strive for greatness in the social sphere due to the inner urgings of
the super-ego. Remember from above that men successfully inherit the
super-ego where women do not, and it is the super-ego that unconsciously
propels men to reclaim their earlier self-subsistence experienced in primary
narcissism. Freud writes, "the young man has to learn to suppress the excess
of self-regard which he brings with him from the spoilt days of his childhood, so that he may find his place in a society full of other individuals
making equally strong demands." Erotic wishes, however, motivate female
fantasy. In women, claims Freud, "the erotic wishes predominate almost
exclusively, for their ambition is as a rule absorbed by erotic trends." Freud
concedes that symptoms might be an imaginative return of the erotic. Perhaps repression plays a part in the psychological portrait of the artist as well.
Yet though repression may generate imaginative symptoms, it does not
channel energy in a productive sense. Freud discusses repression as a withdrawal of energy leaving the female a rigid and less curious character.
Repression may produce imaginative symptoms but not in the cathartic
medium of artwork. These symptoms can become articulated in analysis.
This articulation may not be the new language of the semiotic that, through
its expression, refreshes the artist. The female, in dissolving symptoms,
masters prose and not poetry, the symbolic and not the semiotic. Thus
women who are most afflicted by melancholia are least likely to adopt

Kristeva's counterdepressant cure. Women cannot turn to art to express freely—that is free from the powerful censors of culture—the internal strife that threatens their sanity.

Kristeva choice of a female artist, Marguerite Duras, confirms my suspicions that her theory is too close to Freud's and therefore liable to lead to the conclusion that women cannot produce art. Sadly, according to Kristeva, Duras fails to offer the spectator a refreshing new language within which to banish his/her sadness. Her literature is an "aesthetics of awkwardness" and a "noncathartic literature." Curiously Kristeva's phenomenology of the melancholic artist grants her the authority to become an art critic. The awkwardness comes from the translation of Duras's melancholic affect into the symbolic. The symptom is "dissolved" in her literature without engendering a new language. Kristeva explains, "how can one speak the truth of pain, if not by holding in check the rhetorical celebration, warping it, making it grate, strain and limp?" (p. 225). Duras finds a voice in the symbolic for her pain, yet the symbolic doesn't have the force to match the intensity of the symptom. The symbolic flattens the affect, much like an antidepressant—tying the subject to a referent. Kristeva asserts that "stylistic awkwardness would be the discourse of dulled pain" (p. 226). Kristeva's tendentious claims concerning Duras's work suggest that we do not find the cathartic cure within the feminine artist. On the contrary:

> Her books . . . bring us on the verge of madness. They do not point to it from afar, they neither observe it nor analyze it for the sake of experiencing it at a distance in the hope of a solution, like it or not, some day or other. . . . To the contrary, the texts domesticate the malady of death, they fuse with it, are on the same level with it, without either distance or perspective. There is no purification in store . . . no improvement, no promise of a beyond, not even the enchanting beauty of style or irony. . . . (p. 228)

Without proper distance from the malady of death—a phrase taken from the title of one of Duras's books—this art has "so little cathartic potential," and so brings "madness in full daylight." Such a symbolic articulation of pain, a writing that fuses with the "malady of death," fails to transform it into the sublime or beautiful. Instead, Duras disturbs us. "Lacking catharsis," concludes Kristeva, "such a literature encounters, recognizes, but also spreads the pain that summons it" (p. 229). Duras's writing doesn't even bring about the mild narcosis that Freud and Nietzsche attribute to art production. Duras's talking cure brings her "symptoms," her returned repressed content, into the social and moral arena. Kofman writes that this is "in exchange for a pseudo-cure, a poison-remedy, a 'solution' that cannot help being pernicious since it restores speech to women only in order to model it on men's, only in order to condemn their 'demands' to silence" (pp. 66–67). Duras's rendering of depressed affect into the symbolic—giving voice to female sexuality—brings the reader to madness and infects us with her pain. Thus, when a woman expresses her melancholia, she is not an artist at all, she does not cure us or herself. She merely disrupts the social with her affect that spreads pain everywhere.

Beyond Sublimation

I hope that it is clear at this point that Kristeva's analysis of depression and prescription of the cathartic cure of art production does not provide an account of how we will deal with women's depression, nor how women will become recognized as artists. Women are left helpless to male desire underpinning our theories of intersubjectivity. Luce Irigaray's work is helpful here for clarifying how it is that our social theories are shaped by male desire. For example, she declares that "the social organization we have had for centuries is a patriarchal one. It is a function of civilization constructed by man, a between-men society, with woman being the property of any and everyman; natural property, domestic property" (Irigaray 1996, 44). Women are the property of men, because without a social identity and corresponding ontological status, as different and irreducible to male identity and ontological status, women cannot resist the economy of a mastering subject. The concept of "will" encapsulates the whole of our patriarchal social economy. This "will," or as Nietzsche put it this "will to power," is directed toward the domination and subjugation of objects—most notably nature. Anything not fitting the criteria of subject becomes a possible object of possession or manipulation to a subject. Unfortunately, philosophers from time immemorial bestow upon women a chaotic, mercurial nature. Furthermore, ontologically speaking, women are not subjects, but objects closely resembling animals or young children. That is, women lack reason because they are so ruled by the hormones coursing through their veins. Irigaray argues, "the whole of Western philosophy is the mastery of the direction of will and thought by the subject, historically man" (p. 45). And what it is that man masters is woman. Such a misogynist view of human subjectivity may itself be the very cause of women's depression—that is, their sociologically proven higher rates of depression.

From its inception, Western philosophy privileges the male subject, though it sometimes conceals this in the cloak of gender-neutral subjects that putatively represent the essential human attributes of all human beings. The romantic history of melancholia is a history built on the backs of women so that men appear as the exemplary human subjects. Our cultural memory, on the whole, forgets these women, so their stories do not figure into the distilled and abstracted understandings of what it means to be human. Insofar as philosophy consists of tracts on human agency and subjectivity that ignores at best, or represses at worst, women's stories of their lives, women find no outward evidence, no sign posts, to help them to navigate their journey toward their own self-understanding. Dana Crowley Jack asserts: "the high rates of depression in women can be seen as an almost inevitable response to living in a culture that deeply fears and devalues the feminine" (Jack 1991, 183). Carol Lee Flinders brings this seemingly esoteric notion to our immediate attention in hopes to alert us to the modern crisis of adolescent girls. She writes:

[T]hose who've been working with an on behalf of young girls come gradually to understand how crushingly public representations of girls weigh upon the girls themselves and continue to as they enter womanhood. The source of these representations isn't a government, of course, or any particular institution, but rather a drive for unlimited corporate profit, which has taken the commodification of girls to heights undreamed of in our patriarchal past. The most direct means, pornography, is only the beginning. Highly sexualized representations of young girls are featured in films and music videos and are used to sell all kinds of products, but they also sell the notion that this is what young girls are supposed to look like. Since almost nobody does look like that, insecurity abounds—fertile grounds for marketers of cosmetics, clothing, weight-loss programs, compact discs, soft drinks and more. (Flinders 1998, 301)

Young girls and women threaten to go mad when they are unable to find themselves mirrored in the values and ideals reflected in culture. Instead, corporate greed molds and bends them into consumers and appealing commodities.

Virginia Woolf, as one woman among countless others, explores the motives for why men have denied women an education, an equal wage to support themselves, the right to own property, and the vote. All of these "privileges" are basic conditions for the establishment of a civil identity for women. She surmises that such a wholesale oppression of women stems from a psychological need to raise oneself upon the back of another. She highlights the human need for self-confidence, "without self-confidence we are babes in the cradle" (Woolf 1981, 35). So one way to gain this self-confidence is to feel superior to others, "hence the enormous importance to a patriarch who has to conquer, who has to rule, of feeling that great numbers of people, half the human race indeed, are by nature inferior to himself. It must indeed be one of the chief sources of his power." Flinder's description of the unprecedented corporate pursuit of profit at the expense of young girls encapsulates the current patriarchal quest to conquer, to rule. In this patriarchal psychological prerequisite "women have served all these centuries as looking-glasses possessing the magic and delicious power of reflecting the figure of man at twice its natural size. Without that power probably the earth would still be swamp and jungle." But taming the chaos of the universe through the appropriation of a female materiality, perhaps as in her patriarchal scripted role as either mother or prostitute, leaves women without of sense of their own identity. No one is reflecting her image back.

Instead of looking to age-old theories of sublimation and genial melancholia to find clues for dealing with depression, I suggest, inspired by Irigaray's work, three recommendations for working out a political response to women's melancholia. First, we need to construct not only an objective civil identity for women but also an ontology that posits at least two distinct, sexed ontological subjects that are irreducible to each other. It is important to keep in mind that ontology, after Heidegger, has come to mean something quite different than it did for the ancients and scholastics. Fundamental ontology for Heidegger is a theory about temporality wherein human subjects are projects that live into a future coming toward them from their past. Ontology is no longer, for Irigaray, about laying down essences, but rather about laying down conditions that allow sexed subjects the freedom to live into the rich possibilities of their future and how sexed subjects live together in community. Establishing different trajectories of becoming between men and women will disrupt misogynistic tendencies in Western ontology. One such tendency is Hegel's account of how one becomes self-conscious and self-possessed through a power struggle. A power struggle is the outcome of a subject attempting to tame and subdue objects that threaten him. If we re-envision subjects in relation to other subjects, ruling out the possibility that another subject can ever be made into an object, then the possibility of mastery may drop out. More important, we ought to regard subjects as sexed. Irigaray explains, adopting Hegelian language, "Mastery of, substitution for, thereby become impossible processes given the respect for what is, for what exists. . . . Sexed identity rules out all forms of totality [the drive to master all subordinate objects] as well as the self-substituting subject.... Being a man or a woman already means not being the whole of the subject of the community of spirit, as well as not being entirely one's self" (p. 106). The positive valuation of the "negative"—the limit between one subject and another marked by gender—allows for an opening for women to become. If men pause, in awe, finally recognizing the inappropriable difference of women, then men may come to see how ill-constructed culture is to the other sex. Culture needs to address the needs of two sexes and that these needs may differ. Irigaray sees the actuality of this possibility coming to fruition if men begin to listen to women. She describes:

I am listening to you not on the basis of what I know, I feel, I already am, nor in terms of what the world and language already are, thus in formalisitic manner so to speak. I am listening to you rather as the revelation of a truth that has yet to man- ifest itself—yours and that of the world revealed through and by you. I give you silence in which your future—and perhaps my own, but with you and not as you and without you—may emerge and lay its foundation." (p. 117).

Second, desire needs to be rethought in ways different from the mas- culine model, which Irigaray describes as, "a model of energy involving tension, release, and return to homeostasis" (Irigaray 1994, 20). Such a notion of desire so thoroughly infects the symbolic and imaginary that we can't conceive of a notion of desire that doesn't function to appropriate objects for satisfaction—objects such as women, most notably the mother. Also for Platonists, desire propels a world-weary seeker toward an ecstatic union with his God. Desire begets transcendence—it allows the seeker of truth to transcend the imperfections of his bodily existence in order to live in the pure ether of truth. However, if ontologists begin describing human subjectivity by positing distinct, sexed subjects, then seekers of an Other who is beyond me—who is in many ways ineffable—does not require ecstasy. Irigaray redefines transcendence as the "respect for the other whom I will never be, who is transcendent to me and to whom I am transcen- dent.... Our energy is thence no longer channeled, sublimated, or para- lyzed in a movement towards a beyond I-me, or you, or we. It is the movement and transformation that limits the empire of my ego, of the power of you, or of the community and its already established values" (Iri- garay 1996, 104–105). Desire need not lead us to wish to shed our sexed, bodily identity but rather to embrace these very things as what truly makes transcendence, here and now, possible.

Third, eros could be reconceived as wonder. Instead of love being a tragic journey to recuperate a lost wholeness, love could be precisely that we are always already thrown into relations with other human beings and that these very relations are bountiful. We can never own or possess others for they exceed any category or project that we wish them to fulfill. Wonder perhaps will impel us to recognize a notion of love and intersubjectivity that is not merely reduced to a tragic struggle that brings suffering only redeemed through art and the male artist. Irigaray writes:

The "object" of wonder or attraction remaining impossible to delimit, im-pose, identify (which is not to say lacking identity and borders): the atmosphere, the sky, the sea, the sun. That which he designates as woman-eternity, an other who is sufficiently open, cosmic, so that he can keep moving toward her. Not the eternal feminine if images or representation(s). But a woman-mother who keeps unfolding herself outwardly while enveloping us? And toward whom he moves, without ever getting there, without distinguishing between inside and outside. Going again and again toward her within her? In a movement that precedes desire? Which protects the movement's lightness, its freedom, its continually new impulsion. Always for the first time. (Irigaray 1984, 81)

It is time to conceive of a feminine artist whose productive energy and creative force derives from such a nourishing well-spring of love, rather than continue the masculine, romanticized, theories that great art is born only from struggle—from the pain of existence.

I have argued that Kristeva's contribution to melancholia studies, in the vein of Freud and Nietzsche, offers little hope for women sufferers. Kristeva relies too heavily on sublimation, and maintains the basic insights of Freud's views on women such as to almost naturalize them. Because Kristeva does not imagine a different way of describing our relationship to not only the mother but to others as well, her work itself is melancholy. Though from time to time great men may conquer their depression, and creatively effect the matricide essential to the generation of culture, women will still linger in their sadness. Perhaps more depressing is that women's sadness will be dismissed as an illness in order to frame it as part of their overly emotional makeup. Thus it is the need of philosophy and psycho-analysis to critique the core assumptions that found their respective practices. Perhaps women's depression is more of a symptom of a culture that sacrifices them, than a symptom of their inability to accept their cultural destiny.

172 *Jennifer Hansen*

Notes

1. Julia Kristeva asserts: "For man and woman the loss of the mother is a biological and psychic necessity, the first step on the way to becoming autonomous. Matricide is our vital necessity, the sine-qua-non of our individuation ..." (Kristeva 1989, 27–28).

2. Again, Kristeva writes: "For a woman, whose specular identification with the mother as well as the introjection of the maternal body and self are more immediate, such an inversion of the matricidal drive into a death-bearing maternal image is more difficult, if not impossible. Indeed, how can she be that bloodthirsty Fury, since I am she (sexually and narcissitically), She is I? Consequently the hatred I bear her is not oriented toward the outside but is locked up within myself. There is no hatred, only an implosive mood that walls itself in and kills me secretly, very slowly, through permanent bitterness, bouts of sadness, and even lethal sleeping pills ..." (p. 29).

3. The National Institute of Health's (NIH) ten-year study concluded that women fall into depression twice as often as men "regardless of racial and ethnic background or economic status," and this "same ratio has been reported in eleven other countries all over the world" (NIH 1994).

4. The long list of natural and moral philosophers writing on the subject of melancholia include Theophrastus, who associates this disposition with Heraclitus, Cicero, Plutarch, St. Hildegard of Bingen, Nicholas of Cusa, Marsilio Ficino, Robert Burton, Immanuel Kant, G. W. F. Hegel, Friedrich Nietzsche, Soren Kierkegaard, Sigmund Freud, Martin Heidegger (see Klibansky, Panofsky, and Saxl 1979; Jackson 1986; Kristeva 1989; Schiesari 1992).

5. Freud is a tremendous influence on Kristeva's work. He asserts that "a happy person never phantasies, only an unsatisfied one. The motive forces of phantasies are unsatisfied wishes, and every single phantasy is the fulfillment of a wish, a correction of unsatisfying reality" (Freud 1989, 439).

6. A whole other paper could be devoted to relating this insight to Heidegger's triadic temporal structure of the self as disclosed by anxiety in the face of death, to this insight on the part of Freud.

7. Freud writes in *Civilization and Its Discontents* that: "What he [man] employs for cultural aims [making use of sublimatory techniques] he to a great extent withdraws from women and sexual life. His constant association with men, and his dependence on his relations with them, even estrange him from his duties as a husband and father. Thus the woman finds herself forced into the background by the claims of civilization and she adopts a hostile attitude towards it" (Freud 1961, 51, my emphasis).

References

Aristotle. 1927. *Problemata*. Translated by W. D. Ross. Oxford: The Clarendon Press.

Brennan, T. 1992. *The Interpretation of the Flesh: Freud and Femininity*. London: Routledge.

Freud, S. [1919] 1955. The "uncanny." Translated by J. Strachey. *Standard Edition, XIV.* London: Hogarth Press, pp. 217–52.

Freud, S. [1917] 1957. Mourning and melancholia. Translated by J. Strachey. *Standard Edition, XIV.* London: Hogarth Press, pp. 237–58.

Freud, S. 1959a. Negation. In *Collected Papers.* Edited by J. Strachey. New York: Basic Books.

Freud, S. 1959b. Repression. In *Collected Papers.* Edited by James Strachey. New York: Basic Books.

Freud, S. 1959c. Some psychological consequences of the anatomical distinction between the sexes. In *Collected Papers.* Edited by J. Strachey. New York: Basic Books.

Freud, S. 1960. *The Ego and the Id.* Translated by J. Riviere. New York: Norton.

Freud, S. 1961. *Civilizations and Its Discontents.* Translated by J. Strachey. New York: Norton.

Freud, S. 1989. Creative writers and day-dreaming. In *The Freud Reader.* Edited by P. Gay. New York: Norton.

Flinders, C. L. 1998. *At the Root of This Longing: Reconciling a Spiritual Hunger and a Feminist Thirst.* San Francisco: Harper Collins.

Heidegger, M. 1972. The end of philosophy. In *On Time and Being.* Translated by J. Stambaugh. San Francisco: Harper Torchbooks.

Irigaray, L. 1985. *Speculum of the Other Woman.* Translated by G. C. Gill. Ithaca: Cornell University Press.

Irigaray, L. 1993. *An Ethics of Sexual Difference.* Translated by C. Burke and G. C. Gill. Ithica: Cornell University Press.

Irigaray, L. 1994. *Thinking the difference: For a Peaceful Revolution.* Translated by K. Montin. New York: Routledge.

Irigaray, L. 1996. *I Love to You: Sketch of Possible Felicity in History.* Translated by A. Martin. New York: Routledge.

Kofman, S. 1985. *The Enigma in Freud's Writings: Woman in Freud's Writings.* Translated by C. Porter. Ithaca: Cornell University Press.

Kristeva, J. 1989. *Black Sun: Depression and Melancholia.* Translated by L. S. Roudiez. New York: Columbia University Press.

Kristeva, J. 1999. Maternal politics: An interview with Julia Kristeva. *Studies in Practical Philosophy: A Journal of Ethical and Political Philosophy* 2(1): 133–43.

Jack, D. C. 1991. *Silencing the Self: Women and Depression.* New York: Harper Collins.

Jackson, S. W. 1968. *Melancholia and Depression: From Hippocratic Times to Modern Times.* New Haven: Yale University Press.

Klibansky, R., E. Panofsky, and F. Saxl, eds. 1979. *Saturn and Melancholy: Studies in the History of Natural Philosophy, Religion, and Art.* The Netherlands: Kraus Reprint.

Lacan, J. 1977. The signification of the phallus. In *Écrits: A Selection*. Translated by A. Sheridan. New York: Norton.

Le Doeuff, M. 1990. *Hipparchia's Choice: An Essay Concerning Women, Philosophy, etc.* Translated by T. Selous. Oxford: Blackwell.

National Institutes of Health, National Institute of Mental Health. 1994. *Depression: What Every Woman Should Know*. NIH publication 95-3871. Washington, DC: GPO.

Nietzsche, F. 1967. *The Birth of Tragedy*. Translated by W. Kaufmann. New York: Vintage Books.

Nietzsche, F. 1974. *The Gay Science*. Translated by W. Kaufmann. New York: Vintage Books.

Nietzsche, F. 1989. *The Genealogy of Morals*. Translated by W. Kaufmann. New York: Vintage Books.

Oliver, K. 1995. *Womanizing Nietzsche: Philosophy's Relation to the "Feminine."* New York: Routledge.

Plato. 1961. *Symposium*. In the *Collected Dialogues*. Edited by E. Hamilton and H. Cairns. Princeton: Princeton University Press.

Schiesari, J. 1992. *The Gendering of Melancholia: Feminism. Psychoanalysis, and the Symbolics of Loss in Renaissance Literature*. Ithaca: Cornell University Press.

Woolf, V. 1981. *A Room of One's Own*. Foreward by M. Gordon. San Diego: Harcourt Brace Jovanovich.

9

Depression, Depth, and the Imagination

Jennifer Church

Something most peculiar is happening: my senses—I mean feeling, sight, hearing—are starting to fail me. For instance, I can say that this table is a table, I can see it, I can touch it. But the sensation is thin and dry. . . . It is the same with everything else. Music, scents, people's faces and voices. Everything's getting meaner and grayer, with no dignity.
Mrs. Jacobi, Second Scene, Ingmar Bergman's *Scenes from a Marriage*

When we are depressed, the world looks "meaner and grayer." There is a certain correspondence between how we feel (or fail to feel) and how we perceive (or fail to perceive). Why is this?

The answer may at first seem easy: to the extent that we cease to *care* about what is happening around us, we cease to *notice* what is happening around us. But this overlooks the difference between being preoccupied or absent-minded, where very little is noticed, and being depressed, where what is noticed seems deficient. Mrs. Jacobi, in the quote above, is keenly attentive to the look and feel and sound of tables, faces, voices; she notices her "thin and dry" sensations, and carefully monitors the apparent changes in things. What is striking about her description, of course, is how closely it mirrors the way she is feeling: thin and dry, meaner and grayer, and without dignity. An explanation of the phenomenology of depression must take account of this correspondence between *what* is being felt and *what* is being perceived.

Sartre offers one such explanation. According to Sartre, the depressive projects his own deficiency—a deficiency of the will—onto the world in order to avoid responsibility for it; my problem is made to appear as a problem with the world rather than with myself.[1] If the world is in its very nature a dry, deficient place, there is little reason to think that actions can make any significant difference, and therefore little reason to make the effort.[2] Thus my impoverished perceptions rationalize my inaction; they underwrite my flight from responsibility. But it is highly implausible that we have the sort of control over our perceptions that his account requires; even if I had the thought that a change in my perceptions would absolve me of unwelcome responsibilities, it is hard to believe that I could bring about such a change at will.

Ignoring Sartre's explicit rejection of psychoanalysis and its assumption of an unconscious, one might escape the overly intentional aspect Sartre's explanation by appeal to a more primitive, and less rational impulse to banish bad or unhappy things to someplace outside of ourselves. Just as we react to bad-tasting things by trying to spit them out, so too we react to bad-feeling things by trying to locate them outside of ourselves. This, I think, is on the right track, but it leaves a central problem untouched: How is it possible to transform bad feelings into bad looks? Unlike bad-tasting food that can literally move from inside to outside, the merely felt qualities of my depressed state must be transformed into perceived qualities of the objects around me.

In order to understand this crossover from feeling to perception (and vice versa), from inner to outer (and vice versa), I think we must focus on a more fundamental process whereby the very distinction between inner and outer is articulated. If I am right, certain affective failures and certain perceptual failures are not related as cause and effect so much as they are joint manifestations of a prior failure to adequately distinguish between what is subjective and what is objective. And for reasons that will soon emerge, I consider this more fundamental failure to be a failure of the imagination.

Section I, below, elaborates on the perceptual experience of the depressive to suggest that what it lacks is depth. Then, drawing on Kant, I argue that a failure to see the world as having depth amounts to a failure of the imagination. In section II, I turn to Freud to make a parallel connection between imagination and affect, to show just how the imagination sustains the deflections of desire that are necessary for continued emotional engagement. And, finally, I consider some of the more perverse aspects of depression, as elaborated by both Freud and Kristeva, and suggest that these aspects may also derive from shortcomings of the imagination.

I

Just what does a depressive's world look like? Sartre describes it as a world "in total affective equilibrium," "undifferentiated in structure," with all of its objects "equivalent and interchangeable." He also describes it as a world in which we "dim the lights." These are related notions, for a world that lacks light is a relatively gray world: sharp contrasts between black and white disappear, colors fade, with the result that more objects will appear to be the same color ("equivalent and interchangeable") and fewer objects will stand out to catch one's attention ("affective equilibrium"). Furthermore, with the loss of deep shadows, the three-dimensional character of objects will be less evident, causing the world to flatten out in appearance (to become "undifferentiated in structure"), with the result that less will seem hidden and there will be less to be curious about.

That this is the way the world appears when we are depressed is a well-documented fact: people recovering from depression report that colors and contrasts suddenly seem more vivid, while those entering depression speak of things appearing flatter and grayer. (Note, too, that there is an established correlation between gray skies and gray moods.) Depression is also correlated with a lack of differentiation by other senses: surfaces feel relatively flat and textureless when we are depressed, food tastes flat and interchangeable, and sounds lack resonance and depth. With the elimination or diminishment of each type of differentiation comes the elimination or diminishment of certain types of interest or engagement because being interested depends on being discriminating, and there can be no discrimination without differentiation.

The lack of differentiation in a depressive's world extends over time as well. Past and future seem indistinguishable from the present; it seems that no significant change has taken place in the past or will take place in the future. And, viewed this way, time itself begins to disappear as a dimension; in its place is a kind of continual present. This correlation is also well documented: when we are unhappy, time slows down, and depressives report time coming to a standstill. A depressive's world, then, is a world lacking depth, both in space and in time.

These observations invite the following question: What allows us to respond to information from the world in such a way that the world is experienced as having depth, in both space and time? Assuming that the same sensory information is available to both the depressive and the non-depressive, what sort of failure on the part of the depressive accounts for her failure to experience depth? The question has a distinctively Kantian character, for Kant was concerned with what it takes to have objects of experience (which, he argued, is necessary for experience itself), and he maintained that merely encountering a series of impressions is not enough.

The experience of objects, he argued, requires a recognition of multiple sides to the same thing (i.e., spatial depth) and continuity of the same thing over time (i.e., of temporal depth)—both of which require a variety of impressions to be synthesized into the experience of a single object. And, according to Kant, it is the faculty of imagination that effects the relevant syntheses.

Why imagination? In the first place, imagination brings what is absent into current experience. So, for example, imagination allows me to picture this table as having an underside and a history despite the fact that neither is now present to my senses. This is not merely a matter of memory, since, in many cases, I have not actually observed the surface that my imagination conjures up—and certainly not from the angle that I now imagine it. Such conjurings are, of course, informed by memories, but the imagined surfaces and events extend well beyond what has been observed. In the second place, though, and more important, imagination is what *combines* various impressions, present and past, actual and supposed, into a single experience in such a way that we experience the world as an objective world—as a world with spatial and temporal depth within which we are positioned as subjects with limited powers. Imagination, so understood, not only reproduces experiences in such a way as to ensure continuity in space and time; it effects a synthesis that produces a certain sort of experience—namely the experience of objects as such.[3]

It is important to see how Kant's understanding of the imagination surpasses the more prosaic understanding of Hume. Like Kant, Hume cast imagination in the role of a synthesizer of impressions—the faculty responsible for binding associated impressions together into 'objects'. Hume failed to see, however, that judgments (including perceptual judgments) require not only 'bundle-objects', or objects that are *collections* of spatiotemporal appearances, assembled on the basis of relations of resemblance and contiguity, but 'substance-objects', or objects that *underlie* certain appearances in space-time. Objects that underlie appearances are posited in order to make the world, and our perception of it, intelligible; and if this posit or projection is mistaken, it is nonetheless something we cannot do without. Imagination, on Kant's account of things, must not only collect and re-arrange impressions, it must also project beyond available impressions to something that lies "beneath" or "outside of" impressions—and then back again. Put another way: imagination must not only record regularities in our experience and anticipate more of the same; it must envision a certain *depth* in the world such that regularities in our experience are *explicable* by reference to the objects in that world.

Whereas for Hume an object simply *is* a collection of various impressions or appearances—the various appearances thus being mere parts of the constructed object; for Kant an object must be that which gives rise to various appearances—the underlying source of an infinite number of possible presentations. Kant requires that various presentations of the same object be understood as deriving from different possible relations between that object and a subject. So, to use his example, the house that I now observe has some *depth*, and thus registers as an *object* to me, precisely because I am able to imagine its somewhat different appearance if viewed from some other point in space (or if sensed in some other way, as through some other sense). Likewise a boat's progress down the river has some depth, and registers as an event to me, precisely because I can imagine what must have been observ*able* even when I was not myself observing it, and because I can project a future course on the basis of the underlying causal powers of the objects involved. Imagination, accordingly, in order to give us experience of a world, must not only reproduce and string together the various bits of information we receive, it must structure the information in such a way as to give one the experience of depth.

It makes sense to speak of degrees of flatness or depth. At one extreme is a flatness so complete it precludes the possibility of re-encountering the world, it leaves no room for objects to take shape, and one is left with "blind" impressions—that is, impressions that lack the structure necessary to make them accessible to judgment and to consciousness. (Here one might think of Strawson's "sound world," of only one dimension, and the problems it creates for the possibility of objective experience.) At the other extreme there is a depth so profound it threatens to recede from view entirely, leaving one with concepts or ideas that are "empty"—that is, concepts with no impressions to "fill" them in, no material on which to operate, and thus inaccessible to our senses. (Here one might think of Kant's account of the Ideas of Pure Reason—freedom, God, and the soul, none of which can be experienced through the senses as part of the objective world.) In either case there is a failure of imagination to create the necessary connections between sensation and understanding, intuition and conception. Let us now relate this Kantian account of imagination back to our initial discussion of depression and the experience of the world as an undifferentiated and flat sort of place. As one's capacity to imagine alternative perspectives on the world diminishes, so too does the experienced depth of that world; appearances flatten out to become more and more a mere string of conjoined impressions, and hence less and less appearances *of a world* at all. Or, to the extent that one supposes there to be a world "behind" the flat surface of appearances, that world recedes from view to become an abyss into which all meaningful distinctions disappear.[4]

II

Depression may involve a failure of the imagination, but it also involves an affective or emotional disorder. It is not immediately clear from the above, Kantian, account of imagination why this should be so. Why should an inability to recognize multiple perspectives or to generate multiple alternatives leave one feeling depressed? Couldn't one be happy despite (or even because of) a simple-minded obliviousness to alternatives—experiencing the world only as immediately present, without spatial and temporal depth? Why must the sense that the world has gone flat and that alternative perspectives are no longer possible correspond to a feeling of emotional *loss* or *pain*?

Kant may provide the resources to answer this question, especially if we look beyond his discussion of imagination in the *First Critique* to his discussion of imagination in the *Third Critique*; there he speaks of the special pleasure derived from the free play of the imagination in aesthetic appreciation, and he notes a close connection between enthusiasm and a lively imagination.[5] But I think Freud (who is, in many respects, a latter-day Kantian) offers more help in answering our question. He is more attuned to the vicissitudes of desire, and he has more appreciation of a particular sort of perversity that can sustain depression.

Freud develops the commonsensical observation that when our original desires are thwarted, we must find either new, and less direct, pathways to their satisfaction or we must find substitute satisfactions; that is to say, frustrated desires, in order to continue, must be sublimated or displaced. The ability to deflect one's desires down new paths, or onto new objects, though, depends on the ability to entertain a sufficiently rich array of alternatives—an ability to use one's imagination to construct alternative perspectives on the world. Thus (returning to our question about being happy in a "flat" world), while it is true that someone who recognizes very few alternatives may be content, this will be true only for as long as those alternatives correspond to, and hence satisfy, her desires; she will be in emotional trouble once the available alternatives cease to satisfy—unless the imagination is activated. Well-cared-for babies, with few options, may be happy as long as the available options meet their needs, but they will become first desperate and eventually despondent if their needs remain frustrated. Among other things, a good parent helps to show a child alternative ways to proceed in the face of frustration, helps to identify substitute avenues of satisfaction, and thereby cultivates the child's imagination.[6]

These observations inform Freud's account of depression (or "melancholy") insofar as he emphasizes a certain similarity between depression and grief: in both cases, one is emotionally and motivationally debilitated for as long as one continues to cling to a lost object or a lost opportunity—as long as one views something or someone as the *only* possible (yet, of course, the no longer possible) object of one's desires.[7] In both grief and depression, recovery requires enough imaginative flexibility to effectively deflect one's desires toward other love objects. Such deflection, according to Freud, relies on a kind of "dreamwork" in which the usual criteria of identity are stretched to enable a new object to appear as yet another instantiation of a previous, lost object. It is not enough to decide that person or pursuit A is a good substitute for person or pursuit B; A must be somehow experienced as another manifestation of the *same* B—that is, B must be seen *in* A.[8] And, as we have seen, it is just this collection and synthesis of diverse impressions into experiences of a single object that is the job of the imagination.

When deflection or sublimation is unsuccessful—as when imagination fails to find successful continuations for one's frustrated desires—then, according to Freud, the impulses that underlie one's desires disconnect from the objects one perceives or the ideas one entertains. (One of the very interesting but underdeveloped aspects of Freud's metapsychology, which I don't have time to pursue here, is his theory of repression whereby repression just *is* this disconnection of affect and idea.[9]) Once affect becomes disconnected from objects or ideas, however, it ceases to constitute an emotion, for emotions require objects; it becomes free-floating affect, which is to say it becomes anxiety.[10] On this account, then, depression involves a loss of affective engagement and, precisely because of this loss, it involves a kind of objectless longing—a desire for everything and nothing.

Equally important is the fact that decathected objects or ideas cease to engage one's thinking; the depressive may have many thoughts, but there is nothing to move her from one thought to another—nothing to pull thoughts together into trains of thought, nothing to give the sense that one

thought follows from another. On the assumption that inferential connections are motivated connections binding thoughts to one another, and
on the assumption that inferential connections are necessary to the very
constitution of thought at such, it follows that the loss of motivated connections between thoughts will jeopardize the very occurrence of thought
as such. To the extent that ideas are disconnected from affect, they cease to
be ideas and become empty sounds, shapes, marks. In losing inferential
structure, they lose their depth; in losing their depth, they lose their referents; and in losing their referents, they cease to function as thoughts at all.[11]
This, I suggest, is precisely the predicament of the depressive vis-à-vis
thought; one's own words to oneself, let alone the words of another,
become mere sounds—objects in one's experience rather than concepts by
which experience is organized.

So far, then, we have an account of why a failure of imagination results
in a lack of perceived depth in the world, a lack of motivational attachment
to the world, and a loss of appreciation for the meaningfulness of thought
itself. And we have seen why it is implausible to suppose that someone
lacking (the relevant sort of) imagination could escape these aspects of
depression in the face of the inevitable frustrations that come our way. But I
have not yet addressed the special sort of pain that accompanies most forms
of depression, and I haven't shown that a failure of imagination is necessary
as well as sufficient for such depression.

III

To the seriously depressed, the world appears not only gray but black, not
only flat but suffocating. It could be pointed out that finding oneself without any real alternatives or options—without any way to pursue one's
desires—is painful, but this would not account for the extremity of the
reaction, its dangerous self-destructiveness. The depressive's pain is not just
the pain of feeling cut off from objects of desire, it is a pain that cuts into
and against one's very self. (By focusing on this aspect of depression, we can
begin to understand something of what I earlier called the evident "perversity" of depression.)

Freud notes this self-destructive aspect of depression (versus grief) and
explains it as follows: whereas in grief one feels deprived and wronged by
the world (either by the particular person or part of the world that has been
lost, or by the world at large) and has vengeful impulses in response, in
depression one has so identified with what has been lost that turning against

it, or seeking vengeance on the wrong-doer, amounts to turning against oneself. The depressive, then, is someone who has been narcissistically attached to her lost love object, and the peculiarly debilitating pain she feels is the pain of suffering an attack on one's very self.[12]

Here we might ask: what kind of person becomes narcissistically attached to what kind of object? Freud does not say much beyond suggesting that narcissism involves a regression to the pre-Oedipal stage of primary narcissism in which we treat everything good and everything loved as mere extensions of ourselves. (It is not until the Oedipal triangle is complete that there can be full recognition of an objective world independent of any one subject's perceptions and desires, for it is not until the father intervenes with a competing demand on the mother's attentions that the reality of independent perspectives on the same world becomes evident to the child.[13]) If this is right, though, then it is precisely those who are least able to distinguish subject from object that are most likely to take out their losses on themselves, and insofar as imagination is responsible for maintaining an adequate separation of subject and object, its failure will be responsible for this final aspect of depression as well.

Kristeva, in her book *Black Sun* (1987), develops an interesting variant on this Freudian story. She argues that the depressed person wants to destroy the self not so much because it is a stand-in for what is lost but, rather, because it stands in the way of what is lost—namely that (mythical) oneness with the mother that predates the emergence of the self. Achieving such oneness would require either the separate self or the separate mother to be destroyed—the first route fueling a murderous hatred of the self, the latter an intolerable guilt about one's murder of the mother. And, in either case, it would amount to the obliteration of a subject/object distinction, which would mean the elimination of thought and consciousness itself. Thus, as Kristeva realizes, the severely—one might say "demonically"—depressed person is engaged in a deadly struggle over their own identity and, indeed, over the very viability of intelligible experience.

According to Kristeva, the depressive shuns all objects apart from the undifferentiated mother-object, and since language requires differentiated objects, she shuns language as well. The depressive attempts to immerse herself in silent oneness with the (mythical) mother—insistently, but without success, and without satisfaction. Kristeva calls the sadness of the depressive "the most archaic expression of an unsymbolizable, unnamable narcissistic wound. . . . For . . . narcissistic depressed persons, sadness is really the sole object; more precisely it is a substitute object they become attached to, an object they tame and cherish for lack of another" (p. 12). To leave behind depression and recover language and thought means restoring both a subject/object *distinction* and a subject/object *connection*. Words and experiences must be sufficiently separate from the world to be about the world (and not just about themselves, which would render them flat and meaningless), but the world must also be close enough to our words and experiences to be their referent. In the vocabulary of Kristeva, the realm of the "symbolic" and the realm of the "semiotic" must not lose contact. Sustaining such contact, however, requires an active imagination—for, again, it requires that one treat a variety of experiences as different perspectives on the same world: different ways of talking and thinking about the same things, different ways of working toward the same ends, and different ways of going on from the same past.

The parallels, then, among Kant, Freud, and Kristeva are notable. All three emphasize the importance of imagination in mediating not only sensibility and understanding, pre- and post-Oedipal subjectivity (the naturalistic counterparts to the transcendental and empirical self), but conscious and unconscious mind as well. In order to experience depth in the world that we consciously encounter—a prerequisite for emotional engagement—conscious perceptions and actions must connect up with unconscious impressions and impulses in a variety of ways, and this depends on the ability of the imagination to find symbols (i.e., concepts) that effectively condense (or, in Kantian terms, synthesize) the sensible manifold of unconscious impressions into a structured whole.

The crucial role of imagination, then, is to present a world of many possibilities—a world with real but reachable depths. It won't do to insist on engagement with a world that has lost its appeal and gone flat, and it won't do to insist on taking responsibility or exercising the will when the very existence of a self or a will is in question. The world must open up again, which is to say traversible spaces must be created between subject and object. The central challenge here is the challenge of keeping multiple paths of access open between oneself and the world, for, as I've been arguing, without such multiplicity, both one's self and the world are lost.[14]

Notes

1. Over the course of two pages, Sartre uses four different words to name the emotion whose phenomenology he is describing: *tristesse*, *chagrin*, *morne*, and *douleur* (1948, 64–66). What is important for both Sartre and myself is some characteristics of particular

sorts of sadness, grief, or depression—characteristics which may mark an area in which these emotions overlap.

2. Sartre distinguishes between passive sadness in which the world seems to demand nothing of us and active sadness in which the world seems to demand more than we can possibly give. He claims that both views, however, are designed to justify our inaction.

3. Commentators on Kant are usually careful to distinguish between his conception of a *reproductive* (empirical) imagination as a faculty that merely reproduces past impressions from his conception of the productive (transcendental) imagination that synthesizes impressions into objects of experience. I do not think the distinction is very neat, given reproductive imagination's creative role in "filling in the gaps" of experience, and given the impossibility of reproducing experiences that are not already organized as experiences of objects. Also I would argue that they are both empirical processes that are transcendental requirements on the perception of objects as such.

4. I do not address the question of whether the depressive actually loses the *ability* to entertain alternative perspectives and to synthesize them into experiences of a single world, or only fails to *use* that ability—perhaps through a failure of the will. For my purposes it is enough to establish that some central features of depression are accounted for by a failure of the imagination.

5. Consider, for example, the following two passages from *The Critique of Judgement*: "In a word, the aesthetic idea is a representation of the imagination, annexed to a given concept, with which, in the free employment of imagination, such a multiplicity of partial representations are bound up, that no expression indicating a definite concept can be found for it—one which on that account allows a concept to be supplemented in thought by much that is indefinable in words, and the feeling of which quickens the cognitive faculties, and with language, as a mere thing of the letter, binds up the spirit (soul) also" (Kant 1952, 179). "[F]rom an aesthetic point of view, enthusiasm is sublime, because it is an effort of one's powers called forth by ideas which give to the mind an impetus of far stronger and more enduring efficacy than the stimulus afforded by sensible representations" (p. 124).

6. I take the option of abandoning desire altogether to be unrealistic.

7. Freud's account of depression is put forward in a paper entitled "Mourning and Melancholia" (1917).

8. Here it might be objected that dreamwork operates precisely in order to disguise one's original desires—to allow one one's forbidden desires; to do this, one must locate new objects whose identity with the old are *not* recognized. There is something right about this, but it misses the point. First, in cases of repression, while the identity between the new and the old is supposed to be hidden from the system's consciousness, it cannot be an effective substitute unless the identity is evident to the unconscious.

9. The seeds of such a theory can be seen in many of Freud's metapsychological papers, but it is most fully explored in his 1915 paper "The Unconscious."

10. Recent discussions of drug therapy have noted the close connection between unrelieved anxiety and chronic depression. See Peter Kramer's *Listening to Prozac* (1993) for a thoughtful discussion of the evidence.

11. The assumption that content relies on inferential structure is by no means universally accepted, but as Jerry Fodor and Ernest LePore document in *Holism: A Shopper's Guide* (1992), it is certainly the received view these days. To defend it would take me too far afield here, but I would like to note my belief that this assumption, properly spelled out, is compatible with theories of meaning that assign an important role to causal interactions between mind and world.

12. The idea that the self may turn against itself may seem paradoxical insofar as it seems to require that the self be both subject and object of the attack. I think there are several plausible ways to resolve this paradox. In the case of Freud, it seems to be handled by invoking a distinction between the ego and the super-ego, whereby the super-ego may endeavor to destroy the ego.

13. There are many different ways to spell out this story, of course. Freud thought of the Oedipal triangle as involving a quite literal struggle between father and child over the mother; Lacan took a linguistic turn in emphasizing the self-alienation together with self-recognition that results from the intervention of language as the "law of the father." On both accounts, interestingly enough, the feminine path through the Oedipal complex encounters less of a threat, so achieves less resolution and retains a stronger element of narcissism.

14. Since presenting this paper at the 1997 meetings of The Association for the Advancement of Philosophy and Psychiatry, I have developed some of its ideas in two other papers: "Opening the 'Gap' on Depression: From Monotony to Meaning", co-authored with Beverly Haviland (2001), and " 'Seeing As' and the Double Bind of Consciousness" (2000).

References

Church, J. 2000. "Seeing as" and the double bind of consciousness. *Journal of Consciousness Studies* 7: 99–111.

Church, J., and B. Haviland. 2001. Opening the "gap" on depression: From monotony to meaning. *Psychoanalysis and Contemporary Thought* 24: 153–75.

Fodor, J., and E. LePore. 1992. *Holism: A Shopper's Guide*. London: Blackwell.

Freud, S. [1915] 1957. The unconscious. Translated by J. Strachey. *Standard Edition, XIV*. London: Hogarth Press, pp. 159–216.

Freud, S. [1917] 1957. Mourning and melancholia. Translated by J. Strachey. *Standard Edition, XIV*. London: Hogarth Press, pp. 237–58.

Kant, I. 1952. *The Critique of Judgement*. London: Oxford University Press.

Kramer, P. 1993. *Listening to Prozac*. New York: Viking Press.

Kristeva, J. 1987. *Black Sun: Depression and Melancholia*. New York: Columbia University Press.

Sartre, J.-P. 1948. *The Emotions: Outline of a Theory*. New York: Philosophical Library.

10

The Unconscious as a Hermeneutic Myth: A Defense of the Imagination

J. Melvin Woody

Ever since pre-Socratic philosophers suggested that the planets were not gods, but only stones, one of the primary obligations of philosophy has been to challenge the dominant myths of the day and replace them by more rational forms of explanation. Since the myths of the day are sacred beliefs to their adherents, this mischievous mission is often perceived as an assault upon obvious and unquestionable truths. In our own day, when secular science has displaced mythic religions as the domain of obvious and unquestionable truths, the philosophical obligation to question the obvious and expose the myths is no less important—and no less mischievous.

I maintain that one of the dominant myths of our secular age is the doctrine of the unconscious mind. The existence of the unconscious is a central and nearly sacred dogma for our culture's most prosperous religion: psychotherapy. Although that cult may have "redeeming virtues," I believe that the dogma of the unconscious mind is an obstacle to real understanding, a god to be replaced by a stone. But it is not my purpose to attack psychotherapy as such. Rather, I will attempt to do it a service by clarifying and criticizing its theology. One of the weaknesses of new religious movements is that they tend to be lax about the conceptual clarity of their central beliefs. I hope to show that the psychotherapeutic movement has worshipped at the wrong altar, that the homage it has paid to "the unconscious mind" was properly due to the imagination. Nor is this merely a modern version of ancient disputes about the true name of God—a merely semantic quibble that would make no important difference to practice. For whether one invokes the unconscious or the imagination makes an important difference to therapeutic theory itself and to the application of psychiatric methods to history and to the interpretation of works of art and literature.

I will divide this task into two parts. First, I will undertake to defend the serious point behind my mischievous description of the unconscious as

the "god" of a psychotherapeutic "religion." Second, I will try to show that
no such god exists, that there is no unconscious mind—or, rather, that the
concept of the unconscious mind is a misconception that can be avoided by
recognizing that the functions attributed to the unconscious mind are really
the work of the imagination. The word "unconscious" should be reserved
for referring to states of coma, as James Hillman recommends in *The Myth of
Analysis* (1972, 174). I will try to show that the psychoanalytic doctrine of
the unconscious is a myth due to a hermeneutic error, a misunderstanding
of the nature of interpretation. In order to do that, I will locate the appeal
to the unconscious in psychoanalytic doctrine in relation to other hermeneutic traditions such as history, religion, and aesthetics. The invocation of
the unconscious as an interpretative principle can then be exposed as a myth
that results from a familiar hermeneutic fallacy.

The Unconscious and Religious Hermeneutics

First, then, the serious point behind my theological metaphor. Analogies
among psychoanalysis, myth, and religion were already quite obvious to
Freud and Jung. There are so many rich and inviting parallels to be drawn
that I can scarcely attempt to explore them all. Nor need I, since they have
been provocatively analysed by such authors as Hillman, Lévi-Strauss, and
Eliade.[1] For my purposes, a brief review of salient characteristics of mythic
thought will suffice to provide a background for a more specific comparison
between religious and psychoanalytic strategies of interpreting history.

　　　Students of myth—such as Ernst Cassirer and Mircea Eliade—have
shown that it is characteristic of mythical and religious conception to confuse the distinction between mere metaphor and literal or discursive meaning. It is also characteristic of this mythic way of thinking to treat relations
of meaning as if they were ontological or causal connections rather than
merely semiotic ones. Sympathetic magic and religious ritual seek to exploit
this causal efficacy of metaphor and symbol in practices that range from the
Christian sacrament of communion to sticking pins in a voodoo doll. Third,
it is characteristic of mythic and religious interpretation to explain puzzling
events and numinous experiences by appeal to some hidden purposes or
mental or spiritual agencies at work behind the scenes, whether those be the
gods of archaic myth or the Christian's divine, providential plan, a theme
to which I will return directly. Finally, it is characteristic of this mode of
thought to claim that the priest or shaman commands an esoteric herme-

neutic lore—or art of interpreting signs and omens—which enables him (or her) both to understand those hidden purposes and to propitiate those recondite mental agencies. Eliade presents reams of evidence to show that the method of interpretation employed is typically genetic, based on an appeal to originative acts that supposedly occurred during sacred history, or at the mythical dawn of time. In magical rites and religious rituals the celebrants re-enact those sacred events in order to relieve men of suffering, guilt, or other afflictions. Again, the Christian sacrament of communion offers a convenient example.

For the moment, let us resist the temptation to exploit the inviting parallels with psychoanalysis—that contemporary esoteric art of interpretation that also claims to reveal the meanings and purposes hidden behind overt acts and experiences by a return to the client's origins—and that seeks to relieve the client's suffering and guilt by re-enacting, in the transference, the child's formative relations with godlike parents. Those parallels were noted, even advertised, by Freud and Jung themselves. My task is to focus attention on the *underlying* dogma or myth upon which these parallels depend: the belief in an unconscious mind. A more specific comparison between religious and psychoanalytic strategies of interpretation will help to dramatize the hermeneutic function of that doctrine. To be more exact, I will confine myself to "classical" or "orthodox" Freudian psychoanalysis and the orthodox or traditional Christian view of history.

Psychoanalysis is primarily concerned with interpreting and understanding the history of individuals, though Freud did not hesitate to apply his method to history at large. The Christian view of history is primarily concerned with history as a whole, though individuals may often appeal to it in an effort to understand events in their personal careers. What is important for our purposes is to notice where each finds the ultimate locus of intelligibility. That locus proved to be the unconscious, in the case of psychoanalysis, and divine providence in the Christian view. And we have only to juxtapose the intrepretive functions of the two to see that the idea of the unconscious mind serves a function in psychoanalytic interpretation that is strikingly similar to the role of the idea of divine providence in the medieval Christian understanding of history. That is, "the unconscious" serves a role in the interpretation of individual history—or biography—that is exactly parallel to the function of the idea of divine providence in the Christian interpretation of history at large. This is true at two levels: one popular and one more serious and professional.

At the popular level, each of these ideas functions as an *asylum igno-rantiae*, as the medievals would say: a refuge of ignorance. That is, any event that was remarkable, portentous or inexplicable could always be "chalked up" to the inscrutable workings of providence, the carrying through of God's plan in the world. The untimely death of a son, the loss of a crop—or of a war, the illness or insanity of a ruler—all could be tolerated and understood in this way. Divine providence thus served as a catch-all, omnibus explanation for whatever could not be explained in any other way, or whose importance seemed to transcend the simple causal explan-ations available—hence a refuge of ignorance. The psychoanalytic uncon-scious has come to serve a similar role in our culture in the explanation of individual behavior. It is not invoked to explain what is otherwise intelli-gible, like raising an umbrella when it begins to pour or remembering my own phone number, any more than people invoked God's plan to explain the fact that the streets were wet after a rainstorm. Rather, the unconscious is invoked to explain behavior that is remarkable or portentous and inscru-table: actions and thoughts that seem otherwise inexplicable—bizarre be-havior, physical symptoms for which there seem to be no physical causes, dreams, murders, rapes, and eccentric convictions or habits. Or again, divine providence was invoked to explain historical events that were humanly important, but which no human had intended, such as peculiarly tragic or fortuitous coincidences. Then it would be said that even though there was no *human* intent at work, there was nevertheless a *divine* purpose at work behind the scenes, so that what *appeared* to be accidental was *really* "the will of God." So, too, pop psychology assures us that inadvertent puns and slips of tongue and pen and other apparently accidental behavior, such as fall-ing off a step ladder or hitting my thumb with a hammer—actions that the agent himself insists that he did not *intend* to perform—are really the manifestations of an inscrutable unconscious mind working behind the scenes and using the agent's mouth or hand to achieve its goals, much as providence uses kings and generals as the unwitting instruments of a divine intent.

Moreover this popular version of each doctrine is actually grounded firmly in orthodoxy in each case. For the orthodox clergy—or therapist—would go further and insist that *everything* that happens is due to divine intent, in the one case or, in the other case, that *every* conscious word and deed is determined by the unconscious mind. That is, it is not merely the specific puzzling or anomalous events, to which the ordinary believer points, that have to be explained by referring to an all-powerful, inscrutable mind controlling phenomena for its own purposes and even *in spite of* the conscious human purposes. If the anomalous odd event or act is to be explained in this way, it is because the whole of history—or of an individual's behavior—is determined by such hidden purposes. Or rather, the purposes are hidden and inscrutable *only* to the laity—whereas the clergyman or analyst is distinguished from the rest of us by his ability to explain to the layman just what is the *true* meaning of the events of history—or the individual's words and deeds, thoughts, and dreams. He does this by discovering the *symbolic* or *figurative* meaning of historical or biographical phenomena. The psychoanalyst explains to me, for example, that the true meaning of my present behavior is to be understood only in the light of my attempt to resolve an Oedipal conflict with my father when I was a child. The approach that the medieval interpreter took has been amply explained by the literary historian Erich Auerbach. Auerbach describes the method as follows:

This method of interpretation involves an approach to human and historical phenomena entirely different from ours. We are apt to consider the events of history and the happenings of everyday life as a continuous development in chronological succession. . . . We are able to explain to a certain extent every single historical fact by its immediate causes and to foresee to a certain extent its immediate consequences, moving, so to speak, on an horizontal plane; the figurative approach, on the contrary, combines two events causally and chronologically remote from each other, by attributing to them a meaning common to both; in order to explain the significance of a single historical event, the interpreter had to take recourse to a vertical projection of this event on the plane of providential design by which the event is revealed as a prefiguration or a fulfillment or perhaps as an imitation of other events.

Let one example stand for many: It is a visually dramatic occurrence that God made Eve, the first woman, from Adam's rib while Adam lay asleep; so too, that a soldier pierced Jesus' side as he hung dead on the cross, so that the blood and water flowed out. But when these two occurrences are exegetically interrelated in the doctrine that Adam's sleep is a figure of Christ's death sleep; that as from the wound in Adam's side mankind's primordial mother after the flesh, Eve, was born, so from the wound in Christ's side was born the mother of all men after the spirit, the Church. . . . then the sensory occurrence pales before the power of the figural meaning and a connection is established between two events which are linked neither temporally nor causally—a connection which it is impossible to establish by reason in the horizontal dimension. It can be established only if both occurrences are vertically linked to Divine Providence, which alone is able to devise such a plan of history and supply the key to its understanding. The horizontal, that is, the temporal and causal connection of occurrences is dissolved; the here and now is no longer a mere link in an earthly chain of events, it is simultaneously something which has always been and which will be fulfilled in the future; and strictly, in the eyes of God, it is something eternal, something omni-temporal, something already consummated in the realm of fragmentary earthly event.[2]

For all the fuss that has been made about the originality of the Christian view of history, I submit that this medieval method of interpretation is not so radically different in some respects from the approach of more archaic, mythic religions that see events as meaningful only insofar as they repeat the archetypal deeds of the gods that occurred in a sacred history at the beginning of time, when all things came to be as they are. Mircea Eliade writes that for such societies,

all the important acts of life were revealed *ab origine* by gods or heroes. Men only repeat these exemplary and paradigmatic gestures *ad infinitum*.... Through the paradox of rite, profane time and duration are suspended. And the same holds true for *all* repetition, i.e., all imitations of archetypes; through such imitation, man is projected into the mythic epoch in which the archetypes were first revealed.... insofar as an act acquires a certain reality through the repetition of a certain paradigmatic gesture, and acquires it through that alone, there is an implicit abolition of profane time, of duration, of "history"; and he who reproduces the exemplary gesture thus finds himself transported into the mythical epoch in which its revelation took place. (1959, 32, 35)

The parallels to Auerbach's account of figurative interpretation are so obvious that I need not dwell upon them. Rather, I wish to remind you that the psychoanalyst also grounds the interpretation of the dreams and deeds of the adult by appealing to meanings that dissolve chronological and causal order and project the individual back to the dawn of his life, when parents were as gods and the individual came-to-be who he is—all before the age of five, or perhaps even by the time he was weaned or toilet trained. And just as religious rituals such as those Eliade cites—or the Christian communion or Jewish seder—are understood as repetitions of sacred history and often intended to liberate the individual from the burden of sin or guilt, the analytic process is understood to achieve a similar liberation by "working through a transference," which is a repetition of relations to parents, in order to achieve an epiphany or manifestation of the unconscious that surely invites comparison with the theophany or manifestation of God in the ritual at the moment of the transubstantiation of the bread and wine in the mass or, in more primitive rituals, the identification of the dancer or priest with the god. And if the manifestation of the unconscious takes rather longer, the liberation and purgation accomplished thereby are also expected to be more enduring.

I have not undertaken this extended comparison between psycho-therapy and other forms of religion in order to *discredit* either side of the parallel, though it may well raise some doubts. My primary purpose has been to call attention to the fact that "the unconscious" functions in a system of interpretation, or "hermeneutics," that is entirely comparable to the method of religious interpretation of history employed in the middle ages—and still employed today by the editors of *The Watchtower*, that remarkable publication peddled from door to door by Jehovah's Witnesses. It is a system of interpretation that seeks to explain the meaning of mundane history by a return to myth or sacred history and by reference to intentions and purposes working behind the scenes—and often in despite of the conscious human intentions of the agents themselves.

But except for Jehovah's Witnesses, I assume that even the devoutly Christian historian today would not seriously advocate the use of this method of understanding historical events. And since we no longer seek to understand general history through this method of interpretation, since we insist, for good reasons, upon a more chronological and causal understanding of historical events, perhaps we should hesitate before we adopt that same mode of interpretation in its psychiatric version when we turn to the understanding of *individual* history, or biography—or to allow it to creep back into general history by the back door of psycho-history.

So much for the first stage of my argument, which was to explain the serious point involved in my describing the unconscious as the god of a religion of psychotherapy by locating the hermeneutics of the unconscious in relation to religious interpretation. I now pass to the second stage, which is to argue more positively and vigorously that we should not accept this form of interpretation because there are no unconscious purposes, ideas, or strategies, because there *is no* unconscious mind, and that the problems presented to our understanding by dreams, hysteria, neurotic symptoms, and schizophrenia are better and more simply to be understood as the work—or play—of the imagination and as the conscious expressions of individual personality and feeling. It follows that we should turn the tables upon those Freudians and Jungians who have subjected the masterpieces of art and poetry to psychoanalytic interpretations. That is, instead of treating these other great products of the imagination as mere symptoms or sublimations of unconscious instincts and ideas, we would do better to regard the symbols and symptoms of psychopathology from the standpoint of poetics and philosophical aesthetics. That perspective will reveal the very source of the myth of the unconscious mind.

Aesthetic Criticism and the Hermeneutics of the Unconscious

Briefly, I will try to show that the psychiatric appeal to the unconscious commits one of the most common and elementary fallacies of aesthetic interpretation: that it is guilty of "message hunting"—or, more exactly, of the form of the genetic fallacy that Wimsatt and Beardsley dubbed "the intentional fallacy." The appeal to the unconscious commits that error due to confusion about the relation of image, metaphor, and symbol to literal, discursive thought. As a result it confounds the semiotic and causal orders, which leads to belief in a recondite mental agency at work behind the scenes: the unconscious mind. In so doing, it neatly replicates the primary characteristics of mythic conception and interpretation described earlier. The effect of the appeal to the unconscious is to foster the imperialistic tendencies of discursive reason, its attempt to establish its sovereignty where it has no legitimate right. Indeed, I will try to show that the whole notion of an "unconscious mind" results from confounding *consciousness* with discursive or linguistic thought, with "talking to oneself," to put it in simplest terms.

Every freshman student of literature or art must learn to avoid "message hunting"—the attempt to wrest from the teacher, or to formulate for himself, some little moral homily or grand philosophical profundity that he supposes is *the* nugget of meaning hidden in the poem or play, which he can inscribe in his notebook or memorize so that he need never trouble to look at the painting or read the poem or play again. For now "he knows what it means!" He has discovered the cabalistic secret disguised within the poem's images or the concerto's harmonies—or found the skeleton key to *Finnegan's Wake*. So he no longer needs the poem because now he knows "what the poet was trying to say"—or the painter or dancer. Suzanne Langer's comment upon this effort is a gem of one-line philosophical criticism: "But if the reader can make clear what the poet was trying to say, why cannot the poet say it clearly in the first place?" (1953, 208–209). Even professional or professorial critics are sometimes guilty of more sophisticated versions of this same error. They too may set out to discover the meaning of the poem by discovering the poet's *intent*—or they claim that their interpretations are true *because* they correctly render the poet's intent. They thereby commit the intentional fallacy, which is the fallacy of supposing that the meaning of a work of art is to be sought *beyond* the work itself, in the subjective condition of its creator rather than *in* the poem or painting itself. And in order to resolve any doubts about what the artist intended, they are likely to begin poking into the artist's biography, reading diaries or letters, hoping to find in them a meaning that is not evident in the work of art itself. Wimsatt and Beardsley describe the fallacy involved as follows:

> The Intentional Fallacy is a confusion between the poem and its origins, a special case of what is known to philosophers as the Genetic Fallacy. It begins by trying to derive the standard of criticism from the psychological causes of the poem and ends in biography and relativism. The result ... is that the poem itself as an object of specifically critical judgement, tends to disappear. (1949, 401)

It is easy to see where the fallacy lies. To suppose that the meaning of a work of art resides in some subjective condition of its author is to regard it as a *symptom* or biographical document rather than as an aesthetic object. A work of art only succeeds aesthetically insofar as it clearly displays its meaning. If the meaning of the work is not manifest *in* the work itself, the work *fails* aesthetically. And as for the notion that the standard of meaning is to be sought in the diary or mind of the artist, Socrates noted the flaw in *that* supposition in his *Apology*, where he reported that almost any bystander "could explain the poems better than their authors could" and concluded that poets operate more by inspiration than by knowledge and "say many fine things without an understanding of what they say" (Plato *Apology*, 22b–c). And in fact, the best interpreters of works of art are usually not artists, but critics whose talents are more discursive than creative. In any case, the question, "What did the painter or poet *mean*?" is a question to be asked by the biographer or historian. The question for the critic or general audience is, rather, "What does the *poem* or *painting* mean?"

Now the poet or painter or dancer may very likely *deny* that he ever thought or "intended to say" the things that the critic reads into his work. In reply, the critic may snort, "*He* doesn't know *what* he meant!," thereby echoing Socrates. And he is right! Stuart Hampshire stated the reason succinctly in *Thought and Action*:

> It is characteristic of any considerable work of art that its interest cannot be exhausted in any plain statement of the artist's intention. He always does more than he could previously have said that he was doing. The artist's intention is not clearly detachable from the actual performance to the degree to which it is in any uncreative activity. The power and quality of the work is only known and understood in retrospect, often after many years. ... The intention must be to some degree fulfilled before it is even recognizable. The idea of original art is the idea of an achievement that goes beyond any previous intention and that must always be to some degree unexpected, even by its maker. (1959, 246–47)

Accordingly, the astute critic may rightly insist upon the truth of his interpretation *despite* the artist's denial that he ever entertained the ideas or meanings ascribed to his work in the critic's analysis. But if the critic goes on to insist that the artist *must* have entertained those ideas *unconsciously* nevertheless, then he has gone too far! From the fact that he has discovered a meaning of which the artist was not conscious, it does not follow that he has discovered a meaning that existed "in the artist's unconscious."

Yet that is exactly the reasoning behind the doctrine of the unconscious. The psychologist seeks to formulate the meaning of the symptom or dream in a discursive, propositional "message" and then, like the careless critic, he supposes that his interpretation exposes what the dreamer or client "really meant," or "intended to say." But then, since the dreamer denies that he ever entertained any such thoughts, Freud and his offspring insist that the dreamer must nevertheless have had that message in mind, but that it must have been repressed, buried in the unconscious and represented only in a deviously disguised way in the dream. The same reasoning is applied to somatic symptoms, slips of tongue or pen, and other behavior: all are interpreted as disguised, symbolic expressions of repressed, unconscious ideas—and according to Freud, at least, it is only *ideas* that are supposed to be unconscious, not the affects or feelings attaching *to* them, since those *are* expressed consciously, albeit symbolically, in the dream, somatic symptoms, and so on. Like the freshman or the naive critic, Freud takes the "message" or discursive, propositional product of interpretation to be the *meaning*. But since the dreamer or patient is not aware of ever entertaining such a thought, Freud insists that the dream must be the expression of an *unconscious* idea or wish—an unconscious intent that must be "repressed," since the dreamer denies any knowledge of it even when he finds the interpretation enlightening.

Lest I be accused of exaggeration, I summon Freud himself as my witness. In a celebrated passage in *The Interpretation of Dreams* (2000, 277–78), Freud describes dreaming as just such a process of translating discursive thoughts into images. He describes this "dream work" in the same terms, but still more vividly in *A General Introduction to Psychoanalysis*:

Obviously this achievement is by no means an easy one. In order to get some idea of its difficulty, imagine that you had to replace a political leading article in a newspaper by a series of illustrations; you would have to abandon alphabetic characters in favor of hieroglyphics. The people and concrete objects mentioned in the article could be easily represented, perhaps even more satisfactorily, in pictorial form; but you would expect to meet with difficulties when you came to the portrayal of all the abstract words and all those parts of speech which indicate relations between the various thoughts, e.g. particles, conjunctions, and so forth. With the abstract words you would employ all manner of devices: for instance, you would try to render the text of the article into other words, more unfamiliar perhaps, but made up of parts more concrete and therefore more capable of such representation. This will remind you of the fact that most abstract words were originally concrete, their original significance having faded; and therefore you will fall back on the original concrete meaning of these words wherever possible. So you will be glad that you can represent the "possessing" of an object as a literal, physical "sitting upon" it (possess = potis + sedeo). This is just how the dream work proceeds. In such circumstances you can hardly demand great accuracy of representation, neither will you quarrel with the dream-work for replacing an element which is difficult to reduce to pictorial form, such as the idea of breaking marriage vows, by some other kind of breaking, e.g. that of an arm or leg. In this way you will to some extent succeed in overcoming the awkwardness of rendering alphabetic characters into hieroglyphs. (1960, 183–84)[3]

It is obvious that this whole account assumes that there is a discursive thought in the unconscious, a sentence or proposition, that must be "translated" into a sort of rebus or allegorical code of images. And indeed, this is just the way Freud puts it himself:

[T]he peculiar thing about the way in which the dream-work proceeds is this: its material consists of thoughts, some of which may be objectionable and disagreeable, *but which nevertheless are correctly formed and expressed.* The dream-work transmutes these thoughts into another form, and it is curious and incomprehensible that in this process of translation—of rendering them, as it were, into another script or language—the means of blending and combining are employed. (Ibid., 181)

"Curious and incomprehensible" indeed! For the supposition that there is a latent dream thought, a correctly formed and expressed discursive message, conforming to the interpretation but hidden in the unconscious mind, is as gratuitous and misleading as the notion that the painter must always begin with a discursively expressed intention, which he then proceeds to "translate" into images on canvas. And in fact, when Freud proceeds to show how the supposedly unconscious mind actually *works*, by analyzing dreams and case studies, what he discloses is not at all the logic of discursive language. Instead, he finds what he calls "primary process" thinking, which is quite alien to discursive thought. The salient primary process functions are, first, "visualization" or the use of images, which Freud describes as the translation of thoughts *into* images, as we have just seen. Primary process thinking also employs "displacement," which Freud compares to literary allusion and which replaces the repressed, latent idea by something more acceptable that is metaphorically or metonymically related to it. And, finally, the primary process employs "condensation," which Freud describes as follows:

What condensation can achieve is sometimes quite extraordinary; by this device it is at times possible for two completely different trains of thought to be united in a single manifest dream, so that we arrive at an apparently adequate interpretation of a dream and yet overlook a second possible meaning. (Ibid.)

Condensation results in "overdetermination," by which Freud means that two or more unconscious thoughts may be concentrated in a single symptom or manifest dream.

But what Freud here describes as an "extraordinary achievement" would seem quite ordinary as applied to a work of art of any quality. The better a poem or painting or ballet, the less it is possible to settle upon any single, definitive statement of its meaning. Great works of art seem to overflow with meaning and to support a variety of illuminating interpretations of their import—all legitimately grounded in the work, but none final or definitive. In aesthetics, this observation is a commonplace, almost a cliché. Yet it is evidently just here that Freud encounters that "blending and combination" that he finds "curious and incomprehensible." But if it is curious and incomprehensible, that is because he has *made* it so by assuming that the process *begins* with two or more "correctly formulated and expressed" thoughts repressed in the unconscious, which are then encoded together into a single hieroglyphic image.

But if there are no such well-formed latent thoughts hidden in the unconscious, then the difficulties dissipate, because then no such process of translation or allegorical coding, displacement, and condensation is required. What remains is the use of images, the metaphoric and metonymic allusions, the condensations and the overdetermination—and we can recognize all of these as functions that are characteristic of the *imagination*, that same imagination that is at work in the play of children, in fantasies, fairy tales, and myths, and in the creation of works of art. And indeed, Suzanne Langer has argued forcefully that in his account of the primary process, Freud really discovered and articulated the laws of the operation of human imagination. She noticed that Freud's principles of the dream work neatly matched the principles Owen Barfeld had shown were fundamental to poetic diction. The same principles could also be recognized in the fundamental forms of mythic thought, which Ernst Cassirer had analyzed in

The Philosophy of Symbolic Forms (1955). Langer showed that these are the principles at work in all nondiscursive forms of symbolism. That is, it is only in language and in logically constructed artificial languages, such as mathematics and computer languages, that the mind operates according to the discursive principles of "secondary process" thinking that Freud found to characterize waking consciousness and whose function is to serve the reality principle.

Meanwhile Arieti, Goldstein, and many others have called attention to the striking parallels between mythic thinking and the rather bizarre psychotic thought processes of schizophrenics. There are also interesting parallels to be noted between this "logic" (or illogic) of schizophrenic thinking and Piaget's account of the earlier, more concrete stages in the development of thought in early childhood, and this has suggested that schizophrenia might involve a kind of regression to infancy or early childhood. It might seem more apt to suggest that the schizophrenic has either lost or abandoned forms or levels of discursive thought that the young child has not yet acquired. It would *seem* so—except that mature adults in archaic, mythic cultures *also* seem to think in this way, even though their linguistic functioning is not impaired or distorted as is the schizophrenic's. That is, it would be wrong to see all these nondiscursive forms of thought as prelinguistic or as more childish or primitive or "primary" than discursive, linguistic thought, even though it may be true that *before* the child learns to speak, he or she *can* only think in this way, not having acquired the *means* to think discursively, which depends on learning a language. But that does not mean that linguistic, discursive thinking is superior in every respect and ought always to displace nondiscursive thought wherever possible, though of course we hardly wish to see the world in terms of primitive myths, nor to think as the psychotic thinks. But that need not be the alternative. Cassirer points out that although the forms of mythic thinking eventually yield to more strictly logical forms of thought in the course of history, those same principles reappear in a new and freer medium of expression— as lyric poetry (1946, ch. 6).

All of this further suggests that we are dealing here with the principles of imagination or "free fancy" or "free association," as Langer suggests. What they are free *of*, of course, is the limitations of dictionary definition and grammatical syntax that discipline our use of language—and of the more strictly logical principles that govern discursive reasoning. But that does not mean there are no discernible principles informing these processes of thought and symbolism. We have glanced briefly at Freud's principles of displacement, condensation, overdetermination, and visualization. The same principles are at work in myth and readily recognizable in magic practices. They include the *identification* of two similar things—as when the magician sticks pins in a doll or burns a drawing or photograph of a person in order to cause pain or the death of the person himself. Or again, magic may depend on the identification of the *whole* with one of its parts, as when the magician affects a person by doing something to his fingernail parings or a lock of his hair. Or the magician may get at the person through something associated *with* him—as in the notion that the devil or the sorcerer can come to own a person's soul by either buying or stealing his shadow—or even merely the *length* of his shadow. I will not further explore the resources of sympathetic magic. I hope this is enough to indicate how they illustrate the tropes, or figures of speech, of traditional poetics and rhetoric. I hope it will be obvious that the use of the voodoo doll is a case of metaphor, that the use of fingernails or hair is an example of synechdoche, and that the purchase of the shadow depends on metonymy. But this is also the stuff that dreams are made of—which brings me back from primitive religion to the religion of the unconscious.

For someone might well object at this point and remind me that psychoanalysts do not maintain that the *dream* is unconscious. The dream is a conscious experience, though I am not awake while dreaming. A Freudian or Jungian *might* even concede that the dreaming is a function of the imagination. What is unconscious is not the dreaming but the repressed latent thought or wish, of which the dream is the conscious but disguised translation. And that latent thought only comes to light through the analyst's interpretation.

But I submit that this is simply an instance of the intentional fallacy. It is like the critic projecting his interpretation of a painting into the mind of the artist, insisting that an imaginative, nondiscursive work of art must be the product of a discursively formulated intention. The notion that the dream is a *disguised* unconscious thought is comparable to reasoning that the painter must first formulate his purpose in a clearly formed proposition and *then* attempt to translate it into images by some such process of hieroglyphic coding as Freud describes in that account of the dream-work. There may be painters and composers who work that way. But even if there are, you will note that it leaves the real creative work of translating discursive purpose into artistic result to a process that Freud himself describes as "incomprehensible." So it is an assumption that has no *explanatory* force whatsoever. I believe that there is a much simpler and more satisfying way to understand all this without any appeal to "the unconscious." It is as follows:

The reason that the dreamer or the hysterically deaf or crippled patient or the schizophrenic or the simple neurotic resorts to dream images or to bizarre symptoms or symbolic behavior need not be that all this is a strategy to disguise an unconscious thought in order to smuggle it past the Freudian censor. The reason may simply be that the nondiscursive images and symbols are more adequate, immediate, and eloquent vehicles for expressing his experience of life—that the dream or symptom or schizophrenic symbolism is simply a creative expression of feelings and thoughts that their author has not otherwise been able to express—for any of several reasons. Let's look more closely at each of these claims.

First, the dream or symptom may simply be the most *effective* form of expression rather than a disguised discursive message. This is especially true where the experience or thought involves intense feelings. If we consider the resources that purely discursive language offers for expressing or communicating feelings, we find that they are remarkably scanty and imprecise. What can I say about my feelings? That I am sad, cheerful, anxious, angry, glad, depressed, wistful. . . . Very well, but the list would soon come to an end. Most of us have fewer words for emotions at our command than we do for colors—and the sum available in the English language is not very great. Italian might provide more, I suspect, but Italians would not make such liberal use of their hands if words were adequate. Well, when the names of feelings give out, I can go on to say, "I feel like. . . ." But as soon as I insert that "like" or "as if," I have left the realm of the literal and discursive for the poetic, the domain of metaphor and simile and metonymy and synechdoche. If I want a supple, subtle, finely articulated medium for the expression of emotion, then I must turn to poetry or music or painting or drama or dance—to the arts, which have always been recognized for their ability to "say" more than can be *literally* "said." Here again, Mrs. Langer showed in considerable detail in *Feeling and Form* that these nondiscursive forms of symbolism offer far richer, far more precise resources for formulating and representing the felt qualities of our experience of life than we can find in any language that stops short of poetry. And although we cannot *all* paint or sculpt or write eloquent poetry or dance adequately whenever the need arises to express or think through an intensely felt experience, we *can* all dream—or act out our feelings by slamming doors or sulking or making faces in the mirror—and thereby avail ourselves of the richer, more vivid and dramatic resources of the imagination. And although my dreams may not be works of art—and slammed doors and sulky behavior certainly are not—they may nevertheless communicate my moods and wishes far more exactly than anything I could possibly say by way of a literal description.

Second, I said that we turn to these resources of the imagination to express feelings that we could not otherwise express. By now, it will already be evident that *one* of the reasons we could not otherwise express the feelings is that discursive language as such is such an imprecise and skimpy instrument of expression that we cannot adequately say how we feel unless we resort to poetics—if only the poetics of obscenities and curses. But social circumstances may rule out the use of obscenities, and social proprieties often *prevent* me from expressing my feelings, at least for the moment. So although words may fail me at times, even when they do not, I may have to bite my tongue, shut my trap, swallow my resentment. Afterward, I am likely to kick my tires, drive too fast—or resort to fantasies in order to give shape to my frustrated emotions.

But it is not only the reactions and judgments of others that restrain me. I may be unwilling to say what I am feeling or wishing *even to myself*—at least not in so many words. I may experience feelings and desires that I do not wish to acknowledge, which I choose to disavow, or which I have simply never stopped to formulate reflectively by *saying* to myself: "I am angry—or anxious—or have incestuous desires . . . etc." Yet my frustrated emotions may still find expression in fantasy when I fall asleep and dream—or attain some other form of symbolic or symptomatic expression in my speech, my behavior, or in some physical disability or illness.[4]

But a desire or emotion that is not acknowledged or admitted to *in words* is not therefore *unconscious*. A feeling or mood is not normally an object of awareness at all. Nor is it an introspected subjective *datum* that exists "only in my mind" and has nothing to do with the world. Although not itself an object or *content* of awareness, a feeling or desire is a mode of experiencing objects and persons. It is the "howness" of my awareness of the world as contrasted with the *what* of which I am aware. And I may well be angrily or anxiously aware without ever having *said* so to myself. To *acknowledge* or *admit* how I am feeling is a further step in which I become reflectively aware of my feeling—feeling that was *already* a mode of consciousness, and that is therefore a conscious emotion or desire whether

I *name* it or not. And that conscious feeling may find vivid expression in dream or deed without my being able—or willing—to express it in words.

A psychiatrist may now *interpret* my deeds and dreams to me and convince me that they express or symbolize certain wishes and feelings. I've no quarrel with that—and I gladly concede that I may learn a great deal about myself in the process. But what was not *known* was not therefore *unconscious*. Most of the people and things and events I see are unknown to me, as are most of the scents I smell and sounds I hear. But they are not therefore *unconscious*. It is simply that I cannot *identify* or *name* them—and therefore do not *know* what or whom I am experiencing. The same holds for moods and desires and emotions. But it holds even more frequently in this domain of affects because our names for feelings *are* so inadequate and because feelings are not *objects* of consciousness but modes or ways of being conscious *of* other objects. So through the psychotherapist's interpretation I may acquire a knowledge of desires and fears and wishes that I did not previously acknowledge. But that does not mean that his analyses are penetrating the "disguises" of my dreams and deeds to ideas and wishes that were previously hidden away in some unconscious dungeon of my mind. To suppose that is, again, an example of the intentional fallacy.

And now I am in a position to state my thesis in a final form. My thesis is that the whole idea of an "unconscious" mind is simply the result of confounding consciousness with discursive, linguistic thought. And the consequence of that is that the *rest* of our thought—all the *non*discursive, *non*linguistic, imaginative forms of symbolism and thought that are so much more apt and necessary to full *self*-expression—were thereby placed in limbo and reduced to the status of symptoms of *another* discursive thinker working behind the scenes, or down in the dark dungeon of the unconscious. But that is simply to deprive the imagination of its due—and that is perhaps the most pernicious of all the effects of the Cartesian conception of consciousness—though the identification of thought with inner speech is far older than Descartes.

Of course, it is easy to recognize the assumption at the source of all this tyranny of the word, this imperialism of discursive reasoning. It is, after all, the same assumption that lies at the root of the conviction that there must be some divine providential plan behind the seemingly human and irrational events of history. The root of it all is the belief that, "In the beginning was the *Word*, and the Word was with God, and the *Word was* God."

I submit that this deification of the word is a mistake. It is the ultimate hermeneutic myth—yet another example of that intentional fallacy that transforms the *results of interpretation* into the *cause of creation*. If one must engage in creationist theology, I would prefer that other version that depicts God as *creating* first, and only commenting afterward—or even leaving it to Adam to invent the names for what was already created. And surely it is presumptuous for Adam—or the psychotherapist—to insist that *his* words existed in the mind of God—or the dreamer—even prior to the moment of creation.

It seems only consistent to add an afterword of my own.

After-Word

I have tried to pick a quarrel with one of the giants of modern science, the founding prophet of the religion of psychotherapy. But anyone who has struggled with Freud is aware that Freud always seems to keep a step ahead of his critics, that he has always thought of the criticism first himself. And so it is with my main thesis, that the whole idea of the unconscious mind is simply the corollary of identifying consciousness with discursive, linguistic thought. For that is the conclusion Freud reached at the end of his classic paper on "The Unconscious" of 1915. It is a conclusion to which he was driven, as I was, by reflection on schizophrenia. Freud writes:

What we could permissibly call the conscious idea of the object can now be split up into the idea of the word (verbal idea) and the idea of the thing (concrete idea). . . . It strikes us all at once that now we know what is the difference between a conscious and an unconscious idea. The two are not, as we supposed, different records of the same content situated in different parts of the mind, nor yet different functional states of cathexis in the same part; but the conscious idea comprises the concrete idea plus the verbal idea corresponding to it, whilst the unconscious idea is that of the thing alone. . . . Now too, we are in a position to state precisely what it is that repression denies to the rejected idea in the transference neuroses—namely, translation of the idea into words which are to remain attached to the object. The idea which is not put into words or the mental act which has not received hypercathexis then remains in the unconscious in a state of repression. (1915, 201–202)[5]

So Freud was here first. But if all this is true, then it is not Freud, but Woody who has the last word—or, far better because more expressive, the last laugh. For this would make nonsense of Freud's whole account of the dream-work as a process of translating well-formed latent thoughts from one language into another, from a discursive, linguistic unconscious into a hieroglyphic of images. Indeed, I think that *this* account of the unconscious, which agrees with my own, casts serious doubt upon Freud's actual *use* of that concept throughout most of his writings. But to show that would require another, very different inquiry.

Notes

1. For a particularly interesting recent discussion, cf. Hogensen 1983.

2. This is a composite quotation weaving together parallel passages from Yale French Studies, 5; and Auerbach 1953, 48–49 and 73–74.

3. In general, I prefer to use the Riviere translations, where available. For the same passage in the *Standard Edition*, see (1916–1917, 175–177).

4. Cf. Freud's comment in his "Notes upon a Case of Obsessional Neurosis" (1909, 223) that "the patients themselves do not know the wording of their own obsessional ideas." He goes on to comment, "This may sound paradoxical, but it is perfectly good sense. During the progress of psychoanalysis it is not only the patient who plucks up courage, but his disease as well; it grows bold enough to speak more plainly than before." By "more plainly" Freud obviously means "more discursively." But note also that in this context, he does not seem to insist upon an antecedent verbal "latent thought" in the unconscious.

5. Cf also "The Ego and the Id" (1923, 20), where Freud cites this account of the unconscious with approval at the threshold of his exposition of the "structural model."

References

Auerbach, E. "Typological symbolism in Medieval literature." In *Yale French Studies* 9: 3–10.

Auerbach, E. 1953. *Mimesis: The Representation of Reality in Western Literature*. Translated by W. Trask. Princeton: Princeton University Press.

Cassirer, E. 1946. *Language and Myth*. Translated by S. K. Langer. New York: Harper.

Cassirer, E. 1955. *Philosophy of Symbolic Forms: Mythical Thought*, vol. 2. Translated by R. Manheim. New Haven: Yale University Press.

Eliade, M. 1959. *Cosmos and History: The Myth of the Eternal Return*. Translated by W. Trask. New York: Harper and Brothers.

Freud, S. [1990] 1953. *The Interpretation of Dreams*. Translated by J. Strachey. *Standard Edition, IV*. London: The Hogarth Press.

Freud, S. [1909] 1955. Notes upon a case of obsessional neurosis. Translated by J. Strachey. *Standard Edition, X*. London: Hogarth Press, pp. 153–257.

Freud, S. [1915] 1957. The unconscious. Translated by J. Strachey. *Standard Edition, XIV*. London: Hogarth Press, pp. 159–216.

Freud, S. [1916–17] 1961. *Introductory Lectures on Psycho-Analysis.* Translated by J. Strachey. *Standard Edition, XV.* London: Hogarth Press.

Freud, S. [1923] 1961. *The Ego and the Id.* Translated by J. Strachey. *Standard Edition, XIX.* London: Hogarth Press, pp. 3–68.

Freud, S. 1960. *A General Introduction to Psychoanalysis.* Translated by J. Riviere. New York: Washington Square Press.

Hampshire, S. 1959. *Thought and Action.* London: Chatto and Windus.

Hillman, J. 1972. *The Myth of Analysis: Three Essays on Archetypal Psychology.* New York: Harper and Row.

Hogensen, G. 1983. *Jung's Struggle with Freud.* Notre Dame: University of Notre Dame Press.

Langer, S. 1953. *Feeling and Form.* New York: Scribners.

Plato. *Apology,* 22b–c. Translated by G. Grube in *The Trial and Death of Socrates.* Indianapolis: Hackett Publishing, p. 26.

Wimsatt, W. K., and M. Beardsley. 1949. The Affective Fallacy. In R. W. Stallman, ed., *Critiques and Essays in Criticism.* New York: Ronald Press.

III

Pathologic Imagination Applied to Creative and
Clinical Phenomena

A Phenomenological Psychological Approach to Research on Hallucinations

Amedeo Giorgi

Toward the end of her account of her lapse into mental illness, Barbara O'Brien, the author of *Operators and Things*, gives a brief description of one of her last encounters with her therapist after she had spontaneously recovered. She writes as follows:

"Did you read fantasy fiction?" Dr. Donner asked, "The Operators sound like characters created by a writer of fantasies."

My memories of the Operators were sharp as icicles but searching through the past of sanity was like picking up rocks, every effort devastating.

He tried again. "You exercised remarkable self-control, traveling around the country the way you did for 6 months—considering the condition you were in."

I stifled the impulse to tell him that his statement was absurd. I hadn't been in control. I had been controlled. I said, because I wondered if he had doubts about it, "I want you to understand that all the flukey-lukey has stopped I'm perfectly all right now except that my head was so dry and so empty."

"You've gotten rid of major symptoms You realize that you had schizophrenic hallucinations and that the Operators did not exist." (1958–1975, 14)

Well there you have it, even if a bit indirectly. Hallucinations are interpreted to be the fantasies of schizophrenics. Or, at least, they are the products of the imagination of persons diagnosed as schizophrenic or otherwise mentally ill. Or, perhaps, they are pathologies of the imagination. The last point raises an interesting question. Can the imaginative, that is allowed to be so wild and indeterminate, that is permitted to approach even formlessness and be surprisingly creative, be pathological? How would one know?

Perhaps that's why we're more comfortable in understanding hallucinations as pathological perceptions. Persons, during hallucinatory experience, see things that are not really there. Now, that's clear! However, this procedure is still, at best, a negative achievement. One sees what is not there. How is this possible and why is one so motivated? So let's turn the question around and ask about what the hallucinating person actually sees and how it is possible to have such givens! We notice that difficulties once again emerge. Are they seeing a real thing that is not there, or are they merely seeing a quasi-thing or a pseudothing?

I would like to suggest that the very effort of trying to determine whether hallucinations are pathological manifestations of the imagination or distorted perceptions is already indicative of objective thought, which thus operates on a level that will block a fully adequate understanding of the phenomenon of hallucinations. I prefer to follow Merleau-Ponty and relate hallucinations to the level of pre-objective thought.

It seems to me that Merleau-Ponty has the most comprehensive approach to the clarification of the hallucinatory experience that I have come across, and if this is true, then one would have to research hallucinations from the perspective of the pre-objective level. This would require breaking new ground in scientific methods and in our understanding of the psyche or psychological subjectivity. Traditional science is the child of objective approaches, and we have used these approaches on psychical phenomena rather extensively during the last century with only very limited success. I have made this argument many times before, so I won't repeat it here (Giorgi 1970, 1983). I think that both hallucinations and psychotic disorders are the type of difficult problem that will only yield to solutions springing from a radical change in perspective, assumptions, or approaches. Consequently, in this chapter, I will try to bring into harmony the characteristics of hallucinatory phenomena and the approach required to understand them.

Framework For Analysis of Hallucinatory Experiences of Schizophrenics

First I have to make clear that I am an academic research psychologist and not a clinician. I have never diagnosed pathological individuals nor have I ever tried to cure them. My interest in hallucinations is from the perspective of a researcher interested in all phenomena experienceable by humans—no matter how bizarre—in order to understand humans and their worlds better from a psychological perspective. Thus, for me, hallucinatory experiences are phenomena that have to be explored so that the potentialities and limits of the human psyche can be better understood.

One clear privilege that the above-delineated perspective gives me is the advantage of not having to worry about any actual human being who may be suffering hallucinations. Most clinical practitioners have immediate practical problems to cope with and real, live suffering individuals to heal. Thus the distance academicians have from immediate concerns may give them a certain advantage to entertain novel approaches.

Second, my perspective is phenomenological, and I mean this term in the stricter continental philosophical sense and not in its American usage. Moreover in my phenomenological approach I am inspired by and tend to follow Husserl and Merleau-Ponty rather than Heidegger and his followers. Thus I tend to be descriptive and eidetic in my approach rather than hermeneutic.

Third, as a psychologist, I wish to do purely psychological analyses rather than interdisciplinary ones. Of course, there is nothing wrong with interdisciplinary analyses, and they will certainly be necessary for any ultimate understanding of human beings and their worlds. (I mean by interdisciplinary studies specializations such as psychopharmacology, neuropsychology, and cognitive psychology.) My worry with such combinations, as a psychologist, is always with the potentialities of the psychological contributions. Too often what is considered to be psychological is simply the tail of the dog of the stronger science with which psychology is associated—pharmacology, neurology, and cognitive sciences. I am still worried that psychology has not yet found its proper niche within the family of sciences and has not yet developed its fullest potential as a original and unique science. I worry about it because I believe that it is possible to develop an original and irreducible psychology, but the field keeps being seduced by attractive developments in other disciplines. It used to be only the attraction of the natural sciences, but today literary theory and linguistics also seem to be strong seducers. Psychology's glory, to the extent that is has it, is a reflected glory. And while it is basking in this reflected light of the stronger sciences with which it is associated, the task it was designed to do remains undone. Thus a good part of my work has been designed to orient psychology toward what psychology alone can do.

I mention these three perspectives—academics, phenomenology, and psychology—because they help make sense of the approach I am taking in this chapter. I hope that they will help you understand why I am persistent in pursuing certain leads and not others and why certain emphases appear important to me to the neglect of others. To be sure, other options than those I chose could have been taken, but I want to make clear that a certain logic is being pursued despite the fact that non-logical phenomena are being investigated. However, the guiding logic has to do with the means, and not the content although the latter has its role.

Being phenomenological might carry certain advantages with it to the exploration of the pre-objective realm. Essentially, to be a phenomenological researcher, means to me the following: (1) follow descriptive criteria, (2) operate from within the phenomenological reduction, which means that at least initially not to entertain nonrelevant assumptions and to withhold the existential index from phenomena I am analyzing, and (3) seek the essential structures governing the phenomena, and once discovered, use those structures to account for a phenomenon more systematically as well as to comprehend empirical variations in the data.

Of these three criteria, it seems to me that respecting the guidelines of the reduction might be the most important in analyzing hallucinations. While it is understandable that professionals working within the realm of mental illness usually take a "realistic stance" as a point of departure, one can certainly challenge that perspective when it comes to trying to understand the phenomena experienced by those suffering mental illness. Almost everything about the phenomena of the mentally ill implies falsehood—hallucinations, delusions, illusions, false memories, and so on. That fact implies that their experiences are not "realistic," not in tune with that of most others, and indeed, that is why such persons are classified as pathological. Thus *A Psychiatry Glossary* (1980) describes hallucinations very typically as experiencing as present something that is not really there. It adds that it can happen within any sensory modality. A recent text on abnormal psychology states that a hallucination is a sensory experience without any stimulation from the environment (Davison and Neale [1974] 1994, 392). Thus priority is given to the real, and hallucination is understood in terms of it, as a deviation from it. The same happens when the hallucination is considered a symptom. A symptom is a concept used in a diagnostic framework, and it is understood as a manifestation of a deeper cause that has to be discovered so that the symptom can be removed. Again, causal analysis reflects a realistic framework. From the perspective of the everyday world this makes sense because it marks how pathological people stand out or announce themselves as different or difficult and thus invite the response of care on the part of dedicated professionals. It is a continuation of the perspective of common sense.

However, science often has to break with the attitude of common sense in order to understand the everyday world better than it understands itself. Examples are too numerous and too obvious from the earth being presumed as the center of the universe to the idea that humans may colonize the moon or other planets. In human affairs we are used to the break from common sense that science normally spontaneously provides, that enables us to explore beneath the level of self-awareness and find chemical, neural, or hormonal factors that unwittingly influence us. The discovery of Freudian unconscious is also the result of that strategy. I believe that with the phenomenological reduction, Husserl has given us another kind of break from common sense, but it is one with which we have as yet little experience in application—in part because scholars are still debating if it is even possible. However, I see potential in the use of the phenomenological reduction, especially in the bracketing of the existential index. One way to speak of findings within the framework of the reduction is to speak of presences rather than existences or realities. Its reality status is not necessarily the first thing one would want to know about hallucinations in order to understand them. The issue then becomes one of determining precisely what is given to the hallucinating person. This mode of questioning invites exploration rather than dismissal. The question of the hallucination's reality status is bracketed, and one can try to understand more fully what the nature of the content of the experience is and what function it is serving.

This leads us to the third point, the implications of adopting a psychological perspective. In order to bring about genuine psychological understanding, one has to probe the psychological world, and this presupposes that one knows how to discriminate such a world. The meaning of the psyche in a truly clarifying way is not yet an historical achievement, but that doesn't mean that efforts to advance its understanding should cease. Clearly, the psyche has to do with the structures of experiencing and behaving, but I want to emphasize that for me those terms include subjective dependency. That is, experience and behavior insofar as they are dependent on individuated subjective structures and meanings. These structures can obviously get repeated and become solidified so that they can also lend themselves to certain types of objective analyses, but psychological

analyses should look at them from the perspective of subjective dependence. Primarily this is done through analyses of meaning. Consequently
the key terms for psychological analyses from a phenomenological perspective are structures, presences, and meanings as they relate to the consciousness of an individual subject.

One last thing has to be added, although I hesitate because I could be
accused of taking a nonphenomenological step as this point may look like
an arbitrary assumption. I want to look at those peculiar presences that
appear in the consciousness of persons suffering hallucinations as positive
achievements on the part of such persons no matter how inadequate they
may be or how wrongly motivated they may appear. That is, the question
driving the analysis will be more like—What is the person trying to achieve
by turning to hallucinations? How is he or she trying to help him or herself? I will try to see them as positive contributions that prevent the individual from encountering a bigger problem. I state that this might be a
nonphenomenological step because my experience with hallucinating psychotics is too limited for me to be sure of this step to claim that it is essential. I know that it is certainly true in some cases, I'm just not sure that all
cases and modalities of mental illness would be included. There might be a
better way to phrase this occasional empirical given in a phenomenological
way.

Merleau-Ponty's Perspective on Hallucinations

As I have already implied, if hallucinatory phenomena are going to be
understood, it will have to be from a framework other than that which
produced objective science. But I want to make clear that it is precisely
in the name of science that the shift in framework will have to take
place. The shift is required if we are to obtain results regarding research in
hallucinations as reliable as those of objective science. Merleau-Ponty
([1945] 1962, 334–45) has provided a rigorous analysis of hallucinations
without compromising their essential character. Of course, his analysis
does not provide an answer to every question concerning hallucinations,
nor was that his intention. Rather what Merleau-Ponty provides is a fundamental understanding that establishes the basis for further work with
hallucinations. His understanding can be described in terms of the following
five points.

1.   Hallucinatory Phenomena Are Not to Be Analyzed in Terms of Objective Criteria

From an empirical perspective, Merleau-Ponty ([1945] 1962) points out that the hallucination is not a real thing inserted in a chain of causal events. Hallucinations are not strong enough to function as real links. But Merleau-Ponty shows that the idealistic or intellectualistic opposite isn't correct either, because neither is a hallucination a false judgment belonging to a mode of consciousness that conceives of itself as a transparent and completed totality. Both of these views belong to the level of objective thought. Hallucinatory presence, on the other hand, is not robust enough to be real, nor is the sense involved in it clear and distinct.

To understand how a conscious person can accept a certain quasi-presence as real, Merleau-Ponty ([1945] 1962, 334) points out that the real world itself has to recede as well. This recession of the real world in order to give precedence to the hallucinatory world is indeed a kind of reduction, as Naudin and Azorin (1997) have argued. And if the hallucinatory experience can be seen as a type of phenomenological reduction, it is because it places one squarely in a phenomenal world regulated by rules similar to those that regulate dreams, fantasies, reveries, and so on. When Merleau-Ponty says that hallucinatory phenomena are pre-objective, he means to say that patterns other than those that rule the objective world are in play. He also implies a developmental perspective, since this realm refers as well to what is not yet objective. Thus it could be that those experiencing hallucinations are motivated to stop short of a full objective presence to reality or to develop in a style other than that which will lead to a fully objective given. This may be a misguided motive, but then the phenomenal realm is not guided by rationality. In any case, hallucinatory experience takes place in the pre-objective phenomenal world that has all of the characteristics that phenomenologists have assigned to it. Incidentally, following the strict correlation between act and object that is utilized in phenomenological analyses, one would also have to say that if the noema is not fully developed, then on the noetic side one has consciousness in a pre-actual mode. Its animating activity is weaker than normal, and it does not actualize all the phases required to constitute objectivity. Basically, the hallucinated presence never arrives at the fully articulated real thing or clear idea, and that is what objective modes of thought were developed to deal with. The proper approach to hallucination has to deal with phenomena less objectivated than that. However, lack of full development may not be the only factor. During hallucinatory experience persons may be strongly motivated to accomplish other than objective achievements.

2.   Possibility of Self-Deception

If the experience of hallucination is such that the experience of the real recedes while a quasi-real or pseudoreal takes its place, how is it possible to substitute one for the other? Merleau-Ponty says that this is, in principle, possible if we understand consciousness as developmental in such a way that it includes processes that are lived through without awareness. This idea is no longer difficult for us living in post-Freudian times, but it goes against the old firmly rooted philosophical doctrine that stated that "the existence of consciousness was equal to the consciousness of existing." If one stayed with the old formula, then consciousness would have to be aware of when it was deceiving itself, and hence the task would become problematic. However, both Husserl and Merleau-Ponty allow for the fact that reflective consciousness is not concomitantly aware of all of its prereflective goings on. This would be especially true if there are pre-actual states of affairs leading to that type of presence one would call a pseudo-object While it is difficult to articulate more fully at the moment, the perspective being developed here would call for the understanding of hallucination as a product of the process of experientially living through rather than caused. In other words, the hallucination is a consequence of the dynamics of conscious acts and not the physical stimulus nor physiological, neurological, or even chemical realities.

3.   The Hallucinated Presence Itself

Merleau-Ponty (1945/1962, 339) makes clear that the presences that persons experiencing hallucinations take to be real belong more on the margins of the world than in its center. He describes these presences in many different ways but with stylistic consistency: they belong to a quasi- or pseudoworld, they are thin in duration and in space, they lack the articulateness of the world that the real carries, they are short-lived, they are inarticulate phenomena that lack the relations of true causality, and so on. He (p. 334) also presents a mountain of evidence showing that hallucinators, most of the time, can discriminate between their hallucinations, and their perceptions and the intrinsic quality of hallucinatory presences is one reason why. Indeed, Merleau-Ponty uses an interesting expression to account for this quality. He writes that the presence given in an hallucination is "much less the presentation of an illusory object than the spread and, so to speak, running wild of a visual power which has lost any sensory counterparts" (p. 340). That is, hallucinatory presences are "things" only with respect to "physiognomy and style" (p. 341) that the person can generate without help from the world. What is lacking is precisely sustained contributions from the world. There is no true sensoriness in hallucination, only whatever simulacrum an embodied consciousness can generate. Because this is such a primordial level of subject-world relation, Merleau-Ponty speaks of the hallucinator as one who "exploit(s) this tolerance on the part of the ante-predicative world ..." (p. 343). That is, the hallucinator draws upon that intimate presence to the world that we all have prior to the explicit elaborations of subjectivity that constitute linguistic expressions or perceptual objects except that the process and outcome are different. Because the openness to the world is motivatedly more narrow on the part of the hallucinator, the outcomes are more like the visualizations of after-images or dreams.

4. Role of the Body

One of the reasons that the process of consciousness living through its prereflective modalities is so obscure is that the body is involved. For Merleau-Ponty, it is the body as a subject that is required to summon the presence of the pseudoworld that hallucinators experience. He (pp. 339–40) writes: "Depersonalization and disturbance of the body image are immediately translated into an external phantasm, because it is one and the same thing for us to perceive our body and to perceive our situation in a certain physical and human setting...." Indeed, Merleau-Ponty (p. 340) continues:

Hallucination does not present me with protuberances, or scales, or words like ponderous realities gradually revealing their meaning. It does no more than reproduce for me the way in which these realities strike me in my sensible being and in my linguistic being.[1]

A person's sensible and linguistic being intrinsically involves the phenomenal body. Moreover the last citation leads to an important point. Since in hallucinations the outcome is not so much dependent on how the world is, but on the subjectivity of the experiencer, the completion of the presence—to the extent that it is completed—is almost entirely due to subjectivity. The subject is completing presences according to his or her own motives rather than according to the world's demands. In other words, prior to the animation by intentional acts, the body is the carrier of hyletic data (Husserl [1913] 1931, 226f), namely sensory contents requiring noetic acts to form them. However, the intentional acts of an hallucinator are not so much motivated to present the in-depth articulate objects of the world as presences that are almost entirely dependent on the disturbed state of their subjectivity. As in dreams and reveries these presences may take symbolic forms for reasons still to be understood.

5. Meanings

I stated earlier that the psychology I espouse would seek the analysis of meanings in order to uncover the workings of the psyche. The hallucinations provoked during psychotic episodes can also be analyzed in this way even if these meanings have a different quality. For Merleau-Ponty, the meanings produced in hallucinations are ambiguous, but an understanding of their ambiguity can lead to an understanding of the world of the psychotic. It was mentioned that hallucinatory presences were due to a primordial level of activity on the part on an embodied subjectivity. Because the level of subjectivity that is engaged here is so primordial and because it is relatively incomplete, one ends up with an implicit and inarticulate significance. The task here is not to push this inarticulateness to a level of clarity and explicitness it does not contain, but to understand it as it presents itself, that is, to understand precisely why ambiguity is chosen. Because of the antepredicative level of activity, presences turn out to be more implicit and presumptuous than is ordinarily the case. In Merleau-Ponty's view, all perception is a matter of resolving practically what is essentially an infinite task. In principle, one could continue infinitely with the task of completing and rendering explicit the perceptual object. For most of us, the halting reflects a level of openness to the world that is sufficient for us to negotiate it adequately most of the time. But what if what comes from outside is disagreeable or painful? Then our openness to it might be curtailed or foreshortened, and the presence at which we cease our infinite task will reflect the subject's motivations much more than input from the world. In other words, the presences given to hallucinators are embedded with meanings determined primarily by the animating conscious acts of the hallucinating subjects than the regularities or typicalities of the objective world.

This is where the project I described in the first part of this chapter comes together with hallucinatory phenomena. I began by saying that a phenomenological psychology worthy of its name should be able to give clarifying detailed analyses of lived meanings. Indeed, earlier I argued that a strong component of the authentic meaning of phenomenological psychology was the study of "the noema constituted by subject-dependent acts precisely as they are phenomenally given to the experiencer" (see Giorgi 1986, 63). In these hallucinatory presences, the constitution is almost entirely completed by the experiencing subject. The openness to the objective world as it exists is not taken up by these subjects. The reason for this lack of participation in openness, however, may be discovered by clarifying the meanings that are actually embedded in subjects' hallucinatory givens.

I also mentioned earlier that one has to try to understand the hallucinations experienced by disturbed persons as a type of positive effort on their part. Why would anyone prefer quasi-presences over reality, unless the latter were too horrible to confront? And why would a quasi-reality be appealing to such persons, unless it somehow softened the harshness of the real. In that softness, or any other quasi-quality, one begins to understand the motivation for the disturbed person's world and the understanding of that world can provide clues for how to move out of it. All that is implied in the above is that contemporary research psychologists take up an attitude toward hallucinations that Freud showed with respect to dreams. Recall how dreams were not taken seriously during Freud's era. They were considered to be merely excesses of nervous activity, but Freud insisted that dreams were meaningful and that the meanings were important for understanding the psychical life of the individual. I think that the same is true of hallucinations. Especially within the framework of the phenomenological reduction we ought to take hallucinations as expressions of the psychical life of individuals, not simply as erroneous processes or merely as diagnostic symptoms, but as indicators of motives for choosing an alternative quasi-reality. Of course, medications that eliminate hallucinations are sometimes necessary, but such procedures ought not to be a strategy of cure. If we take them precisely as they present themselves to the hallucinator and truly understand their meaning and dynamics, we can help eliminate hallucinations by meaning transformation instead.

By way of summary, then, Merleau-Ponty's position on hallucinations is that they belong to the phenomenal order because they are pre-objective (or para-objective) presences constituted by embodied subjects that are rich with meanings that need to be deciphered. The presences associated with hallucinators belong to a type of conscious constitution that produces quasi-realities such as dreams, reveries, and other imaginary givens. Their "quasi-character" may be due to the fact that the hallucinators interrupt the process of being present to a real, articulate perception because it leads to painful realities, or it could be due to peculiar animating motivations that contribute to the illness. One implication of these dynamics is that the hallucinatory presences have to be taken as they are given and seen as positive indicators of what is troubling the subjects. If correctly deciphered phenomenologically and psychologically, the hallucinatory presences can tell us a lot about the dynamics disturbing the individuals. For example, it has been observed that the hallucinations of psychotics are not the first symptoms of the illness, but rather their responses to the first symptom, which is withdrawal from the world[2] (Bleuler [1911] 1950). The hallucination might then be interpreted as trying to reconnect to the world, but this time on the subject's terms. That is, the hallucinating subject tries to make the world more comforting, or else, it tries to hear or see characteristics about the world in a distanced way so that his or her responsibility for these qualities is not direct.

An Example from Barbara O'Brien

Since I am neither a therapist nor a clinician I do not have data of my own to present, nor was I able to get the descriptive data I had planned to analyze. Consequently I will use descriptive material from Barbara O'Brien ([1958] 1975), who experienced a psychotic episode and had spontaneous remission about six months later. After she recovered, she wrote up and published a lengthy account of her experiences during the episode.

I believe that one would need to obtain a great amount of biographical data in order to get a precise sense of its psychological meaning, and obviously I cannot present all of that here. In addition there is space only for a limited sense of the meanings expressed, so this example only shows the beginnings of how one might begin to understand the psychological meanings contained in hallucinations.

The hallucinations that O'Brien experienced were both visual and auditory. They started suddenly, as O'Brien reports it, as follows: "When I awoke they were standing at the feet of my bed looking like soft fuzzy ghosts. I tried feeling the bedclothes. The sensation of feeling was sharp. I was awake and this was real" (p. 31). This was O'Brien's first encounter with images whom she called "Operators." Operators revealed themselves to her as human beings with a type of head formation that permits him or her to explore and influence the mentality of others. During her psychotic episode O'Brien was controlled by these operators, and there were quite a number of them, each of whom had special talents and distinct voices. After describing several operators, O'Brien is able to thematize Hinton, the one figure that was always troublesome for her. He was there the morning her psychotic episode started, and she described Hinton as follows:

The third was a real weirdo with hair three inches too long, black, straight, and limp, and with a body that was also long and limp. The face didn't belong with the body or the hair: the features were fine and sensitive, the expression arrogant and unbending.

The elderly man (another operator present the first morning) suddenly cleared his throat. "It is necessary for the good of all concerned that you get to know Hinton better." He turned and looked at the weirdo.

I was positive that I had never seen that face before. The elderly man apparently sensed my thoughts. "You know him well," he said; "you used to know him better."

Later in the book O'Brien gives a more detailed description of Hinton. She writes:

But only with Hinton had I been uneasy, uncomfortable. Certainly, Hinton's appearance would never have inspired a relaxed feeling in anyone. His cavernous face and lean body seemed to be less, rather than more, human. His too long black hair screamed defiance of a social order that accepted barbers as a cornerstone. The stillness of his body and the quiet brooding of his face might just as easily, I should think, have brought a measure of relief to a six month situation in which a half dozen gray wraiths usually were moving busily over the scene and a half dozen voices talking, talking, talking. But there had been no relief in Hinton. He had been around almost all the time but always quietly around, standing in far corners of rooms looking at me out of the corners of his eyes, or sprawled with such relaxation that he seemed broken, in the most comfortable chair. While the other Operators chattered with me, the silent, brooding Hinton observed me. If I occasionally took time to study an Operator, I rarely had the impression that any of them was taking time out to study me. But Hinton was always studying me. It was no great shock to find at the end, when other Operators had disappeared, that Hinton was still on the scene. He had the persistence of the silent. (p. 145)

The description above of Hinton, perhaps not surprisingly, can be applied to aspects of O'Brien herself. In the autobiographical parts of her book O'Brien recalled that she was an odd child and that she stood out in school in math and English for her oddities. She got correct answers, but always in a bizarre way. She summarizes her childhood by saying:

I was, like all children, no conformist. And like most people, I grew up to be the model of conformist adult. The only difference I can see between myself and most people is that in the process of maturing I learned to live separately in different departments. I became, in my early teens, a departmentalized child.... I was an ordinary enough child but I had some oddities. Because I was also a gregarious, adaptable child, eager to become an accepted part of my community, the oddities learned early to manifest themselves in safe places. (p. 148)

Now, if we remember that Merleau-Ponty said that hallucinations are consistent with things in the world, and the world itself, with respect to style and physiognomy, one can see that Hinton very much depicts that compartment of O'Brien's life where her oddities dwelled. First of all, the very fact that several different operators emerged during her illness reflects the compartmentalization of her life. Second, the fact that at the very beginning of her illness Hinton was the one assigned to lead her out of her insanity meant that he represented the aspect of her life that it was most necessary for her to integrate. She wrote that his appearance screamed defiance of the social order, and perhaps that was what she wanted to do but lacked the courage. His body was still and brooding, just as her "odd spirit" was stilled, and she said that no relief was associated with Hinton, just as the "oddities" locked in her compartment were not getting relieved. Of all the operators, she said that Hinton was the most persistent, because his needs were never met.

What I want to indicate here is that a full description of the hallucinatory world is a description of the difficulties of the individual in the psychotic experience. Of course, the psychological meaning is not all handed over to us on a silver platter complete and entire as the above would indicate. That is only a beginning and it lacks depth. But just as with many other presentification modes, interpretation is required as one goes into depth. These are incomplete, symbolic, syncretic, and ambiguous meanings. But the very fact that they have to come back to the individual via quasi-presences indicates a certain distancing or withdrawal of the individual from him or herself and from the world. The "quasi-character" of the subsequent presences could reflect a way of confronting the experienced problems in a less painful way, and that would be the meaning of the distortion.

The account above is a far cry from the solution to the problem of hallucinations and psychoses. However, I was not so much trying to come up with the solution as an approach that would be psychologically fruitful and that could perhaps lead to some gains. A phenomenological psychology that would concentrate on the meanings constituted by the consciousness of such individuals is one way of comprehending the illness. There is a spectrum of presentifying modes of consciousness—namely those modes that create presences without reference to the physical setting—such as imagination, hallucination, delusion, projections, and dreams. Each of these require the phenomenological reduction to be performed. Naudin and Azorin (1997) have made the case for hallucinatory experience, but I think that all presentifying modes require the performance of the reduction. When dreaming, for example, we are rarely present to our bed and bedroom. Sleeping consciousness simply makes the withdrawal easier. When projection is lived through, how could it be possible unless the actual setting receded to make room for the projections? Thus consciousness is doing quite a bit of work in these modalities, yet is rarely probed in a full and systematic way. It is argued here that an analysis of the meanings of the experiences of psychotic individuals will make significant revelations about the conditions of their existence.

Notes

1. Translation of last sentence modified by author.

2. I would like to thank Stephen Rojcewicz for this information and reference.

References

Bleuler, E. [1911] 1950. *Dementia Praecox or the Group of Schizophrenias*. Translated by J. Zinlain. New York: International University Press.

Davison, G. C., and J. M. Neater. [1974] 1994. *Abnormal Psychology*. New York: Wiley.

Giorgi, A. 1970. *Psychology as a Human Science*. New York: Harper and Row.

Giorgi, A. 1983. The importance of the phenomenological attitude for access to the psychological realm. In A. Giorgi, A. Barton, and C. Maes, eds., *Duquesne Studies in Phenomenological Psychology*, vol. 4. Pittsburgh: Duquesne University Press, pp. 209–21.

Giorgi, A. 1986. The meaning of psychology from a scientific phenomenological perspective. *Études Phenomenologique* 2: 47–73.

Husserl, E. [1913] 1931. *Ideas*. Translated by W. R. B. Gibson. New York: Collier.

Naudin, J., and J. Azorin. 1997. The hallucinatory epoché. *Journal of Phenomenological Psychology* 28: 171–95.

O'Brien, B. [1958] 1975. *Operators and Things: The Inner Life of a Schizophrenic*. South Brunswick and New York: Barnes.

Subcommittee of Joint Commision on Public Affairs of American Psychiatric Association. 1980. *A Psychiatric Glossary*, 5th ed. Boston: Little, Brown.

12

Narrative in Play: The Structure of the Imagination in Psychotherapy with Young Children

Robert S. Kruger

Brian Vandenberg reminds us that, "the close association of play and myth suggests that play therapy can also be conceived as a process of providing children with new myths that more directly and successfully address the sources of fear and dread in their lives and offer new hope ..." (1986, 86). In this chapter I explore some of the ways in which young children's play and the imaginative directions it takes can be usefully thought of as narratives. By employing the conceptual structures of "narrative" and "story," the child's psychotherapist can wield a tool to diminish anxiety, depression, and their symptoms in the lives of young children.

Young children imagine and play as naturally as they breathe, suckle, walk, and talk. Indeed, the ability to imagine and to play in certain ways, along with the ability to use language, could be said to be key features that distinguish human beings from other species. As the imagining and playing of young children takes a distinctive, normative shape, so does its deformation when a child is psychologically troubled or aberrant. To understand the structure and significance of these deformations, it is important to explore two somewhat unrelated fields: the natural history of childhood and some terms of literary criticism.

All normally developing human beings learn to speak. Young children (under the age of seven) quickly learn that effective communication with other human beings depends not simply on the utterance of single words but on combining words into a variety of verbal structures. Moreover, as children grow, they find that they are increasingly able to create more and more complex combinations of words from their burgeoning vocabularies. Indeed, parents quickly note that children delight in combining words in a variety of ways that are not always meaningful. Such play with words is characteristic of the developing child (Garvey 1984). Narrative construction is a natural outgrowth of an intersecting group of the evolving abilities in the young child: talking, imagining, and symbolizing.

Narratives are linguistic structures that depend for their creation on the verbal actions of selecting and combining. As Jakobson and Halle (1956, following Saussure) remind us, the actions of selecting items from a range and combining the chosen items in a certain order rest on complementary principles. Brian Wicker elaborates that a selection always implies the possible substitution of a different but similar item in place of the item chosen, without disturbing the functional arrangement, or "context" as a whole (1975, 13–14). By contrast, "the active combination always sets up a functional arrangement or structure such that this arrangement could take a number of different forms without affecting the actual choice of the items included in it" (p. 14). In Jakobson and Halle's terminology, contiguity defines the relation of each item to the items next to it in the "context." Saussure drew attention to the opposition of syntagmatic/paradigmatic. A syntagmatic structure is Jakobson and Halle's combination. A paradigmatic structure is a more formal arrangement reflecting certain rules. Again, reverting to Saussure, this opposition reflects the distinction between language and speech. As Wicker notes, "the 'language' is the treasury of items, or paradigms, from which the user selects, and 'speech' is the act of linking them into a significant chain or syntagm" (Ibid.).

Clearly, in looking at children's narratives in play, we are concerned with syntagmatic relationships. A triad of such relationships governs the work of the child psychotherapist both as diagnostician and clinician who attempts to promote psychological healing. This triad is metaphor, metonymy, and analogy. As we know, a metaphor is a verbal description of a similarity between two apparently dissimilar features or objects. By contrast, metonymy is the use of a part, attribute, or symbolic object for a whole or for the thing signified. Following Wicker, an analogy is a comparison more like a metonymy than a metaphor. However, it clearly implies causal relationships. "For analogical language is concerned with a system of reliable signs" (Ibid., 16). In this sense, analogy is more like metonymy than metaphor. It is in this very fundamental sense that children's play in its construction of narratives reflects analogical structures that link the central themes in the child's emotional life to the central schemas developed in the child's play. How is one to discern these analogies?

As a child's psychotherapist, one must begin with certain fundamental assumptions. Perhaps the most fundamental of these is that the way in which the child plays, and the ensuing narratives the child creates, reflect a perspective that defines what is of significance to the child at that moment. A second, corollary assumption is that a child's pretend play unfolds fictions that have both recursive and creative dimensions.

What is a fiction? Clearly, it is simply a story that tells something that either has not happened or has happened in some way other than the way it is depicted in the fiction. Accordingly, fictions can include myths, legends, fairy tales, novels, and even some biographies and autobiographies (Ibid., 33). Unlike adult stories, however, the child's play-fictions do not usually have a well-developed organization and structure. Frequently the narrative, if it is spoken, is fragmented and contingent with each action-element being determined seemingly on the spur of the moment. Nonetheless, to a skilled observer, there is frequently a recursive underlying structure that can be thematized. A primary diagnostic task of the child therapist is to discern and describe these themes. Much like dreams and fairy tales, pretend play is a pastiche of stories extracted from the ongoing stream of activity in which the child engages in the playroom. Arietta Slade describes the preliminary activity of the therapist in extracting narrative themes from the child's play:

One of the first things that a therapist intuitively does when confronted with play that is disorganized, fragmented, and incomprehensible, is to label characters, objects, or states in play. This may mean naming the objects or toys a child has chosen or asking the child to name them. Thus, when Jimmy grabbed all the duck puppets and began opening and closing their beaks vigorously, I noted that he'd found the ducks, that they were opening and closing their mouths, and that there was a lot of excitement. (Slade 1994, 92)

As Slade goes on the point out, children and the therapist will some-times work collaboratively to develop the narrative.

The goal in labeling is to try to establish who's who, what's what, and what the spirit (excitement, aggression, etc.) of the scene is. In essence the therapist is letting the child know that there is a stage and that he or she is, in effect, setting it. For children who have rarely had a sense of effectance or control, this itself is a dramatic and powerful intervention. (Ibid.)

Thus the psychotherapist often takes the role of collaborator and cocreator with the child in creating a fiction that gives words to the themes the child is enacting in play. Note that the therapist does not create the narrative or define the fiction. Rather, he or she takes the sequence of actions displayed by the child in the child's make-believe and attempts to give some coherent description to it. Nonetheless, for the psychotherapist familiar with the child's life, the child's demeanor, and the concerns of the child's parents, the metonymic and analogic structure thematized in the child's play will not be lost. The themes are metonymic because the psychotherapist assumes that some dimension, emotion, or sequence of actions in the child's play literally stands for some perception or emotional interpretation by the child of the world beyond the therapist's office. One assumes that the child's play has an analogical meaning structure in so far as the narrative that it depicts reflects the type of causality to which the child him- or herself experiences at work in his or her life. Sometimes the metonymy or analogy reflects a desire or wished-for outcome that the child knows to be impossible (and therefore magical or fictional). Thus the child enacts a narrative that reflects both an actual perspective on causality and a wished-for alteration in a perspective.

For example, a young child whom I was treating had a sibling who was dying of cancer. My patient did not clearly know that his sibling was chronically ill and was constantly being taken to the hospital by his parents. He duly but silently noted that his sibling, in the hospital, was subjected to a variety of apparently painful procedures and was growing weaker and more ill by the day. My patient was a youngster unaccustomed to pretend play. He generally wanted to play games or engage in some other activity (e.g., tossing a ball) that tended to allow him to inhibit the expression of his emotion and to avoid taking a particular point of view. On one occasion, however, he expressed an interest in playing with some toy figures that were clearly doctors, nurses, and the accompanying props including an operating table and instruments. In his play he developed a narrative in which a young child was in an automobile accident and was kidnapped, being taken to the hospital by "bad" doctors. This was played out repeatedly. However, the child was "saved" by a superhero (enacted with great vigor by my patient) who came in a large fire truck with sirens screaming and destroyed the hospital, killing the doctors in the process. The anger reflected by the superhero (and, coincidentally, my patient) was palpable. Clearly, his understanding of what had been happening to his sibling was encapsulated in the perspective that the sibling had been taken to the hospital unwillingly and that the bad doctors were harming the sibling. My patient's wish was clearly to free his sibling from this fate and to destroy the doctors in the bargain. I should note that this particular story was played out enthusiastically and in extended form by a youngster who, heretofore, had rarely engaged in very much dramatic play. The moral of this narrative was clear: my patient wished to be a powerful, mythical hero who, in his fairy tale narrative, could free his sibling from the illness that was so destructive and from the evil doctor-demons who were working their wicked black magic.

Had I, as a psychotherapist, been unaware of the accompanying life context of my patient, I would only have seen an elaborate fictional narrative that reflected some evil powerful adult figures who harmed children and this child's anger about that. My hermeneutic efforts would have laid bare the recursive theme of my patient's story (as he played this out on several occasions over several psychotherapeutic sessions). However, the full context and significance of the story was only clear to me in my role as natural historian. Through gathering details about this child's life from his concerned parents, I was attuned for expressions of what I would expect to be normal emotions in those circumstances: anger, grief, frustration, anxiety. For the most part, the expression of these feelings was markedly missing, and when questioned, my patient generally denied them. Nonetheless, from time to time in his dramatic play, he reflected a different point of view. This example illustrates the necessity for the psychotherapist to understand both the wider context of a child's life (and therefore not to treat the child in isolation from his/her familial context). However, it also illustrates the necessity to be attuned to the analogic and metonymic narratives that may reflect the child's immediate concerns.

I wish to address two further aspects of narrative creation by young children that the child psychotherapist often puts to good use. These are the use of replicas in pretend play and perspective-shifting that the utilization of these replicas requires. Both replica use and perspective-taking follow a developmental course and evolve in stages as the child's understanding of social action, causality, and moral responsibility evolve.

All developmentally normal children engage in metonymic transformation from the beginning of their imaginative play activity. Thus a broom can be a horse, a block can be a dinner, a stick wrapped in a blanket or a leaf can be an infant. Wolf and colleagues have described these five stages of the symbolization of human action in replica play (Wolf, Rygh, and Altschuler 1984, 195). In the most fundamental, primitive stage, the child treats the figure as if it were a representation of a human being, "talking to it, feeding it, placing it in chairs or swings. However, the figure remains the passive recipient of the child's actions; the child makes no attempt to make the figure act as an independent agent" (Ibid., 203). At the next stage the child describes the figure as an independent agent and ascribes speech and action to it, but there is no evidence that the child attributes any internal, especially emotional, states to the figure. Subsequently the child ascribes sensations, and perceptions, and physiological states to the figures progressing through a stage in which this child ascribes emotions, obligations, simple moral judgments, and elective social relations to the figure. In the most sophisticated stage of imaginative development, the child ascribes cognitions like thinking, planning, wondering, and knowing to the figure, thereby making it appear to be an independent actor who is able to portray dramatically the child's imaginary narratives (Ibid.). Moreover it is at this most complex stage of imaginative development that the child is able to depict an imaginary figure who can take a perspective other than his or her own. Accordingly, to achieve this stage of development and the imaginary play that accompanies it, the child must intuitively develop a "theory of mind" that includes the conception of human agents who can act, think, and assume moral responsibility.

Wolf and colleagues' research clearly indicates that, between the ages of one and five years, "children begin to represent to aspects of human behavior. First in action and then through representational behaviors, children begin to apprehend themselves and others as independent agents. In a parallel fashion, children recognize that, beyond performing actions, human actors also undergo internal experiences" (Ibid., 205). It is just such representation and the cognitive and emotional development that accompanies it which form the basis for what, as adults, we think of as empathy. Not surprisingly, children who have difficulty in engaging in pretend play with replicas and in developing the types of narratives common to such play often have difficulty in understanding other human beings as feeling, thinking agents like themselves. Autistic children are well known to lack the type of theory of mind that evolves concurrent with such play. It is not clear whether teaching autistic children explicitly to develop narratives that are analogic fictions depicting different types of emotional experience and reciprocal social action would assist them in developing a greater degree of empathy and understanding of the emotions of others. It is clear that young children are quite attuned to the emotional states and concerns of others, especially their caretakers. Their pretend play, through the use of replicas, may often reflect their perception of another's point of view. This is especially true of their narratives about attachment figures.

For example, a young girl whom I once treated was from a foreign country. Her father traveled frequently on business with the result that her mother was frequently left alone in a strange country with two young children. This child frequently played out narratives in her psychotherapy sessions that could best be characterized as reflecting themes of anxiety on separation. However, I noted that in her narratives, two structural components stood out: the figures leaving (and therefore abandoning) the families were not mothers but fathers and the figures who were left, or abandoned, were never children but mothers. After my patient had played out this type of narrative several times, I simply commented that the mother must be very sad when the father leaves. My patient enthusiastically agreed that she was. More as a matter of curiosity than a suggestion, I asked, "Do you think the mother will tell the father how she feels and ask him to stay?" This question received little comment from my patient and so I persisted (as therapists are wont to do), "Perhaps the mother will say, 'Please don't go.'" To this, my patient abruptly responded and said, with great intensity, "Oh no! She doesn't want the man to know." Initially I was puzzled by this response and went on to question my patient about why the mother wouldn't want the father to know how she felt. It became quite clear that, in my patient's understanding of her mother's perspective, her mother was quite sad every time her husband left on business but did not want to burden him with her feelings, and so, quite simply, kept them to herself. As an adult treating a child, I initially assumed that this was the child's understanding of her father's leave-taking and that perhaps she herself was saddened by his absence. Through subsequent play and conversation it became very clear that, while she missed her father, she was not bereft when he went away on business. Since it is my practice to speak periodically to parents when I am treating a child (in this case, for anxiety and social inhibition), I subsequently mentioned to the child's mother during one of the sessions that her daughter seemed to have the idea that she, the mother, was extremely distressed by her husband's departure when he went away on business but that she hadn't disclosed to her husband the intensity and depth of her feelings. At this, the mother looked, in rapid succession, surprised and sad. She acknowledged that the child's depiction of her experience of her husband's frequent separations was accurate and that, indeed, she had been reluctant to tell him about it because he was burdened with many other responsibilities. It became quite clear that the child's anxiety, particularly around separation, closely mirrored the mother's anxiety at separation from her husband. In this instance the child was able to depict accurately in a relatively elaborate narrative the emotional perspective of someone to whom she was quite close. The analogical structure of her play clearly reflected the cause–effect sequence which she observed in her mother's and father's interaction when her father departed on one of his frequent trips. No doubt, she had also closely observed her mother's state following her father's departure and drew her own conclusions. Since her mother's sadness and anxiety was clearly of concern to the child, the recursive theme of being abandoned but concealing the fear about it found its way into the child's repeated metonymic narratives.

In sum, we see that the child's play can be conceptualized as a series of fictional narratives of greater or lesser length. These narratives are composed of contiguous fragments selected from the child's store of developing verbal symbols. They are combined syntagmatically in narrative structures that are fictional and are closest to metonymy and analogy. They are rarely metaphorical in a formal sense. The metonymic and analogic relationship refers to significant emotional features in the child's life beyond the playroom. Where these features are powerful traumatic forces creating feelings of anxiety and helplessness, the narrative may take the form of a fairy tale in which the protagonist (usually enacted by the child) plays out a mastering of the danger that the child perceives to threaten him or her. The psychotherapist, by being attuned to the metonymic structure of the child's play narratives, can often discern the child's perspective and the threat that dominates it at that moment. Through collaborative play, the therapist is able, hopefully, to assist the child in feeling empowered to master the threat.

References

Garvey, C. 1984. *Children's Talk*. Cambridge: Harvard University Press.

Jakobson, R., and M. Halle. 1956. *Fundamentals of Language*. The Hague: Moulton.

Slade, A. 1994. Making meaning and making believe: Their role in the clinical process. In A. Slade and D. Wolf, eds., *Children at Play*. New York: Oxford University, pp. 81–107.

Vandenberg, B. 1986. Play, myth and hope. In R. van der Kooij and J. Hellendoorn, eds., *Play, Play Therapy, Play Research*. Berwin, The Netherlands: Swets North America.

Wicker, B. 1975. *The Story-Shaped World*. South Bend: University of Notre Dame Press.

Wolf, D., J. Rygh, and J. Altschuler. 1984. Agency and experience: Actions and states in play narratives. In I. Bretherton, ed., *Symbolic Play*. New York: Academic Press, pp. 195–217.

13

On the Dialectics of Imagination: Nijinsky's Sublime Defeat

Pascal Sauvayre and Barbara Forbes

Imagination, the heart of the creative process, is described here as the product of a dialectical tension of becoming, in line with the central Hegelian concept. This core dialectical movement can be conceptualized in any number of ways. When applied to imagination, the dialectic is seen as a tension between primary and secondary process, between the verbal and the nonverbal workings of the mind, and between raw emotional experience and its symbolic representation in the work of art.

The creative movement of imagination must rely on keeping the dialectic alive. If either side of the dialectical tension takes precedence over the other, what ensues is a break, or the 'collapse' of the dialectic, and therefore the death of creativity and becoming. The creative movement is lost whether the mind's collapse is into the realm of cold logic and secondary process (as in Wordsworth's famous quote, "we murder to dissect"), or into the raw unformulated world of primary process. Madness and creativity can therefore be seen as incompatible results of the same core dynamic.

The case of Vaslav Nijinsky, who is considered to be the most brilliant dancer in history, but whose career ended prematurely in mental illness, illustrates both the creative tension and its collapse. Using his diary, accounts of his performances and choreography, as well as a number of biographies, we will trace significant aspects of his development, placing emphasis on the ways in which he attempted to solve his problems through the creative use of his imagination. An essential feature of his dancing was his extraordinary leap, which gave the illusion not only that he left the ground to an exceptional height but also that he hovered, suspended over the earth for an instant, before deigning to return to it. However, it seems he was defeated by his inability to integrate the imaginary world he danced into with the real one he returned to at the end of every leap.

Koestler and Polanyi also present accounts of creativity built on a core dialectical tension between primary and secondary process that respect the integrity of both the poles and the opposition between them. This approach discards a view of mind that upholds the dominance of logically structured verbalizations, of reason, and of intellect as refinements of the 'lower' and more 'primitive' workings of the mind. For instance, a bias is embedded in the psychoanalytic dictum "regression in the service of the ego," in which primary process is put in the service of the 'superior' secondary process. From our perspective neither side of the tension 'serves' the other; each equally maintains the other in this lively "ever progressing motion," as Hegel put it. The formality of secondary process language must therefore be mastered in order to maintain the tension with the sensorial languages of primary process.

A thesis advanced here is that an essential ingredient in the creative process is the neutral yet active presence of the other (either actual or internalized) in the unfolding of the self, and in the maintenance of the dialectic of opposition. In Nijinsky's case, his sister was the catalyst for this presence. His life and work exemplify both the creative brilliance and turbulence of the dialectic during his ten-year productive period, as well as the collapse of its tension into his long chronic period of insanity that lasted from age thirty until his death in 1950 at sixty one. His leap, extraordinary even for dancers, serves as a fitting metaphor for his existential conflict and for the theoretical considerations we develop.

Is There a Correlation between Madness and Creativity?

An ancillary but relevant issue is the question of whether creative genius and psychopathology are correlated. This possibility has been a source of fascination in Western civilization since the Greeks. Reflecting on the essence of creativity, Plato declared, "for the poet is a light and winged holy thing, and there is no invention in him until he has been inspired and is out of his senses and the mind is no longer in him" (1937, 289). Aristotle (1979), taking a more empirical approach, made the observation that there was a tendency toward melancholia in those who achieved eminence in philosophy, politics, poetry, and the arts. "Modern" science's struggles with this issue can be said to begin with Cesare Lombroso's pioneering studies in the late nineteenth century which systematically categorized the mental symptoms of creative geniuses (Rothenberg 1990).[1] The common assumption that underlies all of the explorations on this topic is that "both creative people and mad people have mental experiences which the ordinary person finds incomprehensible or does not share" (Storr 1976, 261). Or, in more psychoanalytic parlance, both groups have greater access to the "prominence of primary process mechanisms" (Arieti 1976, 355).

Frieda Fromm-Reichman writes about Nijinsky that "the nature of his mental illness may really be considered as one of [the] very sources of the impressive specificity of his art" (1990, 69), clearly suggesting that his madness and his creativity were linked in an essential way. A few paragraphs later, referring to creative geniuses, she explains that "their creativity can allow them to spend many years without becoming psychotic" (p. 70), thereby suggesting an essential incompatibility between creativity and madness.

This incompatibility is consistent with Langer's (1953) perspective. She points out that the "widely popular doctrine that every work of art takes rise from an emotion which agitates the artist and which is directly expressed in the work" misses the fact that "the feeling in a work of art is something the artist conceived as he created the symbolic form to present it, rather than something he was undergoing and involuntarily venting in an artistic process." Art is a healthy representation of intense and 'deep' experience. Langer uses Wordsworth's apt expression, "emotion recollected in tranquillity" to clarify this distinction.

But equating a symptom of mental illness with completely unformulated experience doesn't hold up because in the symptom itself is enfolded an intricate symbolic representation—as Anna O. originally helped us understand. This simplistic equation would indeed be a misreading of Langer, or of Fromm-Reichman. Suffice it to say for now that the symptom's symbolic nature remains accessible or distant. On the other hand, the more powerful the artistic representation, the 'closer' it is to the agitating emotion. How then is creative 'work' to be understood that it can be simultaneously consistent with and antithetical to madness? What the work of art does that the symptom does not do is communicate; it conveys meaning. We would then look at a symptom as an as yet unsuccessful attempt to convey meaning.

By exploring the difference between the success of the work of art and the failure of the symptom to convey meaning, we will argue that artistic expression is characterized by the maintaining of a core dialectical tension. This tension can exist between, for instance, the agitating emotion and the symbolic representation, between the artist and the work, or between the speaker and the listener. In contrast, the symptom, madness, and meaninglessness, are conceptualized as the collapse of that tension—implosion instead of an unfolding of the self.[2]

What is necessary for the unfolding of the self, and absent in the case of its implosion, is the presence of the other. Whereas the work of art speaks to someone who hears, the symptom does not. The 'someone' is not necessarily an actual audience but, more important, an internal one, or an internalized other. However this 'other' is conceived, it is the essential ingredient in the dialectical unfolding of the self, or of the agitating emotion, or of the unformulated experience (whatever terminology we use), othering itself through the work of art. As we will see in Nijinsky's case, it was the special relationship with his sister that served as the catalyst for this internal audience necessary for the unfolding of the self. When Nijinsky lost his sister, he also lost the ingredient of his internal audience, and so his attempts at communication repeatedly failed at reaching an 'other,' and they became symptoms of mental illness. The symptom lacks precisely this capacity for meaningful othering, and so symptom and work of art are two completely different, yet mutually related, experiences and processes.

Dialectical Tension and Its Collapse

While it is true that the symbolic representation is not the agitating emotion but a representation of it, the representation must 'carry' something of the thing it represents in order for it to be an effective representation, in order to 'speak.' The work of art must therefore be *from* the emotion, and simultaneously, *about* the emotion.

This paradox of creativity is also to be found in Freud, ever the master of contradiction. On one hand, he notes (1920/1968) that the "true artist" elaborates the artist's internal life in such a way that it modifies the material sufficiently so that its "origin in prohibited sources is not easily detected" (p. 385) and that the personal notes are discarded. The work of art is therefore quite different from its internal sources. In the very next sentence, however, he notes that the artist possesses the "mysterious ability" to represent these internal so "faithfully" that they provide "so strong a stream of pleasure that, for a time at least, the repressions are out-balanced and dispelled by it" (Ibid.). The urge is simultaneously transformed, hidden, and yet fully there in the work.

It is crucial to capture both sides of this opposition. Understanding the interplay between the agitating emotion and the work of art as a dialectic does just that. The symbolic representation *is* the agitating emotion othering itself, objectifying itself into something different that simultaneously negates, confirms, and articulates its nature. By being about the agitating emotion, the work must to some degree be different from it and stand against it. It is the maintenance of this tension of opposition that brings the work "alive." This opposition is captured well in Wordsworth's description of the artistic process as a *tranquil* recollection of emotional *agitation*. The agitation finds its completion in the tranquility that simultaneously opposes and deepens the expression of the emotion.

In turn, the work of the artist can also be seen as an ongoing process of formulating him/herself in, against, and through the work. As an instance of Hegel's vision of a fundamental rhythm to all becoming, art and the artistic process are in an "ever progressing motion" of the unfolding of the self through its own opposition. The self is thus "a movement and unfolded becoming;... this unrest is the self" (Hegel 1807/1965, 34, II.1).

[The self's] movement of positing itself ... [is a] mediation between a self and its development into something different ... its own double and opposition, a process that again negates this indifferent diversity and its opposite: only this sameness which reconstitutes itself, or the reflection into itself in being different ... is its own becoming the circle that presupposes its end as its aim and thus has it for its beginning. (1807/1965, Preface, II.1, 28–30)

The tension between the artist and the work—his/her otherness and opposition—is the integrated self. The integrated self completes and continues the circle. Or rather, it completes and continues the spiraling development of the self as a refinding of the simplicity of the undifferentiated self through the sublimation of the differentiated self. "That which has returned into itself is the self, and the self is the identity and the simplicity that relates itself to itself" (1807/1965, Preface, II.1, 34). It is important to note here that the integration of the opposition does not mean the dissolution, nor even the weakening, of opposition. On the contrary, integration is itself maintained through the tension of the opposition.[3]

Koestler and Polanyi provide particularly illuminating takes on this dialectical opposition at the heart of creativity as the interplay of conscious and unconscious, of secondary and primary process, and formal and sensorial languages, capturing central features of both creativity and madness. As we will see, this particular annotation of the opposition captures central features of both creativity and madness.

Koestler (1964), for instance, refers to this dialectical opposition as "bisociation" which he defines as the "perceiving [of] a situation or event in two habitually incompatible associative contexts" (p. 95). Polanyi, in turn, explains that all manner of discovery and creativity "proceeds by a see-saw of analysis and integration similar to that by which our understanding of a comprehensive entity is progressively deepened" (1969, 129–30). The seesaw metaphor effectively conveys the mutual and simultaneous inhibition and support that each side of the opposition does to and for the other. An addition to the metaphor that includes the forward motion of creation is that of the handcar, which is powered along the train tracks by a seesaw motion.

Polanyi refers to "focal" and "subsidiary awareness," akin to conscious and unconscious, as mutually negating and defining each other. The interplay between the two allows the mind to articulate what had been undifferentiated, such as Langer's 'agitating emotion,' for instance. The creative work, then, involves a "two way traffic between conscious and unconscious" (Koestler 1964, 181) that is based on the tension of "something hidden that may yet be accessible, . . . a knowing of more than you can tell" (Polanyi, 131). As Jung put it, creative persons "often can't think at all, because they never intentionally use their brain" (1968, 190). In Koestler's terms, it is only by "thinking aside" that we can know more than we do.

Unconscious and primary processes provide a comparatively infinite field, or ground, from which the riches of creativity and originality are mined. In "each case the creative act consist[s] in a new synthesis of previously unconnected matrices of thought; a synthesis arrived at by 'thinking aside,' a temporary relinquishing of the rational controls in favor of the codes which govern the underground games of the mind . . . forging new combinations of seemingly incompatible contexts" (Koestler, 182). This aspect of the bisociative mechanism is natural to the primary processes of the unconscious.

Primary processes provide the ground *from* which, and *out of* which, the leap of creativity originates. Koestler captures this phenomenon quite effectively with the phrase *reculer pour mieux sauter*—a regression into the unformulated. A somewhat weaker version of this notion can be found in the psychoanalytic concept of "regression in the service of the ego." Interestingly Nijinsky's innovative choreography seems to have been permeated by this subsidiary awareness of the unknown. Jacques Riviere's observations on *Le Sacre du printemps*, which was premiered in 1913 to an uproar of praise and criticism, vividly convey this awareness of the unconscious.

This is spring as seen from the inside; spring in all its striving, its spasms, its partition.... There is a profound quality of blindness in this dance. An enormous question is borne by all those beings that move under our eyes. It is in no way different from them. They carry it along with them without comprehending it, like an animal that keeps turning around in its cage, without tiring of touching the bars with its forehead. They have no other organ than their entire organism, and they use it in their seeking.... And little by little, by the sheer patience and obstinacy of their questioning, a kind of solution is created which, once again, is no different from them and which likewise interflows with the mass of their bodies that is life. (Kirstein 1975, 168)

Wrestling with questions about his relationships and life, he sought a solution through his body. From his grounding in classical ballet, he created movement that was criticized as not being dancing but that gave full expression to his vision.

On one hand, because of its exclusive reliance on formalized languages, secondary process is woefully insufficient in the creative process. In contrast, the unconscious uses languages, such as pictorial and other sensory-based languages, that, thanks to a fluid syntax, have access to a deeper level of reality, and in particular to inner reality. "In images and other primary process phenomena, the energy is free (i.e., it shifts from one image to another), whereas in secondary process mechanisms it remains tied to the object on which the attention of the individual is focused" (Arieti 1976, 52). In other words, in secondary process mode, the creator (artist or scientist) can never see more than he/she sees. The rigidity of crystallized formal language cannot bend or mold itself to the subtleties and idiosyncrasies of reality, just as the Procrustean bed of theory breaks reality so effectively. If it remains unaided by pictorial and other nonverbal representation, "language can become a screen which stands between the thinker and reality. This is the reason that true creativity often starts where language ends" (Koestler, 177; Singer and Pope 1978). Only imagistic language and other sensory-based languages are the appropriate "vehicles of thought," as Koestler puts it, to maneuver effectively in the unpredictable terrain of the depths of the mind and of reality. "Whoever speaks in primordial images speaks with a thousand voices" (Jung 1970, 202). Only with imagery can we speak more than we say. Koestler illustrates in convincing detail how the creative leaps in the fields with the most formal and rigid languages, specifically physics and mathematics, have all been grounded, in part, in the looseness and fluidity of imagery.

At the same time, however, the artist must master the formality of language and secondary process in order to use it as an effective communicative tool. The poet must first master the rules of the word in order to break them creatively to gain symbolic access to the world of the underground. The tension between formal and sensorial language must be maintained.

Nijinsky mastered the rigorous training of formal dance to such a degree that he was able to transcend its limitations, and through the sensory language of the body, to give expression to his emotional life. Nijinsky would warm up for each performance with a specific sequence of rhythmic leaps. He would bounce gradually from small to bigger and bigger leaps, reach his maximum elevation, and then reverse the process by decreasing the height of his jumps until he was again at a standstill. Using his body as an instrument on which he regularly practiced the scales of leaping, Nijinsky was refining an emotional palette from which to play the chords of his body and to convey the strength and subtlety of his emotions. There can be no clearer physical image of integrated opposites and dialectical movement than that of this repeated motion from the earth into the air and back again, or of this extraordinary dancer epitomizing the tension between the freedom of the human spirit and the extreme adherence to a rigid discipline.

These considerations do away with the hierarchical and stratified view of mind, as in the tip of the iceberg metaphor. From this perspective, secondary processes are not sublimated or improved variations of primary ones. Both processes stand on equal footing on the dialectical see-saw. The creative act emerges as much out of the unruliness and chaos of primary process as it does out of the formality of secondary process. Both equally support and negate each other.

The dialectical tension can therefore be lost as much in the direction of the deadness of secondary process, as it can in the direction of primary process. Instead of *reculer pour mieux sauter*, Koestler aptly uses Blake's *reculer sans sauter* to refer to this type of collapse—emotional agitation that can no longer be recollected. Much like the deep-sea diver, the artist's ability to work depends on his ability to move back and forth between the surface and the depths.

[They] are prone to fall victims to the "rapture of the deep" and tear their breathing-tubes off.... The capacity to regress, more or less at will, to the games of the underground, without losing contact with the surface, seems to be the essence of the poetic, and of any other form of creativity. "God guard me from those thoughts men think / In the mind alone, / He that sings a lasting song / Thinks in a marrow bone" (Yeats). (Koestler, 316–17)

Nijinsky's underground games took place at the height of his jump, which carried him in flight from the stage to his depths in space. To whichever side of the dialectical see-saw the fall occurs, whether it is on the more disorganized and flamboyant "rapture of the deep" side, as in "madness," or whether it is on the emptier dead side of analytic dissection that begins at the surface, the results are equally pathological—madness in the larger sense. The un-othered self fails to become a self just as the self stuck in otherness, the alienated self, fails to do so as well. When Nijinsky lost the presence of his sister, both internally and externally, he also lost the ability to recognize his other. The tension collapsed, and he recoiled into his own "empty depth" (Hegel's phrase) which was unutterable, incommunicable. He could only think in his mind alone. He became mad. As we will see, Nijinsky's leap is a powerful metaphor for an artist's creative brilliance, which in turn is linked to the psychosis he fell into—the rapture of his own depths.

Ogden (1989) aptly coins the term "collapse" to refer to psychopathology as the break of the seesaw. What collapses is the tension between the poles of opposition, the same tension from which the leap of creativity is generated. "Psychopathology can be thought of as forms of collapse of the richness of experience generated between these poles" (1989, 46). All poles must remain equally present to carry this momentum. In this sense creativity and madness are incompatible yet rooted in the same dynamic.

An important aside as a final theoretical note. In using the image of the break of the dialectical seesaw of creativity, we do not mean to imply that all creative tension is absent. The symptom, whether "neurotic" or "psychotic," is itself a creative attempt, however unsuccessful, at communicating meaning, as Sullivan has so effectively argued. His distinctions among prototaxic, parataxic, and syntaxic levels of experience (1953) can be useful here. Prototaxic experience would be completely raw unformulated experience, a sort of ineffable 'thing-in-itself' or noumenal experience that, as soon as we think we can recognize it (whether in words, behavior, or other), implies that we are talking about something that has already risen out of its unformulation, that would include symptoms of course.[4] Symptoms reside *primarily* at the parataxic level, and art at the syntaxic one, but as with all human interactions, they both have a foot planted at each level. There is always madness in art, and art in madness. We could in fact approach the distinction between madness and art from the perspective of dialectical opposition we advocate.

Vaslav Nijinsky (1889–1950)

One of the greatest choreographers of this century, George Balanchine, who choreographed for Diaghilev's Ballets Russes as did Nijinsky, put Nijinsky's artistic talent in dance into perspective when he commented that whereas others' talents are restricted to doing one thing well, he believes that "Nijinsky could do them all! He could do everything! And that was his secret" (Volkov 1985, 214). He played an instrument, his body, so masterfully that he was capable of funneling and transmuting his own raw and unbridled energy toward the audience, stirring in them the same passionate life force that propelled his dance. Like any great artist, "he enthralls and overpowers, while at the same time he lifts the idea he is seeking to express out of the occasional and transitory and into the realm of the ever-enduring" (Jung 1953, 202).

The Incident at the River

To understand Nijinsky, a critical life incident serves as a powerful metaphor for both of the interconnected extremes of his life; his artistic strength and his spiritual defeat.

As a young child of no more than six or seven years old, time and again Vaslav, irrepressibly physically active, would wander off only to be found after a prolonged search. After one disappearance, when he returned home in tears of terror at being punished, his father pushed him away, saying: "Get out of my sight.... I will deal with you tomorrow morning!" (Nijinsky 1973, 53). Instead of the usual punitive ritual, which consisted of threats, humiliation, and mounting turmoil with the entire family in a state of distress until the father finally relented, and sent the child to a corner; this time, Vaslav's father took him for "swimming lesson" in the Neva river. He demonstrated to the boy how to swim, and when Vaslav was reluctant to follow his direction and get into the deep water, his father picked him up and hurled him in. Nijinsky remembers that once submerged, a burst of physical strength came to him which enabled him to thrust himself, as if he were leaping, to a rope, and by grasping it, to save himself.

The incident seems to have left an indelible memory of almost being killed by his father, and of the superhuman feat by which he saved himself. He had to jump, he had to perform, or he would have died. He writes in his diary, a succession of autobiographical recollections written at the onset of his illness, "I was a boy of six or seven, but have not forgotten the story." He then associates to an anecdote told him by his doctor at the time, who was encouraging him to be gentle with his daughter ". . . because (according to the doctor) the child does not forget how the mother and father treat it. He told me that his father was once angry with him and he cannot even now forget his anger until today. . . . I almost cried. I was sorry. I do not know who to pity more, the son or the father. They both are miserable. The child has lost his love for the father and the father the love of God" (1973, 43).

What he powerfully and tragically identifies as the mutual misery of father and son, unable to love each other, is reflective of a more pervasive disconnectedness and deadness that permeated every facet of his life. As we will describe, his art can be seen as a successful attempt to articulate this core experience of bestial tragedy into a coherent physical movement. An example the path from trauma to art can be seen in his powerful leap which became a central feature of his oeuvre. His sister explained that it "caused a sensation" (B. Nijinska 1981, 296) when "Nijinsky shot out of his room like an arrow from a bow . . . the actual effect was as though he leaped from a crouching position, the kind of leap a tiger might make" (Kirstein, 99). This central experience othering itself in dance is Nijinsky himself, thrusting himself into life through his art with the strength of every fiber in his body.

Eventually, however, he became unable to find himself even in his art; he became opaque to himself. The tension that had kept his spirit afloat collapsed, and he drowned, claimed by the rapture of his own depths.

Significant Life History

His childhood was replete with neglect, violence, and instability. The middle of three children, Nijinsky was born to parents who were both Polish dancers. His mother had been orphaned when she was seven years old, and Vaslav describes her as fearful and anxious about life, which resulted in a tendency to react to stress with either helplessness or rage. The father, a handsome and athletic man with a reputation for impetuous and violent behavior, had persuaded his wife to marry him by producing a revolver (at whom it was pointed is not clear), and declaring that this was the last time he would ask her. He was five years her junior.

During their early childhood, the Nijinsky children were constantly "on the road," in Poland or Russia, staying for only a short time in each of the places their parents found work dancing, and then moving on to the next theater. Also contributing to Vaslav's sense of insecurity was the ongoing turmoil of his parent's marriage. When he was eight years old his father finally left his family to live with his mistress in Moscow, and his departure prompted stormy and disobedient behavior in Vaslav. His older brother, Stanislav, entered an asylum a few years later and was hospitalized for most of the remainder of his life. Although their father maintained contact with his family, he provided for them only sporadically over the years.

The children moved with their mother to St. Petersburg, where the two youngest were enrolled in the Imperial Theatrical School. His natural talent for dance was encouraged by both his parents from an early age (he began performing at the age of four), and his mother's narcissistic investment in his dancing eventually also became a concrete vested interest. Vaslav contributed significantly to the family income even as a young boy because students at the Imperial Theatrical School were paid for their performances. In an ironic twist, Vaslav was holding together his disintegrating family through his leap, just as he was holding his sense of self together.

Nijinsky progressed rapidly in his dancing, but he was an outcast. He had difficulty in his academic studies, and he was often in fights with his peers, who would easily provoke him with their teasing. His Polish accent, his high cheekbones and slanted eyes (they earned him the nickname *japonczek*), and his dancing (it inspired jealousy and criticism, "are you a girl, to dance so well?" they would tease; B. Nijinska, 85), all set him apart from his peers as an oddball. Lacking the verbal and emotional skills to confront their teasing, he relied on the language of his physicality to establish himself through fights and through daring feats.

Nijinsky's recollections of a critical incident with his mother indicate a relationship with her as tortured as the one with his father. And as in the recollections of his father, they also suggest a path from his unformulated experience to his art. After a schoolboy prank (it involved a spitball), for which Nijinsky took the blame, his mother resorted to beating him with branches, and he recalls this experience with an urgent explanation of how much love he felt for his mother: "I loved my mother and was therefore pleased that everyone knew about [the beating]" (Nijinsky 1973, 61). As a result of the beating, he continues, he then began to get good marks at school.

To this he associates that he was in tremendous conflict about masturbation, and that his dancing suffered because he masturbated too much. He gives his love for his mother as the reason he gave up masturbation because if his dancing deteriorated, he would not earn the money his mother relied on to support the family. At age fifteen, he made the conscious decision to redirect his energy into dance. As a result "I grew thinner and started dancing like God" (1973, p. 62). The connection between God and his father, which he makes explicitly in his recollections of the swimming lesson (see above) should not be lost on us. Nijinsky here makes the connection between his mother's dependency on him, his sexuality, his art, and even the rivalry with an absent father, a connection that matured into work renowned for such powerful eroticism that it left audiences either ecstatic or enraged, but nothing in between.

A rapid succession of parental figures appeared in Nijinsky's life leading to Sergei Diaghilev, the impresario who organized Les Ballets Russes and who launched Nijinsky onto the international scene as both a dancer and choreographer. Finally, Nijinsky gave in to the advances of a beautiful and wealthy Hungarian aristocrat and amateur dancer, and proposed to her by asking with typical hesitancy and verbal awkwardness, *Voulez-vous, avec moi?* (B. Nijinska, 485). Romola became his wife in 1914. Eventually she would win the definitive battle of the protectors against Diaghilev, who dismissed his protégé when he heard of his marriage, and it was with her that Nijinsky spent the rest of his life. Afraid, and not "knowing life" as he put it, Nijinsky found refuge in the self-serving and exploitative love of protectors very much like his mother.

In a surprisingly insightful passage he writes, "I was afraid of life, my mother was also afraid of life, and I had inherited this fear from her" (1973, p. 134). Just as he did with his mother as a boy, he sacrificed his independent strivings to guarantee the integrity of the person to whom he submitted himself. He calmed his anxiety by protecting his mother from her fear of life, and also entrusted her with the responsibility of reassuring him in his own fears—which in turn were fanned by hers.

Parental figures provided Nijinsky with more than his fair share of unformulated traumatic experiences to inform his work, but with none of the necessary tools to articulate that experience. To understand his creative process better, one must, in our opinion, look past his protectors to the steady presence of his sister, which provided him with a means of formulating his experience.

Role and Support of Sister

Throughout their childhood, Vaslav and his younger sister, Bronislava, were constant companions. They had an intimate relationship in which she looked up to him, enamored of his vitality, yet also mediated between him and their youthful world. From their earliest years Bronia was his ally at all times. After one summer vacation, for instance, when Vaslav was overwhelmed by resuming the task of homework, Bronia did it for him, writing his "How I Spent My Summer" essay by imagining herself into his every activity (B. Nijinska, 150). When Nijinsky's prowess as a dancer was evident, he began to give his sister lessons, and this role as her coach continued when they were both dancing with the Ballets Russes. In fact it was he who convinced Diaghilev to hire Nijinska for the initial Paris season of Les Ballets Russes in 1909.

In all his interactions with people other than his sister, Nijinsky is constantly described as somewhat withdrawn and uncommunicative, even awkward. It seemed that he "felt out of place ... [and] seemed listless and uncommunicative. Usually he had little to say and remained silent, or merely smiled. When Nijinsky did open his mouth, he seemed clumsy, struggling for words, almost disorganized" (Ostwald 1991, 36). This inability to communicate verbally permeated his interpersonal relations and is certainly consistent with his family's pattern. For Nijinsky, the successive assimilation of different languages, necessitated by his childhood relocations, deprived him of the use of his mother tongue—Polish—and bred an insecurity with verbal expression. Also typical of his family, however, was the use of physicality as the only means of expressing intensely felt emotions. When this was integrated in dance, Nijinsky was capable of conveying the full depth of emotion. In effect it seems that Nijinsky's inability to communicate verbally was in inverse proportion to his ability to communicate through dance. It is as though only through dance was he able to come alive and embrace life rather than be afraid of it.

Bronia became a vital ingredient in his work as a choreographer, for it was with her, at home, that he demonstrated every step of the choreography and tested the possibilities before presenting them in the dance studio to the company—and then he relied on Bronia to demonstrate for him. He literally penned his ballets on her body. All of his ballets departed radically from any previously created, and elicited extremes of praise and criticism from audiences, whose boos and fervent applause were mixed. To the dancers, whom he asked to move in ways for which their classical ballet training had not equipped them, his works were incomprehensible. Nijinsky's temper would flare when he came upon their resistance, and so he became dependent on his sister as a negotiator/translator in rehearsals as well.

As the one person in his life who was a neutral witness to his family traumas, Bronia can be seen as an early external other who would allow him to be himself without interfering, without the destructive power of his parents, and so give him room to become himself; to express himself. She was a catalyst, not only for the development of his internal other, but also for his interaction with actual others who were essential in the creation of his work. We see here how Bronia concretely articulated Vaslav's presence, acting as both his mirror and his pen, and so enabled him to be in dialogue with himself. It was through this reciprocal reflectiveness between Vaslav and Bronia that the oeuvre that was Nijinsky emerged. The result was choreography of incredible emotional power.

The brother and sister's collaboration culminated in the work they did together on the third work he choreographed, *Le Sacre du printemps*, which Bronia says "proceeded fast and easily" (B. Nijinska, 450). She was to dance the central role of the sacrificial virgin and Vaslav took "only two rehearsals to create the solo for me ... as he watched me he was radiant" (p. 450). Structurally images of circles within circles became integral to the choreography. The work's first of two acts is dominated by an asymmetry in both the arrangement of dancers on the stage and in their movements. This gives the effect of disparate elements coexisting in an effort toward harmonious interaction, a theme that we are suggesting is found at the heart of the creative process.

As Millicent Hodsen (who re-created the ballet for re-staging by the Joffrey Ballet in 1988) points out, this is not a story of a young girl dancing herself to death, but of the act of faith this represents: "The young woman dances in order to save the earth. There is this marriage between a member of the ancient tribe, and the Sun God" (Kinberg and Grimm 1989). "Significantly, only the Chosen Virgin danced alone" (Garafola 1989, 69), in a solo consisting of repeated leaps—but she cannot escape except by marriage with God in death. Nijinsky ends her desperate dance with a fall to the ground, a moment of contraction, in which her supplicating palms and exposed, surrendered throat mimic orgasm; and the rush of the six "bears" as they lift her overhead, an offering to God—life in the throes of death. Here we can see Nijinsky create order from chaos and give a positive, tangible shape to his inner struggle. Through the strength of the circle of life, he can be seen leaping toward life in the midst of death. Indeed, we must imagine him to be most fully alive, most completely himself, through his work.

However, midway through the company rehearsals of *Sacre*, which the dancers endured with overt hostility, Bronia announced that she was pregnant and would not be able to dance. "He did not let me continue but screamed at me, 'There is no one to replace you. You are the only one who can perform this dance, only you, Bronia, and no one else!'" Apparently he flew into a rage of homicidal intensity. Bronia's departure from rehearsals of *Sacre* was the beginning of a gradual separation between the siblings, and Bronia actually avoided him because "I found something frightening in Vaslav" (B. Nijinska, 462). Without her, his internal other was gradually slipping away from him, and so was his life.

Illness

The tours became more of a burden than life-giving, he was more and more quiet and absentminded, gradually developing a suspiciousness toward everyone around him. At the start of World War I, Romola rented a villa in St. Moritz, and Nijinsky acquiesced to a life cut off from ballet and isolated in the mountains, devoting himself to planning new ballets. With the exception of one, these never came to fruition.

At this time he also directed his artistic energies into sketching costume designs, portraits, and abstract works (drawings, pastels, and watercolors). But at this time his art is less powerful, although it gives indications of his inner turmoil. The impression of a chronological viewing of the later drawings was "as if you see the eye of the mind closing as you watch, and it is an eye in each case, and in each last drawing the eye seems to grow tighter and tighter, and then the vision is sealed, nothing more is seen" (Hartley 1977, 72).

In his ongoing struggle to articulate his experience, he worked on a solo in which he wanted to "play the role of a lunatic," and he named it *Marriage avec Dieu*. On January 19, 1919, he performed it for an invited audience in an elegant hotel in St. Moritz. He asked his pianist to play Chopin and then, wearing white silk pajamas, sat in a chair facing the audience and stared at them as the pianist played on and on. The awkwardness of the situation, filling everyone with an eerie feeling, highlighted the centrality of alienation in human experience, as his theme. This was his last performance.

The diary Vaslav had been writing now became the focus of his energy, and he wrote feverishly in it every day. He describes the incident that is given as evidence of his final, unequivocal, descent into madness, in which he wandered through the village of St. Moritz with a cross, blessing all those whose paths he crossed. A maid in his house had been in service to Nietzsche, and warned Romola that she had observed similar behavior in this former employer before he was removed to the "madhouse." Nietzsche's parable of the misunderstood madman, or of Zarathustra, who comes down from the mountain in a state of feverish enlightenment to announce the death of God, presaged his own destiny. Indeed, Nijinsky had been reading Nietzsche, whom he felt "would understand me" (1973, 5), and with a similar absence of any viable communication, he became (as he described himself) a "Clown of God" (p. 74).

Not until the whole diary is published in a translation that is true to the idiomatic Russian in which it was written, will we have a full picture of what it was he wanted so desperately to communicate. Sadly Romola edited out fully one-third of the contents of his notebooks which included erotic and scatological poems, and details of his childhood masturbation. There is a bitter irony in our contemplation of the notebooks that make up his diary. In his last effort to communicate, Nijinsky finally chose words as his medium, and attempted to use the language of the society that had failed to understand him. This prose poem, the last tragic example of how he coped with his inner conflicts, inspires and saddens, even in its edited form. As the eye of the mind was closing shut, we find in the diary, replete with odd and incomprehensible associations, the distance between art and symptom disappearing, and art dissolving into symptom. This diary exemplifies the gradual collapse from art to symptom. The madness in the art is not to be found in its flamboyance but in its decreasing ability to inspire, to touch both himself and others.

Nijinsky was treated by Eugen Bleuler, who then referred him to Ludwig Binswanger, but improvements were limited at best. Any attempt to investigate his childhood led to silence or protestations that it was of no importance. He showed susceptibility to paranoid thinking which grew into a fear of death. He would beg his doctors to help him with his sick thoughts, and he alternated between states of catatonic stupor and agitation. In 1921, after not seeing him for seven years, Bronislava visited Vaslav in the sanitarium. He "showed no emotional reaction ... [and] remained impassive, but when I said ... 'I have already devised two ballets,' Vaslav suddenly turned his head and looked straight into my eyes. He said very firmly, as if instructing me, 'The ballet is never devised. The ballet must be created'" (B. Nijinska 1981, 514). Moments later, he was "again staring into the distance." It is as though he was thoroughly aware of the very interplay of processes of which we are talking here. He knew that conscious 'devising' alone is not sufficient in order to create.

Eventually, insulin shock treatments were administered, and finally, after 180 of these, when his speech had become a word-salad, and he became incontinent, they were stopped. To Romola, his withdrawal was a sign of his "past" illness, so she removed him from the hospital. For the remainder of his life, a residual schizophrenic, he lived with her and a devoted male nurse, occasionally having brief contact with his old colleagues from the world of ballet and with his two daughters. Over the years of his mental illness, Nijinsky gradually put on weight, developed high blood pressure and progressive arteriosclerosis, and had what appeared to be several mild heart attacks. In 1950 he suffered renal failure, lapsed into a coma, and died.

In a sense, his spirit had died long before, and he was fully aware as it was happening. He had been desperately calling out to God, his father, "I feel near death and I ask God to help me" (1973, 143), but as had been the case so many times, his call went unanswered, misunderstood. He did not know how to be. "No artist can deceive God" (p. 148). That is, if God is listening. Nietzsche, whose life struggles were so similar to Nijinsky's, aptly wrote "living off 'my own oneself' and drinking one's own blood entails the danger of losing the 'thirst for oneself' and drinking 'oneself dry'" (1881, Letter to Rohde). Without the presence of the other, one cannot become a self, and as Nietzsche did before him, Nijinsky imploded into himself. In this unloved, disconnected state, it was only with God that Nijinsky felt he could communicate. A parallel can again be drawn between Nietzsche, who signed his last letters "The Crucified One," and "Dionysus," and Nijinsky, who ended his diary by signing off "God and Nijinsky." As Nijinsky put it, "I am the one who dies when he is not loved" (1973, 98). Or, in W. H. Auden's words:

What mad Nijinsky wrote
About Diaghilev
Is true of the normal heart;
For the error bred in the bone
Of each woman and each man
Craves what it cannot have,
Not universal love
But to be loved alone.

From *September 1, 1939*

Notes

1. Parenthetically, it is interesting to note that Lombroso was the specialist whom Romola, Nijinsky's wife, first wished to consult when he became ill, convinced that no other than he would have the understanding of genius necessary to help her husband. He was, however, no longer alive at the time.

2. We do not mean to imply that the implosion of the self is ever an absolute one, that symptom can be equated with the absolute absence of symbolic representation. The symptom is best viewed as an attempt out of that imploded state, and conceptualizing 'symptom' and 'art' as mutually exclusive entities would be succumbing to the very compartmentalized and 'undialectical' thinking we are critiquing. We will return to this difficulty when the 'collapse' of the dialectical tension is discussed.

3. This point is central to our understanding of madness as the collapse of that tension. Conflict and opposition are essential to any forward progress. Progress must be the result of respecting the integrity of both poles of the opposition, not of a dampening or minimizing of the differences. If the latter were so, we would be left with a leveling of reality to the smallest common denominator, whatever the context may be.

4. From this perspective, it could also be argued that symptom is itself the creative product of a dialectical interplay of opposing modes of experience, and so on and on.

References

Arieti, S. 1976. *Creativity: The Magic Synthesis.* New York: Basic Books.

Aristotle. *Problems II: Books XXII–XXXVIII.* Translated by H. Apostle. Iowa: Peripatetic Press, 1979.

Auden, W. H. 1945. *The Collected Poetry of W. H. Auden.* New York: Random House.

Freud, S. 1968. *A General Introduction to Psychoanalysis.* Translated by J. Riviere. New York: Washington Square Press. London: Liverwright Press, 1920.

Fromm-Reichmann, F. 1990. The assets of the mentally handicapped: The interplay of mental illness and creativity. *Journal of American Psychoanalysis* 18: 47–72.

Garafola, L. 1989. *Diaghilev's Ballets Russes.* New York: Oxford University Press.

Hartley, M. 1977. The drawings of Nijinsky. In P. Magriel, ed., *Nijinsky, Pavlova, Duncan: Three Lives in Dance.* 1977. New York: Da Capo Press.

Hegel, G. W. F. 1965. *Phenomenology of the Spirit.* Translated with Commentary by W. Kaufman. New York: Anchor Books.

Jung, C. G. 1966. *The Spirit in Man, Art, and Literature.* Translated by R. Hull. Princeton: Princeton University Press.

Jung, C. G. 1968. *Analytical Psychology.* Edited by R. Hull. New York: Vintage Books.

Jung, C. G. 1970. *Psychological Reflections.* Edited by J. Jacobi and R. Hull. Princeton: Princeton University Press.

Kinberg, J., D. Grimm, and T. Prod. 1989. The search for Nijinsky's "Rite of Spring." *Dance in America.* New York: Danmark Radio and WNET/Thirteen.

Kirstein, L. 1975. *Nijinsky Dancing.* New York: Knopf.

Koestler, A. 1964. *The Act Creation.* New York: Macmillan.

Langer, S. 1953. *Feeling and Form.* New York: Scribner's Sons.

Nietzsche, F. 1969. *Selected Letters of Frederich Nietzsche.* Edited and translated by C. Middleton. Chicago: University of Chicago Press.

Nijinska, B. 1981. *Early Memoirs.* Edited and translated by I. Nijinska and J. Rawlinson. New York: Holt, Rinehart and Winston.

Nijinsky, V. 1973. *The Diary of Vaslav Nijinsky.* Edited by R. Nijinsky. Berkeley: University of California Press.

Ogden, T. 1989. *The Primitive Edge of Experience.* Northvale, NJ: Jason Aronson.

Ostwald, P. 1991. *A Leap into Madness.* New York: Carol Publishing Group.

Plato. *Ion.* Translated by B. Jowett. *The Works of Plato,* vol. 4. New York: Tudor Publishing, 1937.

Polanyi, M. 1969. *Knowing and Being.* Chicago: University of Chicago Press.

Rothenberg, A. 1990. *Creativity and Madness.* Baltimore: Johns Hopkins University Press.

Singer, J., and K. Pope, eds. 1978. *The Power of Human Imagination.* New York: Plenum.

Sullivan, H. S. 1953. *The Interpersonal Theory of Psychiatry.* New York: Norton.

Storr, A. 1976. *The Dynamics of Creation.* Harmondsworth, Middlesex, England: Penguin.

Volkov, S. 1985. *Balanchine's Tchaikovsky.* Translated by A. Bouis. New York: Simon and Schuster.

14

Was St. Anthony Crazy? Visionary Experiences and the Desert Fathers

Greg Mahr

The desert fathers were fourth-century Christian ascetics who abandoned urban and rural society for lives of prayer, solitude, and fasting in the deserts of Egypt and the Near East. Widely emulated, the desert fathers were also known as "athletes of God" because of their amazing capacities for fasting and continuous prayer. Saint Anthony was the most influential of the desert fathers. Anthony's example led thousands of young men and women, from provincial Egyptian villagers to urbane Romans, to the wilds of the desert. His biography, *The Life of Anthony*, became a bestseller of the late classical world. Harnack said that "no book has had a more stultifying on Egypt, Western Asia and Europe than *The Life of Anthony*" (quoted in Waddell 1957). By 394 travelers reported that the population of the desert in Egypt equaled that of the towns. Anthony, the solitary ascetic, had founded a mass movement that ultimately became medieval monasticism.

Ascetic life had a vivid inner focus. In prayer and solitude the desert fathers became keen observers of mental states and inner experiences. They had important insights into psychological and psychopathological issues, including the origins of depressive symptoms and the nature and meaning of asceticism and sacrifice.

In this chapter I will describe the complex visionary experiences of the desert fathers, especially Anthony. Although the desert fathers can sound very modern in their terse descriptions of depressed moods, they also offer accounts of visions and battles with demons that to modern readers sound quite bizarre and psychotic. An understanding of Anthony's visionary experiences can help broaden our understanding of psychosis.

Before describing the Anthony's visionary experiences in detail, it is necessary to describe the everyday life of the ascetics, as well as the demonology that pervades the desert experience. The desert monks adopted a lifestyle remarkable for its simplicity and austerity. Solitary monks would live in one- or two-room cells made of sun-dried brick, simple enough to be constructed in a single day. They restricted both sleep and food intake. The hermit John began his ascetic life by spending three years in uninterrupted prayer, not sitting at all or lying down to sleep, but simply snatching some sleep while standing (Russell 1981). Although monks might fast for long periods, they typically ate one light meal of dry bread soaked in water and seasoned with salt and green herbs. Vegetables like lentils might supplement the diet of bread and water. Monks rested on the ground on simple mats of reeds.

Although monks prayed and chanted much of the day, they also raised their own herbs and vegetables and performed simple crafts, like weaving baskets of palm leaves. Manual labor was valued to relieve boredom and as a good in itself. Solitude and silence were the rule, even for monks that lived communally in monasteries. Monks would remain in their cells much of the week, perhaps sharing a meal once weekly with their comrades. The cells of solitary monks were often in the wilderness, miles from any other habitation. For urbane and sophisticated monks like Evagrius, desert life was a sharp contrast to aristocratic life in imperial Rome. For poor Egyptian monks, the contrast was less stark. In the *Sayings of the Desert Fathers*, a poor monk admitted that his life in his cell was actually more comfortable than his past life as a shepherd (Ward 1981, 10).

Although some monks like Anthony and Evagrius were erudite and educated, many were simple and illiterate. The Scriptures were considered the only relevant reading, and monks made popular the use of bound texts instead of scrolls, so that scriptural passages could be more easily referred to and committed to memory.

Despite the harshness of desert life, the desert fathers lived long lives. Anthony reportedly lived to be 105 (Athanathius 1980), and monks are frequently described to be in their nineties. Specific ages are the stuff of legend and not literal truth, but descriptions of sickness and infirmity among monks are rare.

Demons, sins, and mood states were conceptually linked in the minds of the desert fathers. A crucial sin/mood state/demon was acedia. Acedia is the transliteration of a Greek word which means "non-caring state." John Cassian describes it "a torpor, a sluggishness of the heart; consequently it is closely akin to dejection (*tristitia*); it attacks especially those monks who wander from place to place and those who live in isolation. It is the most dangerous and persistent enemy of the solitaries." He continues "it begets in the monk's mind a horror of his convent, disgust with his cell and aversion for his brethren." The monk "leaves his cell and returns ceaselessly." He longs for visits to distract him, he loses all his "force and ardor." (Kuhn 1976, 50–51). Finally acedia can lead to despair and suicide.

Acedia is referred to as the "demon of noontide," from Psalm 91. "Thou shalt not be afraid for the terror by night; nor for the arrow that flieth by day; nor the pestilence that walketh in darkness; nor for the destruction that wasteth at noonday." In the view of the ascetics, the symptoms of acedia peaked at noonday, in contrast to our modern view of the diurnal variation in depression.

The desert fathers, specifically Evagrius, were the first to catalog the capital sins (Ponticus 1981). Foremost among Evagrius's eight deadly sins was acedia. Mastery over other vices left one vulnerable to further temptation. If one mastered concupiscence, for instance, one was vulnerable to gluttony. Acedia, once mastered, is replaced by joy. Associated with every sin was a demon. This demon was not just a symbolic personification of the sin but an actual fallen angel that tempted with that sin. Modern moral stigma about depression may have its origins in this equation of sin, demon, and mood state. This moral perspective, while stigmatizing depression, also sanctified it. Acedia was not only sin, but also a stage of spiritual growth, an accepted phase of ascetic life.

The visionary experiences of the desert fathers are structured by their demonology. The capacity for accessing visionary experiences appears to have been most highly developed in the early ascetics. The demonic visions of later monks like Evagrius are much less detailed and have a conceptual quality, as if one were seeing the embodiment of a vice, not an actual demon. Even the great Anthony, reflecting on his precursors in the desert, lamented that "God does not allow the same temptations and warfare to this generation as he did formerly, for men are weaker now and cannot bear so much" (Ward 1981, p. 6).

Athanasius's *Life of Anthony* is the most vivid account of visionary experiences among the desert fathers. According to Athanasius, Anthony was called to ascetic life at the age of eighteen or twenty. His parents had died six months earlier, and he was left as the sole caretaker for his younger sister. At church he heard the Gospel passage, "If you would be perfect, go, sell what you possess and give to the poor." Immediately he donated all his possessions, turned his young sister over to a convent, and began to live in the desert, visiting those wise men who were already living in the wilderness. Demons first tempted him with memories of his sister and his possessions. Then the demon "advanced against the youth, noisily disturbing him by night, and so troubling him in the daytime that even those who watched were aware of the bout that occupied them both" (Anthanasius 1980, 34). The demon beguiled him various forms, including that of a voluptuous woman. While his friends supplied him with bread, Anthony locked himself in a tomb. There he was flogged by a multitude of demons and found by his friends lying as if dead. The next night he returned to the tomb, daring the demons with shouts of "Here I am—Anthony! I do not run from your blows." "The demons, as if breaking through the buildings four walls, and seeming to enter through them, were changed into the forms of beasts and reptiles. The place was immediately filled with the appearances of lions, bears, leopards, bulls, and serpents, asps, scorpions, and wolves" (p. 38). Anthony again mocked the demons, and finally a vision of the Lord comforted him.

Visions of plates of food and piles of gold followed, then Anthony again locked himself in an abandoned fortress for an extended period. "Since he did not allow them to enter, those of his acquaintance who came to him often spent days and nights outside. They heard what sounded like clamoring mobs inside making noises, emitting pitiful sounds and crying out.... At first those who were outside thought certain men were doing battle with him ... but when they stooped to peek through a hole, they saw no one, and they realized then that the adversaries were demons" (p. 41).

For twenty years Anthony lived in this way. Finally his friends and followers tore down the walls of the fortress by force. Anthony emerged unaged, at great peace. "The state of his soul was one of purity, for it was not constricted by grief, nor relaxed by pleasure, nor affected by either laughter or dejection" (p. 42). He preached, purged demons, healed the sick.

In his preaching Anthony offers further insight and observations on demons, and draws clear connections between demonic visitations and depressive symptoms. "They are treacherous and prepared to be changed and transformed into all shapes. Frequently without becoming visible, they pretend to chant with sacred songs, and they recite sayings from the Scriptures. And even when we are reading, they are able to say right away and repeatedly, as if in an echo, the same things we have read. While we are sleeping they arouse us for prayers, and they do this incessantly, hardly allowing us to sleep.... They do these things that they might bring the simple to despair ..." (p. 50).

Contagion was not an important issue for a solitary monk like Anthony, but later ascetics who lived communally had to be continually vigilant against the contagion of demonic visions and acedia. A central concern of Cassian's *Foundations of the Cenobitic Life* was protecting the monastic community from the contagion of demonic influence (Cassian 1894). Monks who were victims of acedia were isolated and prescribed stringent regimens of prayer and work to prevent their malaise from infecting the community at large.

Despite the dangers of visionary experiences, the capacity to experience visions was highly valued. Visions conferred status and validated the desert experience. Visions helped monks see the future, distinguish right from wrong, and affirm their connection with the spiritual world. While valued, visions were never actively sought. Visions were never the goal of fasting or deprivation but an anticipated and welcomed outcome. Visions were not seen as pathological but were potentially dangerous, contagious, and subject to misinterpretation. For Augustine, who lived just after the time of the desert fathers, visionary experiences were the highest form of knowledge, and sense data the lowest.

How are we to make sense of these experiences of Anthony and the other desert fathers? How can their experiences be understood and "mapped" onto modern categories of mental phenomena and psychopathology? Any mapping must incorporate key elements, namely the powerful meaning of visions in the context of desert life, their capacity for contagion, and their association with acedia and depressive symptoms.

Naturalistic explanations are obvious enough. Robert Burton, in the *Anatomy of Melancholy*, attributes both the depressive symptoms and the visionary experiences of the desert monks to fasting and social isolation (discussed in Jackson 1986). The diurnal pattern of acedia has been attributed to the relentless noonday African sun and to hunger from eating one meal only (Kuhn 1976, 42).

Naturalistic theories, however, do not account for key aspects of Anthony's visions. Visions induced by starvation or dehydration are rarely well remembered by patients. In delirium, the brain is rarely capable of storing memories. The visual hallucinations that occur in delirium are fleeting and primitive and lack detail and structure. They rarely have meaning or personal relevance for the patient and never have a broader social meaning or carry risk of contagion. Furthermore delirium is a grave medical symptom. Even a single episode of delirium carries substantial risks of mortality and morbidity, repeated episodes suggest a degree of ill health that is inconsistent with the historical record. Kroll, in a study of visionary experiences in the Middle Ages, could relate only 5 percent to starvation and 11 percent to stress-related syndromes or states (Kroll 1982).

Schizophrenia is among the most common causes of psychosis. Anthony's history does not suggest schizophrenia. His visions were consistent with those of his subculture. Despite his asceticism, Anthony remained involved with society throughout his life. He visited monks regularly, taught, and preached. In the context of his chosen lifestyle he was very functional and successful.

Elements suggestive of depression are prominent in Anthony's history. His asceticism begins soon after the sudden loss of both parents. He is thrust at a young age into a caretaking role for his sister. He abandons that role by placing his sister in a convent. Demons haunt him with memories of home and loved ones, suggesting guilty self-reproach. Chanting voices of demons wake him from sleep, he battles acedia and despair. Like someone suffering from depression, he stops eating.

Delusions and hallucinations can certainly accompany severe depression. In depressive psychosis hallucinations and delusions are mood congruent. The content of the psychotic experiences typically centers on guilt, self-reproach, and nihilistic fantasies. Self-reproach and guilt were certainly an element of Anthony's visions. Yet Anthony, the great visionary, is described as a happy man. "His soul being free of confusion, he held his outer senses also undisturbed, so that from the soul's joy his face was cheerful as well ... he was never troubled, his soul being calm, he never looked gloomy, his mind being joyous" (Athanathius 1980, 42). It is common to read of monks who did appear sad. The monk Arsenius, a Roman of senatorial rank, had "a hollow in his chest carved out by the tears which fell from his eyes all his life while he sat at his manual work" (Ward 1981, 18). To consider Anthony's visions purely as a product of depressive psychosis is inconsistent with the descriptions of his cheerful demeanor. The contagious quality of his visions and the power they had to influence others are also difficult to explain according to a depressive model.

This very power of Anthony's visions and the influence he had over Western culture for centuries suggest not only the weak claim that Anthony was not delirious, crazy, or sick but the stronger claim that his visions gave him powerful insight. His insight, colored by his visions, resonated so powerfully in the culture as a whole that he was able to reshape that culture. His visionary experiences must not only be de-pathologized but reconsidered as examples of human creative power.

Anthony visions occur near the dawn of the Christian era. Constantine was baptized a Christian on his deathbed in AD 337; Anthony died in 356. Christianity, in relation to the classical world, meant a new sense of time, a new kind of salvation, and a new psychology. In Christianity, more so than ever before, the inner life is crucial. Christ's teachings changed the definition of sin. Before Christ, one could do wrong in action; after Christ, one can sin in the heart without doing an evil act. "Ye have heard it said by them of old time; Thou shalt not commit adultery: But I say unto you, that whosoever looketh on a woman to lust after her hath committed adultery with her already in his heart" (Matthew 5:27). Anthony experienced through his visions an inner world where good and evil were palpable and alive, where salvation was a daily battle against evil, where life literally hung in the balance. This newly perceived inner life was experienced as a hallucinatory reality; seeing it made it more powerful than thinking it ever could have.

The sudden prominence of the mental state called acedia may also be related to this new and vivid experience of the inner life. Ennui and acedia are minor cultural concerns until the fourth century. Both Stanley Jackson and Reinhard Kuhn note that after the time of the desert fathers the bored, spiritually tinged depression that is acedia becomes a central cultural concern. The inner life has its dangers.

Keeping in mind that we have de-pathologized Anthony's visions, is there anything in modern psychiatric nomenclature that is reminiscent of the experiences of Anthony? Similar states might suggest a mechanism for such visions. The family of "culture-bound" syndromes listed in the appendix to DSM-IV include contagious visionary, nearly psychotic phenomena. Qi-gong, pibloktoq, spell, and zar involve contagious culturally sanctioned near-psychotic episodes in individuals who may not have other evidence of psychopathology. DSM-IV does not attempt to explain the mechanisms involved in such behavioral syndromes, and does not identify them as pathological, instead referring to culture-bound syndromes as "patterns of aberrant behavior" (APA 1994, 844).

In fact we need not journey to exotic lands or distant times to find examples of contagious near-psychotic experiences. Pilgrims by the thousands, including large numbers from our own society, journey to Ireland and Bosnia to visit the sites of the most recent Marian apparitions. At those sites large crowds have seen collective visions of the Virgin Mary, as well as hallucinatory experiences of the sun moving in strange patterns, and base metal rosaries turning to gold. These individuals are not psychotic nor mentally ill by other standards, yet they see things that we do not see and might be considered to suffer from "culture-bound syndromes."

Another family of illnesses reminiscent of the experiences of Anthony are the somatoform disorders, specifically conversion disorders. Conversion disorders occur when emotional stressors or conflicts are "converted" into somatic symptoms. In a conversion paralysis, for instance, a patient may present with an inability to move or feel the arm, although there is no evidence of nerve injury. The patient has symbolically expressed emotional conflicts in a somatic language. Conversion disorder is an "as if" illness. The person with conversion unconsciously pretends to be sick, enacts a story of illness to symbolically express an emotional conflict.

Similarly patients consciously or unconsciously feign psychiatric symptoms. In factitious psychiatric illnesses patients will pretend, not for any ulterior motive like time off work but simply for the sake of pretending, that they are crazy or depressed or suicidal. They are not, though they believe they are, in a manner analogous to the patient with a conversion disorder.

Interestingly a kind of contagion also operates in conversion disorders. Patients will typically base their conversion symptoms on someone they have known with an actual illness. A patient with a conversion paralysis will often have someone close to them who actually suffered from paralysis; a patient with conversion seizures will base their seizure symptoms on someone they have known with seizures or even on their own actual seizures.

The mechanism that operates in conversion disorders is dissociation. Dissociation is a poorly understood phenomenon first described by Pierre Janet in 1889. Dissociation occurs in a continuum from normal forms like daydreaming to pathological forms like dissociative or conversion disorders. In dissociation feelings, memories and perceptions that would normally be associated are "dissociated" or split off from awareness. To use metaphorical language, in dissociation some parts or levels of consciousness are split off from other parts. A person with a conversion paralysis knows on some level that they can move and at times will move, especially when they are distracted or in special mental states like trance. The part that can move and knows it is somehow split off from that part that really believes it can't move. Dissociation involves different and discontinuous narratives of the self and can be thought of as a kind of autohypnotic state.

Contagion is central to trance and dissociation. Patients under a trance are "suggestible" and can be induced to have powerful believed feelings and experiences. For instance, in a standard technique for trance induction, an induced hallucinatory experience is used as a measure of the depth of a trance. Under trance a person is asked to imagine that a helium balloon is attached to their index finger. The more a person's finger and hand are pulled upward "involuntarily" by the imaginary balloon, the deeper they are under trance. In trance people who are not crazy can experience vivid and contagious hallucinations.

I propose that the mechanisms involved in dissociative phenomena and conversion symptoms are operative in psychotic experiences like Anthony's. These mechanisms involve a splitting of consciousness or a "willing suspension of disbelief" that allows visions to be experienced as real, as well as a symbolic or expressive aspect of the visionary experience that makes the visions contagious and socially meaningful. These visions can be distinguished from hallucinations seen in delirium, which are meaningless, and from the hallucinations seen in schizophrenia and depression, which may have idiosyncratic meaning to the sufferer but do not infect or influence others.

Anthony's visionary experiences are prime examples of this special kind of psychotic experience. They might be termed culture-bound hallucinations if we focus on the social and cultural aspects of the phenomena, "conversion" psychosis if we use conversion as a model for the psychological mechanisms involved, or dissociative psychotic experiences if we use language borrowed from the study of analogous dissociative phenomena in hypnosis and trance. Certain culture-bound hallucinations unleash powerful emotional forces. In the case of Anthony the creative power of his visionary experiences drove a generation of urbane young men to live in abject poverty in the wilderness. This emotional power can be profoundly dangerous, as witnessed by the bizarre ascetic excesses of later ascetics like Symeon Stylites or modern millenarian cultist visionaries like Jim Jones or David Koresh.

References

American Psychiatric Association. 1994. *Diagnostic and Statistical Manual of Mental Disorders*. DSM-IV, 4th ed. Washington, DC: American Psychiatric Association Press.

Athanasius. 1980. *The Life of Anthony*. Trans. by R. Gregg. New York: Paulist Press.

Cassian, J. [1894] 1955. *Conferences and Institutes*. Trans. by E. Gibson. Grand Rapids, MI: Eerdmans.

Jackson, S. 1986. *Melancholia and Depression: From Hippocratic Times to Modern Times*. New Haven: Yale University Press.

Kroll, J. 1982. Visions and psychopathology in the Middle Ages. *Journal of Nervous and Mental Disease* 170: 41–49.

Kuhn, R. 1976. *The Demon of Noontide*. Princeton: Princeton University Press.

Ponticus, E. 1981. *The Praktikos*. Trans. by J. Bamberger. Kalamazoo, MI: Cistercian Publications.

Russell, N., trans. 1981. *The Lives of the Desert Fathers*. London: Mowbray.

Ward, B., trans. 1981. *The Sayings of the Desert Fathers*. Kalamazoo, MI: Cistercian Publications.

Waddell, H. 1957. *The Desert Fathers*. Ann Arbor, MI: University of Michigan Press.

Index

Abraham, Nicholas, 52, 53
Acedia, 254–55, 257, 259
Adolescence, 139–40, 142
Adolescent girls, commodification of, 168
Ambiguity
  in hallucinations, 218
  Merleau-Ponty on, 103
  and psychopathology, 99–100
  tolerance for, 93, 102–103
Amnesty, 62
Analogy(ies), 226
  between child's life and play, 226–32
Anatomy of Melancholy (Burton), 257
Ancient cultures, madness in, 3–5
Anna O., 106, 235
Anthony, Saint, 17, 253, 255–59
  illnesses reminiscent of experiences of,
    260
  longevity of, 254
Anticipation
  and imagination, 43
  thetic character and temporal mode of,
    77
Apollinian drive, 151–53
Apology (Plato), 195
Aporias, of imagination-in-use, 8
Archaic psychiatry, 3
Arieti, Silvano, 199
Aristotle, 5, 65, 158, 234
Arlow, Jacob, 126
Arsenius, 258
Art, 13. See also Creative process
  and artist's internal life, 236
  depression conquered by, 149
  dialectical tension in, 233, 235–36, 237–
    38, 240

and emotion, 236–37
  Langer on, 235
  in Nijinsky, 246
  expression of feelings in, 201
  Freud on, 13, 150–51, 159–60
  and Freud on primary process, 198
  and intentional fallacy, 194–96
  for Kristeva, 149, 158, 161
  love as well-spring of, 171
  Nietzsche on, 13, 152–54, 160
    and Dionysian impulse, 152, 153, 159
  and social transformation, 126
  and women, 166
Ascetic life, 253
Assertability conditions, 22, 24, 32
Auden, W. H., on Nijinsky, 251
Auerbach, Erich, 191
Augustine, St.
  on time, 97–98
  and visionary experiences, 257
Auschwitz, and remembrance, 67
Autistic children, 230

Balanchine, George, 242
Barfeld, Owen, 198
Barthes, Roland, 10
Beardsley, M., 194, 195
Beckett, Samuel, 53, 56
Belief
  and fantasy, 85–85
  in hallucinatory experience, 76–79
  and imagination, 26, 29, 32, 33, 78
  and memory, 70–72, 87n.15
Bend for Home, The (Healey), 54–56
Bergman, Ingmar, Scenes from a Marriage,
  175

Binswanger, Ludwig, 250
Birth of Tragedy (Nietzsche), 151–52
Bisociation, Koestler on, 238
Black Sun: Depression and Melancholia
(Kristeva), 148–49, 183
Blake, William
and collapse of dialectical tension, 240
on Locke, 17n.2
Bleuler, Eugen, 89n.39, 250
Body, and hallucinations, 217–18
Body-mind problem, 6
Borrowed fantasy, 124, 125
Boundaries
aesthetic play with vs. pathological loss
of, 100–101
Dionysian blurring of, 152
Bruner, Jerome, 123
Buddha, and transcendence, 138
Bunuel, Luis, 31–32
Burton, Robert, 257

Cartesian conception of consciousness,
203
Cartesian dualistic paradigm, 41, 43, 44
Cassian, John, 254, 257
Cassirer, Ernst, 3, 6, 14, 188, 198–99
Cavell, Stanley, 24
Certainty, political extremists' demand
for, 103
Cervantes, Miguel de, *Don Quixote*, 125
Child abuse, memories of, 10, 57–58
Childhood games, 115
Children, young
and narrative construction, 225–32
and play, 225
analogical structures in, 226–32
Christ, and transcendence, 138
Christianity, 259. *See also* Desert fathers
Christian view of history, 189–193, 203
Civilization and Its Discontents (Freud), 149,
163, 165, 172n.7
Clinical situation, 15–17. *See also*
Psychiatry; Psychoanalysis;
Psychotherapy
vs. academic researchers, 211
children's play in, 226–32
and conscious fantasies, 113
frog-in-room case, 23

imagination in, 29–30, 32–36
and phenomenological model, 45, 47–
49
and treatment as conversion to clinician's
way of thinking, 40
Clinton, Hillary, 144
Coherence theory of truth, 45, 48
Coleridge, Samuel Taylor, on Locke,
17n.2
Collective imagining, 131n.23
shift in, 126
Commodification, of girls, 168
Comparative phenomenology of mind, 65
Complementary fantasy, 123
Compulsives, tolerance for ambiguity
lacking in, 103
Condensation, Freud on, 198, 200
Congreve, William, 143
Congruent fantasy, 123
Conscious fantasy. *See under* Fantasy
Consciousness
confounded with discursive, linguistic
thought, 203
and hallucination, 216
imagination in structure of, 44
Constantine (emperor of Rome), 259
Continental philosophy, 8–9. *See also*
Phenomenology
Conversion disorders, 260, 261
Correspondence theory of truth or
validity, 9, 39–40, 41, 45, 48
Creatively productive imagination, 5
Creative process, 233, 234. *See also* Art
dialectical tension in, 233, 234, 235–36,
237–38, 240
and madness, 17
and Nijinsky, 233, 234 (*see also* Nijinsky,
Vaslav)
and pathologic imagination, 15–17
and primary process, 233, 234, 237, 238,
240
and psychopathology, 234–36
and secondary process, 233, 234, 237,
239, 240
Creative tension, 16–17. *See also*
Dialectical tension
"Creative Writers and Daydreaming"
(Freud), 159

Creativity, paradox of, 236
Crime, and memory as witness, 60–61
Crucible, The (Miller), 58
Cultural fantasy, shared, 124
Culturally transmitted fantasies, 123–26
Culture-bound hallucinations, 17, 260, 261
Culture-bound syndromes, 259

Daydreaming. *See* Fantasy
Delirium, hallucinations in, 261
Delusional beliefs, 33
Delusions
  in depressive psychosis, 258
  DSM–IV on, 2–3
  empiricist understanding of, 40, 47
  phenomenological understanding of, 47
Depression. *See also* Melancholia
  as affective or emotional disorder, 180–82
    self-destructive aspect of, 182–84, 186n.12
  and Saint Anthony, 258
  hallucinations in, 261
  and imagination, 181, 183, 184
  and inner-outer distinction, 176
  as lack of differentiation or depth, 177, 179–80
    and Kant's account of objective experience, 177–79
  phenomenological description of, 13–14, 175
  Sartre on, 175–76, 176–77
  and sin of acedia, 255
  tolerance for ambiguity lacking in, 103–104
Descartes, René, 203
Desert fathers, 253–55
  Saint Anthony, 17, 253, 254, 255–59, 260
Desire, masculine model of, 170
Diaghilev, Sergei, 242, 245, 246
Diagnostic and Statistical Manual of Mental Disorders, fourth edition (DSM–IV), 2, 6, 39, 259
Dialectical tension, creative (artistic) process as, 233, 234, 235–36, 237–38, 240

Diamond, Cora, 21, 22, 23, 24
Dictionary of Psychoanalysis, on fantasy life, 11
Dionysian festivals, 150, 152, 154
Dionysian impulse, 152, 153, 159
Discursive reason
  consciousness confounded with, 203–204
  and appeal to unconscious, 194
Displacement, Freud on, 197–98, 200
Dissociation, 260–61
Don Quixote (Cervantes), 125
Dora, Freud's case history of, 10, 57, 59–60
Double injunction, 62
  in *Hamlet*, 52, 54, 62
  and history, 56
  as poetic exigency, 56
  in psychotherapy, 57
Dream-image, and hallucination, 75–76
Dreaming (nightdreams), 28
  as effective expression of feelings, 201–202
  vs. fantasies, 112–13
  Freud on, 75–76, 128n.11, 196–98
  and hallucinations, 219
  hallucinatory dream-images, 72–73, 74
  and intentional fallacy, 200–201
  interpretation of as identification, 202
  Merleau-Ponty on, 98–99
  and unconscious, 200
Dream model of fantasy (Freud), 115–16
DSM–IV (*Diagnostic and Statistical Manual of Mental Disorders*, fourth edition), 2, 6, 39, 259
Dualistic paradigm, Cartesian, 41, 43, 44
Duras, Marguerite, 166–67

Ego and the Id, The (Freud), 163
Eliade, Mircea, 188, 189, 190
Emotion, and art, 236–37
  Langer on, 235
  in Nijinsky, 246
Empathy, in children, 230
Empiricist tradition. *See also* Science
  and hallucinations, 15, 40
  on the imaginary, 8–9
  and Locke on madness, 2

Empiricist tradition (cont.)
  in model of imagination, 39–42, 44,
    48
  and psychiatry, 6, 7
Enigma of Woman, The (Kofman), 164
Erikson, Erik, 101–102
Esquirol, Jean-Étienne, 77
Essay concerning Human Understanding
    (Locke), 1
Ethical consciousness, 140, 141, 142–43,
    145
  sexual dimension of, 141
Ethics. *See also* Morality
  and mother–infant relationship, 137
  of remembrance, 53, 60–62
Evagrius, 254, 255
Existential phenomenology, 94
Experience, and truth/falsity of
    perception, 40
Experiential domain, clinicians' goals in,
    47

Fairy tale, child's narrative as, 232
Faith, Merleau-Ponty on, 10. *See also*
    Perceptual faith
False memory syndrome, 57–58
Familiarity, in memory, 69–70
Fantasy, 79–85
  as autistic, 89n.39
  conscious (daydreaming), 11
    adaptive aspects of, 114
    benefits of, 116
    classification criteria for, 116–17
    culturally transmitted, 123–26
    elements of, 121–22
    example of lifelong effect of, 130n.18
    examples of through woman's life,
      119–22
    Freudian models of, 11–12, 115–16
    generative, 118–19, 130n.19
    hiddenness of, 112–15
    about medications, 129n.15
    as multilayered, 130n.19
    and play, 129n.14
    repeating, 117–18, 130n.19
    shared, 122–23, 124
    transient (fleeting), 117, 130nn.17,19
  as creative and adaptive, 11

Freud on, 11–12, 81–82, 83, 113, 115–
    16, 123, 127n.5, 129n.12, 162, 172n.5
  female, 165
  and hallucination, 65, 79–80, 82–83, 84,
    858888
  and imagination, 65, 79–80, 81–82, 84,
    85, 112–16
  unconscious, 113, 114, 129n.14
  as valuable achievement, 111
Faurisson, Robert, 61
Feeling and Form (Langer), 201
Feelings. *See also* Emotion
  dreams and symptoms as expression of,
    201–202
  and truth/falsity of perception, 40
Ficino, Marsilio, 155, 162
Fiction(s)
  in child's pretend play, 227
  vs. history, 56
  memory in
    and *The Bend for Home*, 54–56
    and *Hamlet*, 51
  reinvention in, 62
Fictional narratives, child's emotional
    themes in, 226–32
Figure-ground/theme-horizon structure,
    95
Finnegan's Wake (Joyce), 56
"Flashback," 88n.27
Flaubert, Gustave, 125
Fleeting (transient) fantasies, 111,
    130nn.17,19
Flinders, Carol Lee, 168, 169
Frenkel-Brunswik, Else, 102, 103
Freud, Anna, 88n.39
Freud, Sigmund
  and analogies to myth or religion, 188,
    189
  on art, 13, 150–51, 159–60
  on belief in reality, 71
  on castration, 144
  childhood-seduction theory of, 57, 113–
    14, 127–28nn.8,9,10
  on death drive, 163
  on depression, 180–81, 182, 184,
    186n.12
  on dreams, 75, 128n.11, 196–98
  and hallucinations, 219

hallucinatory dream-images, 72, 73–74
and intentional fallacy, 200–201
and fantasy (daydreaming), 11–12, 81,
   83, 84, 113, 115–16, 123, 127n.5,
   129n.12, 162, 172n.5
   female, 165
on festivals, 159
on fixation, 141
on girls, 164
on hallucination, 77
on *Hamlet*, 52
on hardships of life, 149, 154
on hate, 143
on hysteria, 113–14, 127nn.4,6,7
   and case history of Dora, 10, 57, 59
on infantile development, 12, 133–34,
   135–36
on infantile sexuality, 137
on intersubjective relations, 155
and Kristeva, 149, 166, 171, 172n.5
on latency period, 139
on love, 135, 136, 138, 140
on negation, 161
on Oedipus complex, 147–48, 186n.13
on originary wholeness, 155
on paradox of creativity, 236
and pathologic imagination, 7
phallocentric view of, 13
on play, 129nn.12,13
and psychoanalysis of history, 189
on repression, 164–65, 181, 204
   in case of Dora, 57
on retentiveness, 69
Ricoeur on, 145n.2
on sexuality, 135, 142, 144
on sleep, 75
on sublimation, 13, 14, 138, 163, 180,
   181
on super-ego, 154–55, 159
and unconscious, 196–98, 200, 204–
   205
on women, 156, 165–66, 172n.7
   Kofman on, 164
"Freud and Dora: Story, History, Case
   History" (Marcus), 60
Freudian case histories, and modernist
   fiction, 60
Fromm-Reichman, Frieda, 235

Fuentes, Carlos, 125
Future-directedness, and imagination, 43

Galileo, 25
Gallop, Jane, 60
Gavigan, Melody, 58
Gay Science, The (Nietzsche), 153
Gender differences. *See* Women
Genealogy of Morals (Nietzsche), 154
General Introduction to Psychoanalysis, A
   (Freud), 196–97
Generative fantasies, 118–19, 130n.19
Gestalt psychology
   and Merleau-Ponty, 93
   and *Prägnanz*, 94–96
   and subjective/objective status of
      perceptual phenomena, 106n.5
Golden rule, 137
Goldstein, Kurt, 199
Greece, ancient, Dionysian festivals of,
   150, 152, 154
Greece, Homeric, 4
Green, André, 53

Halle, M., 226
Hallucinations, 15–16, 72–79, 209–10
   and St. Anthony, 17, 258
   contagious, 261
   "culture-bound," 17, 260, 261
   in depressive psychosis, 258
   empiricist understanding of, 15, 40
   and fantasy, 65, 79–81, 82–83, 84, 85–
      86
   framework for analysis of, 210–14, 223
   and imagination, 65, 74, 85, 209
   meanings in, 218–20, 222
   and memory, 65, 85
   Merleau-Ponty on, 15, 210, 211, 214–
      20, 222
   O'Brien's account of, 209, 220–22
   psychotic patients' stance toward, 99
   as responses to first symptom, 220
   thetic character and temporal mode of,
      77–78
Hallucinatory belief, 10
Hamlet, and memory, 51–54, 62
Hampshire, Stuart, 195
Harnack, Adolf von, 254

Healey, Dermot, 54–56
Heaney, Seamus, 56
Hegel, G. W. F., 169, 234, 237, 241
Heidegger, Martin, 9, 43, 99, 147, 158,
   169, 211
Heisenberg's uncertainty principle, 45
Hermeneuticists, 48
 and correspondence theory, 40
Hermeneutics, of religion and the
   unconscious, 188–93
Hierarchical levels of theoretical inquiry,
   37, 38, 39
 and model A, 42, 48
 and model B, 46, 48
Hillman, James, 188
Historical crime, and memory as witness,
   60–61
History
 Christian understanding of, 189–93, 203
 vs. fiction, 56
 need to let go of, 61
 proper recollection of, 51
Hobbes, Thomas, 1, 65–66
Hodsen, Millicent, 247
Holocaust, and remembrance, 10, 60–61
Holocaust Testimonies: The Ruins of Memory
   (Langer), 61
Homer, 4
Hume, David, 5, 66, 70, 74, 86n.7, 178,
   179
Husserl, Edmund, 43, 69, 70, 71, 97, 211,
   213, 216
Hysteria, Freud's theory on, 113–14,
   127nn.4,6,7
 in case of Dora, 59–60

Identity
 and adolescent sexuality, 142
 sexed, 169–70
 women's lack of sense of, 169
Illusions
 empiricist understanding of, 40
 Freud on, 150
Imaginary/real relationship, 9–10, 54. See
   also Subjective-objective relation
 aesthetic vs. pathological uncertainty
   over, 100–101
 in empiricist/dualist model, 39, 42
 and James on pluralistic faith, 106n.9

and Merleau-Ponty, 10–11, 94, 96, 97,
   98–99, 104–105
 and infant's object constancy, 101
 in narrative memory, 60
 and psychopathology, 7, 104
 and Rorschach testing, 102
Imagination, 7, 30
 as adaptive tool, 112
 authority for what is imagined, 28–29
 and belief, 26, 29, 32, 33, 78
 as "belonging" to person, 27–28, 30–31
 Bunuel on, 31–32
 in clinical situation, 29–30, 32–36
   frog-in-room case, 23–24
 and depression, 181, 183, 184
 dialectical tension as producing, 233
 and empiricist philosophy, 8–9, 39–42,
   48
 in expression of feelings, 181–82
 and fantasy, 79–80, 81, 82–83, 84, 85,
   111–12
 and hallucination, 65, 74, 85, 209
 in Kant, 5, 184, 185n.3
   on aesthetic appreciation, 13–14, 180,
   185n.5
   on objective experience, 13, 106n.11,
   177–179, 180
 Kierkegaard on, 1
 life-roles of, 24, 31
 and melancholia (Kristiva), 161–62
 and memory, 65–72, 74, 85, 86n.7
 Merleau-Ponty on, 93–94, 96 (see also
   Merleau-Ponty, Maurice)
 models of, 37, 49
   and hierarchy of levels of theoretical
   inquiry, 38, 39
   model A (empiricist/natural-scientific),
   39–42, 44, 48
   model B (phenomenological), 42–49
 in modern period, 5–6
 mimetic vs. creatively productive, 5
 pathological, 1–3, 5, 7, 8–17 (see also
   Psychopathology; Psychosis;
   Schizophrenia)
 and perception, 25–27, 30, 31, 65, 75–
   76
 and phenomenologically oriented
   philosophy, 8–9, 10–11
 and primary process, 198–99

and principles of mythic thinking, 199
and psychiatry, 6–7
and psychoanalysis, 11
and psychopathology, 6, 7
and Rorschach tests, 102
and subjective-objective distinction, 28, 176
synthetic (Kant), 106n.11
and telling, 26–28
temporal position of, 86n.9
thetic character and temporal mode of, 77–78
and unconscious, 14–15, 187, 188
Wittgenstein on, 25, 26, 28
in young children, 225
Imaginative production, 13
Imagining: A Phenomenological Study (Casey), 86n.1
Individuation, principle of, and Appollinian drive, 151–52
In Dora's Case (Kahane), 59
Infant development, 12, 136–37. *See also* Mother-infant relationship; Oedipus complex
Freud on, 12, 133–34, 135–36
and perceptual faith, 101–102
withdrawal of mother in, 139
Ingram, Paul, 58
Integrated self, and artistic tension, 237
Intentional fallacy, 14, 194–96
and deification of word, 204
and dream interpretation, 200–201, 203
Intentionality-based model of human being, 43, 44
Interdisciplinary studies, 211
Interpretation, religious, 188–89
and explanation in terms of unconscious, 189–93
Interpretation of Dreams (Freud), 52, 115, 196
Intersubjective relations, 155. *See also* Other
Freud on, 155
Merleau-Ponty on, 97
and shared fantasies, 122–23, 124
Involuntariness, of hallucinations, 76, 88n.26
Irigaray, Luce, 12, 13, 167, 169, 170
Irving, David, 61

Jack, Dana Crowley, 168
Jackson, Stanley, 259
Jakobson, R., 226
James, William, 69, 70, 87n.12, 102–103, 106n.9
Janet, Pierre, 260
Jaspers, Karl, 6
Jehovah's Witnesses, 193
John (hermit), 254
Jones, Jim, 261
Joyce, James, 56
Jung, Carl
and analogies to myth or religion, 188, 189
on creative persons, 238
and dreaming, 200
on fantasies, 85

Kahane, Claire, 59
Kant, Immanuel, on imagination, 5, 184, 185n.3
in aesthetic appreciation, 13–14, 180, 185n.5
in objective experience, 13, 106n.11, 177–79, 180
"Keys to Dora" (Gallop), 60
Kierkegaard, Søren, 1, 99
Klinger, Eric, 115
Knowledge of other minds, Merleau-Ponty on, 97
Koestler, A. 234, 237, 238, 239, 240
Kofman, Sarah, 164, 166–67
Koresh, David, 261
Kripke, Saul, 22
Kristeva, Julia, 12, 13, 148–49
on art, 161
on Duras, 166–67
and Freud, 149, 166, 171, 172n.5
on melancholia (depression), 13, 156–59, 160, 183–84
and antidepressants, 160–61
and imagination, 161–62
inadequacy of, 167, 171
on narcissistic sadness, 155–56
on sublimation, 160, 161, 163, 164, 171
on women, 162–63
and melancholia, 167
and sublimation, 163–64

Kroll, J., 258
Kuhn, Reinhard, 259

Lacan, Jacques, 52, 155
Laing, R. D., 99
Langer, Lawrence, 61
Langer, Suzanne, 14, 194, 198–99, 201,
 235, 238
Language
 and creativity, 239
 Wittgenstein on, 21–23
Lévi-Strauss, Claude, 188
Life of Anthony, The, 253, 255
Literary tales, and fantasies, 81–82
Locke, John
 and "experience," 94
 and hallucinations, 15
 and imagination, 7, 8, 17n.2
 on madness, 1–3, 5
Lombroso, Cesare, 234
Love, 136, 138–39
 betrayal of, 143–44
 Freud on, 136, 138, 140
 development of, 135
  and sexuality, 135, 142
 Mother as primal object of, 134–35
 as wonder, 171
Lyric poetry, 199
Madame Bovary (Flaubert), 125
Madness. *See also* Pathological
  imagination; Psychopathology;
  Psychosis; Schizophrenia
 in ancient cultures, 3–5
 and creativity, 17, 234–36
 Locke on, 1–3, 5
 reformers on, 2, 18n.3
Madonna, as culturewide myth, 126. *See
 also* Mother
Magic, sympathetic, 200
Mania, tolerance for ambiguity lacking in,
 103
Marcus, Stephen, 60
Marriage avec Dieu (ballet), 249
Mattoon, Illinois, "phantom gasser," 1, 6,
 8
Meaning(s)
 in hallucinations, 218–20, 222
 and symbol vs. symptom, 235
 Wittgenstein on, 21–23

Melancholia, 148
 and intellectual/artistic achievement
  (Aristotle), 234
 Kristeva on, 13, 157–59, 160, 183–84
 and antidepressants, 160–61
 and imagination, 161–62
 as inadequate analysis, 167, 171
 of women, 149, 172n.3
 and attempts at art, 167
 and culture, 171
 political/ontological responses to, 169–
  71
Memory, 51
 double injunction on, 62
 in *Hamlet*, 52, 54, 62
 and history, 56
 as poetic exigency, 56
 in psychotherapy, 57
 and ethics, 60–62
 and fantasy, 85
 in fiction
  and *The Bend for Home*, 54–56
  and *Hamlet*, 51, 52, 54, 62
 and function of narrative remembrance,
  62
 and hallucination, 85
 and imagination, 65–72, 74, 85, 86n.7
 James on, 87n.15
 narrative, 56, 62
 and perception, 65, 67, 71, 73
 recovered, 57–59, 61
 Reich on, 61
 suppressed, 57–59
 temporal character of, 67–68
 thetic character and temporal mode of,
  77–78
"Memory of Suffering, The" (Ricoeur),
 61
Merleau-Ponty, Maurice, 10, 43, 93
 on ambiguity and openness, 103
 and Frenkel-Brunswik on psychological
  rigidity, 102
 and hallucinations, 15, 210, 211, 214–
  20, 222
 on imaginary/real relationship, 10–11,
  94, 96, 97, 98–99, 104–105
 and imagination, 93–94, 96
 on perceptual faith, 10, 96–98
  developmental account of, 101–102

psychopathology as breakdown of, 99–101

and *Prägnanz*, 94–96

and psychiatry, 104

"Message hunting," 194–196

by Freud, 196

Metaphor, 226

and child's fictional narrative, 232

and magic practices, 200

Metonymy, 226

and child's fictional narratives, 228, 229, 232

and magic practices, 200

MidSummer Night's Dream, A (Act V), quoted, 111

Millenarian cultist visionaries, 261

Miller, Arthur, *The Crucible*, 58

Models of imagination. See *under* Imagination

Modernist fiction, and narrative of Freud's Dora case, 60

Molloy (Beckett), 53

Monks, life of, 253–54

"Monster in the Mist, The: Are Long Buried Memories of Child Abuse Reliable?" (Reich), 58

Mourning, over son's renunciation of mother, 147–48

Montaigne, Michel de, on philosophizing, 158

Morality. See also Ethical consciousness; Ethics

Freud on, 154–55

Nietzsche on, 154, 155

Moses, 4

Mother, 145

and adolescence, 140

and depressives, 183

and Kriszeva on sublimation, 164

need for, 140

need to leave, 140–41

as primal love object, 134–35

as primary object of loss, 157

rejection and pain from, 143

Mother-infant relationship, 12, 133, 136–37, 143. See also Infant development; Oedipus complex

Freud on, 12, 133–34, 135–36

for girls (Kristeva), 164

negativity in, 139

Muriel's Wedding (film), 118

Myth(s), 126

challenging of, 187

from play therapy, 225

unconscious mind as, 187

Myth of Analysis, The (Hillman), 188

Mythic religions, 192

Mythic way of thinking, 3, 188–89

and Freud's primary process, 198–99

and lyric poetry, 199

and schizophrenia, 199

Narcissism, 12, 133–34

in depression, 183

Freud on, 183

and Kristeva on lost love, 156

of puberty, 140

Narrative(s), 226

child's emotional themes in, 226–32

in fantasies, 80–82, 89n.36

in Freud's theory of hysteria, 57

and case of Dora, 59–60

Hamlet as tragedy of, 52–53

and young children's play, 16

Narrative construction

imagination as, 9–10

for young children, 225–26

Narrative memory

literary vs. nonliterary forms of, 56

two functions of, 62 (*see also* Double injunction)

Natural science. See Science

Natural-scientific understanding of imagination, in model of imagination, 39–42, 44, 48

Near-psychotic experiences, 260

Nietzsche, Friedrich

on art, 13, 151–55, 160

and Dionysian impulse, 150, 153, 159

on forgetting history, 61

and Kristeva, 149

on man as sick animal, 7

and Nijinsky, 249, 250–51

on originary wholeness, 155

on will to power, 167

and women, 147

Nijinsky, Bronia (sister), 236, 241, 246–48, 250

Nijinsky, Romola (wife), 245, 248, 249, 250, 251n.1
Nijinsky, Stanislav (brother), 244
Nijinsky, Vaslav, 16–17, 233, 240, 242
    and awareness of the unknown, 239
    and dialectical see-saw, 241
    diary of, 249
    father's "swimming lesson" for, 242–43
    and Fromm-Reichman on madness-creativity link, 235
    illness of, 248–51
    leap of, 233, 241, 243
    life history of, 243–46
    and sister, 236, 241, 246–48
No's Knife (Beckett), 56

Object constancy, 101
O'Brien, Barbara, 209, 220–22
Obsessives, tolerance for ambiguity lacking in, 103
Odyssey (Homer), madness portrayed in, 4
Oedipus at Colonus (Sophocles), 151
Oedipus complex, 133, 137, 147–48
    and Freud on girls, 164
Oedipus story or triangle, 141, 186n.13
    and depression, 183
Ontological doubt, 100
Ontological faith. *See* Perceptual faith
Ontological insecurity, 99
Ontology, 169
Operators and Things (O'Brien), 209
Organizing fantasies, 117–18
Other
    and artistic expression, 236
    Nijinsky's sister as, 247, 248
    and self, 250–51
Other minds, knowledge of, Merleau-Ponty on, 97
Overdetermination, Freud on, 198, 200

Paradox of creativity, 236
Paranoid delusional system, 99
Paranoid persons, 33, 34
    tolerance for ambiguity lacking in, 103
Paranormality, of hallucinations, 73–74
Participation, in fantasy, 81–82

Pathological imagination, 3, 7. *See also* Psychopathology
    control lacking in, 10
    and creative or clinical phenomena, 15–17
    Locke on, 1–3, 5
    and philosophical reflection, 8–11
    and psychodynamic thought, 11–15
Patriarchy, Irigaray on, 167
Pendergast, Mark, 58
Perception
    as false, 40
    and fantasying, 65
    and gestaltists, 95
    and hallucination, 65, 72–79
    and imagination, 25–27, 30, 31, 65, 75–76
    and memory, 65, 67, 71–72
    and Merleau-Ponty, 88, 105n.4, 212
    in phenomenological model, 45
    and Rorschach tests, 102
    thetic character and temporal mode of, 77–78
Perceptual (ontological) faith, 93, 105n.1
    ambiguity sustained by, 103
    Merleau-Ponty on, 10, 96–98
    developmental account of, 101–102
    psychopathology as breakdown of, 99–101
    and natural science (Merleau-Ponty), 104
    psychopathology as breakdown of, 99–101
Perceptual inflexibility anxiously demanding absolute certainty, 103
Personal relationships. *See* Intersubjective relations; Other
Perspective-taking, in child's narrative creation, 229–230
"Phantom gasser," 1
Phenomenological description of depression, 13–14
Phenomenological reduction, 212, 213
    and hallucinatory experience, 215, 223
Phenomenology (phenomenological tradition), 8–9, 10. *See also* Merleau-Ponty, Maurice
    and correspondence theory, 40

existential, 94
and hallucinations, 15, 211, 212
limits of (Merleau-Ponty), 104
in model of imagination, 42–49
Phenomenology (Merleau-Ponty), 97
Phenomenology of mind, comparative, 65
Phenomenology of Perception (Merleau-Ponty), 95, 96
Philosophical reflection, and pathologic imagination, 8–11
Philosophy of Symbolic Forms, The (Cassirer), 198–99
Piaget, Jean, 101
Picturing, 25
Pinel, Philippe, 2
Plato, 5, 135, 147, 156, 195, 234
Play
  and fantasy, 129n.14
  Freud on, 129nn.12,13
  in young children, 225
    narratives in, 226–32
    with words, 225–26
Play model of fantasy (Freud), 115–16
Play therapy, 225. *See also* Children, young
Pleasure, from fantasies, 84
Plotinus, 155
Poetic exigency, 56
Poetry, lyric, 199
Polanyi, M., 234, 237, 238
Postmoderns, and correspondence theory, 40
Pragmatic theory of truth, 45, 48
Prägnanz, 94–96, 104
Pre-objective level
  and hallucinations, 210, 215, 219–20
  and phenomenological research, 212
Presentifying modes of consciousness, 223. *See also* Delusions; Dreaming; Hallucinations; Imagination
Pretend play, 227. *See also* Play
  and empathy, 230
Primary process thinking, 197–98
  and creativity, 233, 234, 236, 238, 240
Projectedness, of hallucinations, 75–76, 88n.25
Prophets, and social transformation, 126

Prototaxic experience, 241–42
Psychiatry. *See also* Clinical situation; Psychoanalysis; Psychotherapy
  and imagination, 6–7
  and Merleau-Ponty, 104
Psychiatry Glossary, A, 212
Psychical reality, 84–85, 113–14
Psychoanalysis. *See also* Clinical situation; Psychiatry; Psychotherapy
  and imagination, 11
  myth and religion analogous to, 189
Psychodynamic thought, and pathologic imagination, 11–15
Psychological memory, 58
Psychology, in family of sciences, 211
Psychopathology. *See also* Pathological imagination
  as breakdown of perceptual faith, 99–101
  and creativity, 234–36, 241–42
    as collapse of dialectical tension, 241, 251n.3
  as demand for absolute certainty, 103–104
  and imaginary-real relationship, 7, 104
  and imagination, 6, 7
  as lack of correspondence with external reality, 40
  and Merleau-Ponty, 11, 93
  from perspective of poetics and philosophical aesthetics, 193
  and young children's narratives, 16
Psychosis
  analysis of meanings of, 223 (*see also* Hallucinations)
  and Saint Anthony's visionary experiences, 253 (*see also* Anthony, Saint)
  depressive, 258 (*see also* Depression; Melancholia)
Psychotherapy. *See also* Clinical situation; Psychiatry; Psychoanalysis
  double injunction in, 57
  as identification of affects, 203
  verbal dimension vs. creative imagination in, 14–15
Puberty, 139–40
  Freud on, 142

Reality. *See also* Belief; Imaginary/real
  relationship
  disregarding vs. denying of, 89n.39
  and Merleau-Ponty on natural science,
    104
  and Merleau-Ponty's perceptual faith,
    97, 104
Recovered memories, 57–59, 61
Reflective self-representation, 82
"Regression in the service of the ego,"
    234, 238
Reich, Walter, 58, 61
Relationships, personal. *See*
    Intersubjective relations; Other
Religion, primitive, 200
Religious interpretation, 188–89
  and explanation in terms of unconscious,
    189–193, 203
Remembered child abuse, 10
Remembering Satan (Wright), 58
Repeating fantasies, 117–18, 130nn.17,19
Replica use, in child's narrative creation,
    229–30
Representation, verbal vs. nonverbal
  forms of, 14
Repression, Freud on, 164–65, 181, 204
  in case of Dora, 57
Retentional fringe, 69
Retentiveness, 69, 87n.12
Ricoeur, Paul, 56, 61, 135, 145n.2
Riviere, Jacques, 239
Romantic movement, and Kant, 5
Rorschach, Hermann, 102
Rorschach testing, 102, 104
Rosen, George, 1
Russell, Bertrand, 70

Sachs, Hanns, 123
Sacre du printemps, Le (ballet), 239, 247–48
Samuel, Book of (I, 16:23), 4
Sartre, Jean-Paul, 13, 43, 76, 80
  on depression, 175–77, 184–85nn.1,2
  and Merleau-Ponty, 94
Sass, Louis, 100
Satanic rituals, and recovered memories,
    58
Satisfaction
  from fantasies, 84

of imagination, 26
Saussure, Ferdinand, 226
Sayings of the Desert Fathers, 254
Scenes from a Marriage (Bergman film), 175
Schizophrenia
  and Saint Anthony, 258 (*see also*
    Visionary experiences)
  in frog-in-room case, 23–24
  hallucinations in, 17, 76, 209, 261 (*see
    also* Hallucinations)
  and mythic thinking, 199
  of Nijinsky, 16, 250 (*see also* Nijinsky,
    Vaslav)
  symbolism of, 201
Science. *See also* Empiricist tradition
  Merleau-Ponty on, 104
  and psychical phenomena, 210
  and study of hallucinations, 214
Secondary process, and creativity, 233,
    234, 237, 239, 240
Self
  integrated, 237
  and love, 145
  and other, 250–51
Self-confidence, and Woolf on
  suppression of women, 168–69
Self-deception, and hallucination, 216
Self-esteem, and betrayal of love, 143–44
Semiotic, Kristeva on
  and depression, 184
  and women, 162, 165
Sense of participation, in fantasies, 81–83
Sensory vivacity, of hallucinations, 66,
    74–75, 77
Sensuous imagery, 67
Sex differences. *See* Women
Sexed identity, 169–70
Sexuality, 141–42
  feminine, 162–63
    Kofman on, 164
  and Freud, 135, 142, 144
  and infant-mother relationship, 137
  in puberty, 139–40, 142
  and quest for identity, 142
  thematic, 139, 142
Shared fantasies, 122–23, 124
Simpson, Eilene, 125
Simpson, O. J., 143

Singer, Jerome, 80–81
Slade, Arietta, 227
Socrates
  on artists' understanding, 195
  and transcendence, 138
Somatoform disorders, 260
Sophocles, 151
Spence, Donald, 10
Strawson, P. F., 179
Subjective dependency, 213–14
Subjective-objective relation. *See also*
    Imaginary/real relationship
  in empiricist/dualist model, 40, 41
  and imagination, 28, 176
  and Kristeva on depression, 183, 184
Subjectivity, 6
  empiricist position's devaluing of, 41
  and hallucinations, 217–18
Sublimation, 12, 135, 148, 156
  Freud on, 13, 14, 138, 163, 180, 181
  Kristeva on, 160, 161, 163, 164, 171
  and social dimension, 157
  women thought incapable of, 148, 156–
    57, 162, 163
  Kristeva on, 13, 163–64
Suggestibility, in confessions, 58
Suggestion, and Fred's case of Dora, 59
Suggestions of Abuse: True and False
    Memories of Childhood Sexual
    Trauma
*Suggestions of Abuse: True and False
    Memories of Childhood Sexual Trauma*
    (Yapko), 57–58
Sullivan, H. S., 241
Super-ego
  for Freud, 154–55, 159
  Kristeva on, 159
  of men vs. women, 165
Supernatural, the, 3
Suppressed memory, 57–59
Sweeney Astray (Irish saga), 4–5
Symbolic play, 16
Symbolic speech, 165, 184
  and Duras, 166, 167
Symeon Stylites, 261
Sympathetic magic, 200
Sympathetic view of nature, Cassirer on, 3
Symposium (Plato), quoted, 156

Symptoms
  as attempt to communicate meaning,
    241
  as collapse of dialectical tension, 236
  as effective expression of feelings, 201–
    202
  hallucinations as, 212
  at parataxic level, 242
  symbolic representation in, 235
Syntagmatic relationships, 226
Synechdoche, and magic practices, 200

Telling
  and imagination, 26–28
  question of completeness of, 51, 56 (*see
    also* Double injunction)
Terr, Lenore, 58
Testimonial memory, 57–59, 61, 62
Theory of mind, child's development of,
    230
Thought, in depression, 181–82
Thoughts concerning Education (Locke),
    17n.2
Tolerance for ambiguity, 93, 102–103
Tomkins, Silvan, 111
Thought and Action (Hampshire), 195
"Throwback," 88n.27
Tragedy, as double injunction, 54
Trance, 261
Transcendence, 170
Transference fantasies, 113, 117, 129–
    30n.16
Transient (fleeting) fantasies, 117,
    130nn.17,19
Treatise of Human Nature (Hume), 66
Truth
  coherence theory of, 45, 48
  correspondence theory of, 9, 39–40, 41,
    45, 48
  poetic lies as, 54
  pragmatic theory of, 45, 48
  and shared standards or rules, 35–36
Tukes, Samuel and William, 2

"Uncanny, The," 159
Uncertainty, and psychopathology, 99–
    100
Uncertainty principle in physics, 45

Unchained Memories: True Stories of Traumatic Memories Lost and Found (Terr), 58
Unconscious
of artist, 196
belief in as imperialism of discursive reasoning, 203–204
and Christian view of history, 189–93, 103
and desire or emotion, 202–203
discovery of as break from common sense, 213
Freud on, 196–98, 200, 204–205
vs. inability to identify or name, 203
language of, 239
as misconception and myth, 187, 189, 193
appeal to as "message hunting," 194
and imagination, 14–15, 187, 188
"Unconscious, The" (Freud), 204
Unconscious fantasy, 113, 114, 129n.14

Vandenberg, Brian, 225
Vico, Giambattista, 6, 66
Victims of Memory: Sex Abuse Accusations and Shattered Lies (Pendergast and Gavigan), 58
Virgin Mary, 141
Visible and the Invisible, The (Merleau-Ponty), 96, 97, 105n.1
Visionary experiences
of desert fathers, 255
of Saint Anthony, 17, 253, 257–59, 261
Visualization, Freud on, 194
Voltaire, 74

Wachtler, Sol, 143
War and Peace (Tolstoy), reinvention in, 62
War of the Worlds, The (Wells), 1
Waywardness, in fantasy, 83
White, Hayden, 10
Wicker, Brian, 226
Wilde, Oscar, quoted, 147
Willing suspension of disbelief
in dissociation or conversion symptoms, 261
in fantasies, 84

Wimsatt, W. K., 194, 195
Wish fulfillment, in fantasies, 83–84
Wittgenstein, Ludwig, 8, 21–23, 24, 25, 26, 28, 30, 32
Women
Freud on, 156, 165–66, 172n.7
Kofman on, 164
Kristeva on, 162–63
and melancholia, 167
and sublimation, 163–64
melancholia of, 149, 172n.3
and attempts at art, 167
and culture, 171
political/ontological responses to, 169–71
and mourning for mother, 148
and sexuality, 162–63
Kofman on, 164
sublimation held impossible for, 148, 156–57, 162, 163
Kristeva on, 163–64
suppression of, 167–69
and commodification of girls, 168
Western tradition's view of, 147, 167
Woolf, Virginia, 168
Words, Wittgenstein on, 21–23
Wordsworth, William, 233, 235, 237
Wright, Lawrence, 58

Yapko, Michael, 57
Yeats, William Butler, on Locke, 17n.2
Young children. *See* Children, young